ACTIVE
LEARNING

A C T I V E
LEARNING

A Study Skills Worktext

RORY DONNELLY
Northeastern Illinois University

HOLT, RINEHART AND WINSTON, INC.

Fort Worth   Chicago   San Francisco   Philadelphia   Montreal
Toronto   London   Sydney   Tokyo

Publisher/Acquisitions Editor:	Charlyce Jones Owen
Developmental Editor:	Tod Gross
Senior Project Editor:	Charlie Dierker
Manager of Production:	Tad Gaither
Art & Design Supervisor:	John Ritland
Text and Cover Design:	Patrice Mozelewski

Copyright Acknowledgments

From *Arts and Ideas,* seventh edition, by William Fleming. Copyright © 1986 by CBS Publishing, 1980, 1974, 1963, 1955 by Holt, Rinehart and Winston, Inc. Reprinted by permission.

From *Explorations in the Arts* by G.M. Pinciss and Marlies K. Danziger, et. al. Copyright © 1985 by Holt, Rinehart and Winston, Inc. Reprinted by permission.

From *The World of Biology,* third edition, by William Davis and Eldra Pearl Solomon. Copyright © 1986 by Saunders College Publishing. Reprinted by permission.

From *Understanding Human Behavior,* fifth edition, by James J. McConnell. Copyright © 1986, 1983, 1980, 1977, 1974 by Holt, Rinehart and Winston, Inc. Reprinted by permission.

Photo Credits

Page 286: Copyright © 1968 Metro-Goldwyn-Mayer, Inc.
Pages 277, 280, 282, 283, 288: Courtesy of the Museum of the City of New York.

ISBN: 0-03-005982-8

Address editorial correspondence to: 301 Commerce Street, Suite 3700, Fort Worth, TX 76102
Address orders to: 6277 Sea Harbor Drive, Orlando, FL 32887
1-800-782-4479, or 1-800-433-0001 (in Florida)

Printed in the United States of America

0   1   2   3   016   9   8   7   6   5   4   3   2   1

Holt, Rinehart and Winston, Inc.
The Dryden Press
Saunders College Publishing

PREFACE

The aim of this textbook is to enable you to become an active learner—a person who takes control of learning during college. You will be an active learner when you:

▲ Play an active role in making decisions that affect your education
▲ Accept responsibility for learning in each of your classes, even under difficult conditions, and
▲ Use learning strategies that actively engage you in the learning process

To achieve this aim, *Active Learning* teaches the academic skills needed in each class you take during your college career, skills such as time management, active reading, test taking, and using a college library. Since college is a new and rather specialized environment, you will need these skills whether you are a traditional 18-year-old freshman, a returning student, a non-traditional student in a special program, or a non-native speaker of English.

The organization of this textbook follows the cycle for a typical term. Part One presents skills needed at the beginning of the term, such as sizing up your classes and time management. Parts Two and Three cover the language skills needed in your daily class encounters, including listening, notetaking, and textbook reading strategies. Parts Four and Five cover strategies used in studying for and taking tests, and Part Six presents skills related to doing oral and written assignments for class. However, since the parts are self-contained, they do not need to be read in a particular order. So if you are given an assignment in the college library the first week, skip ahead to Chapter 16 and read it on your own.

In order to learn or master any skill, whether it's serving a tennis ball, making chili, or changing a tire, it's not enough to read about it; you need hands-on experience. Since the aim of this book is to teach you a set of skills, it is organized as a worktext. After each strategy or skill is presented, an *exercise* is provided so you can practice it. Also, at the end of each chapter, you'll find *journal writing* exercises and *academic writing* assignments. Use the journal writing exercises to reflect on the skills you've been practicing or to relate new ideas to your own experiences. Use the academic writing assignments to synthesize the skills from the chapter, or to apply the skills to one of your classes.

Since you'll be reading this textbook for class, you'll want to become familiar with the study aids provided in each chapter and to use them as aids to reading comprehension. At the beginning of each chapter you'll find a list of *learning objectives*. Use them to set your own learning goals for reading. Within each chapter, you'll find many *figures* and *illustrations*. Refer to them as you read to deepen your understanding of the ideas they illustrate. Also note that *technical terms* related to college and academic skills are presented in boldface and defined the first time you encounter them. These terms are also included in a *glossary* in the appendix. Finally, each chapter ends with a *summary*. As you read the summary, check your understanding of the chapter as a whole and reinforce your learning.

During this term, you'll want to practice the learning and study skills you're studying by applying them in other classes. If you practice these skills consistently, this should be a strong term academically for you. To help you see how these skills can be used in other classes, three typical undergraduate general education courses are used as running examples throughout the textbook: an introductory psychology course, a general biology course and a general humanities course. Many sample passages used in this book are taken from four Holt, Rinehart and Winston college textbooks often used in these courses: *Understanding Human Behavior* by James McConnell, *Arts & Ideas* by William Fleming, *Explorations in the Arts* by G. M. Pinciss et. al., and *World of Biology* by P. W. Davis and E. P. Solomon. A chapter from *Explorations in the Arts* is included in the appendix for you to practice reading and marking a textbook reading assignment.

As you will discover, many projects you work on in college are collaborative efforts. This principle of cooperation also holds true for work you do after college in a professional career. For example, a book like this is the product of collaboration with many other instructors and editors. I would particularly like to thank Carlo Annese, Bergen Community College; J. W. DeGrendele, Montgomery County Community College; Ceil Fillenworth, St. Cloud State College; Sev Garcia, Porterville College; Barbara Gold, Westchester Community College; Chuck Harkins, Gloucester County College; Richard Higginbotham, Northeastern Illinois University; Heather Huseby, University of North Dakota; Barbara Henry, West Virginia State College; Dennis Nelson, Willmar Community College; Solveig Nelson, Grand View College; Marion Perry, Erie Community College; Vonnie Ross, Lane Community College; Doris Snyder, Northeastern Oklahoma A&M; Daniel Strumas, Indian River Community College; and Donna L. Swartz, Essex Community College, who read earlier drafts of the manuscript and offered suggestions about how to improve it.

I would also like to thank the editorial and production team of Holt, Rinehart, and Winston who worked with me, especially Charlie Dierker, Tod Gross, Lisa Moore, Kate Morgan, and Charlyce Jones Owen. Finally I'd like to thank the boys: David, Matthew, and Douglas Stephens. You are always there to support me, and you are active learners all.

R. D.

TABLE OF CONTENTS

PART FOUR   Studying

PART FIVE   Taking College Exams

PART SIX   Doing Academic Assignments

P A R T

ONE

STARTING THE TERM

CHAPTER

1

SIZING UP YOUR CLASSES

In this chapter you will learn:

▲ what information you need to know about each of your classes from the start
▲ how to evaluate whether the classes you've selected are right for you
▲ ten steps to a strong start this term

The first academic skill you need to master your first week of the term is to find out as much as you can about your classes during the first class sessions. These first classes are your chance to get an overview of the course and to learn the course requirements. They also are your chance to verify that the classes you've registered for are good choices for you.

STUDYING A COURSE SYLLABUS

A **syllabus** is a handout summarizing important information about the class. A syllabus lays out what the instructor plans to teach and what your responsibilities are if you are to be a successful learner. Use it to get an overview of the class and to get a sense of the amount and kind of work the class will require. Figure 1.1 is a sample course syllabus from an introductory psychology class. It shows the types of information usually contained in a syllabus. Since some instructors prefer to outline the course requirements orally during an orientation lecture, be sure to take notes during these first class sessions. If you need information that you don't learn from the syllabus or from the instructor's comments, ask the instructor directly.

Figure 1.1

Syllabus: Introductory Psychology

Purpose: The purpose of the course is to introduce students to the field of psychology, and to give them an understanding of the methods psychologists use to learn about human behavior.

Text: *Understanding Human Behavior* by James V. McConnell, 5th edition, Holt, Rinehart and Winston, 1986.

Supplemental readings will be assigned.

Outline:

Week	Topic	Chapter
UNIT I	BIOLOGICAL BASES OF BEHAVIOR	
1	Introduction	1
	The Brain	2
2	Altered States of Consciousness	3
	Structure and Function of the Brain	4
3	General Systems Theory	5
	First Test	
UNIT II	SENSATION AND PERCEPTION	
4	Touch, Taste, Smell, Hearing and Seeing	6 and 7
5	Visual Perception and Speech Perception	8
	Second Test	
UNIT III	MOTIVATION	
6	Introduction to Motivation	10
7	Sexual Motivation	11
8	Emotion, Stress, and Coping	12
	Third Test	
UNIT IV	LEARNING AND MEMORY	
9	Conditioning and Desensitization	13
	Operant Conditioning	14
10	Memory	15
	Fourth Test	
UNIT V	MATURATION AND DEVELOPMENT	
11	Physical and Emotional Development	17
12	Cognitive Development	18
UNIT VI	PERSONALITY THEORY	
13	Survey of Personality Theories	19
14	Individual Differences	20
15	Abnormal Psychology	21
16	Psychotherapy	22
17	FINAL EXAM	

Evaluation: Grade for the course will be based on performance on the four tests (60%), performance on the final (20%), and two written assignments (20%).

Policies: You may make up a test only if you have made arrangements with me before the date the test is given. If written assignments are late, they will receive a lower grade. Attendance will be taken.

Please come to class on time, take notes on all lectures, and do reading assignments prior to the class in which that topic will be discussed.

If you are having trouble in the class, tutoring is available at the Tutoring Center (room 2048).

■
E X E R C I S E   1

Complete this worksheet for one of your classes. Get the information from the course syllabus, from the instructor's orientation lecture, or, if necessary, by asking the instructor directly.

1. Title of the class
2. The instructor's name
3. The instructor's office location, office hours, and phone number
4. Books and materials to be purchased for the class
5. Is an outline of the course provided?
6. Are the goals for the course named? If so, where?
7. Is a list of reading assignments and when they are due provided?
8. Are some books and materials for the class held on reserve in the library?
9. What homework do you need to prepare for class? (Give type and how and where assignments are given.)
10. Exams: how many, what type, when given, what percent of grade?
11. Written assignments: description and when due
12. Outside work required, such as labs or field trip
13. Grading criteria
14. Classroom policy on attendance
15. Policy on alternate grades (such as an "I" [incomplete] grade)
16. Policy on lateness
17. Policy on late or missed assignments
18. Other course requirements (e.g., classroom participation, conferences with the instructor)
19. Is extra help available? From where?
20. Other important information about the course

Note that you can use this list as a checklist for gathering information about your other classes as well.

ARE YOU RIGHT FOR THIS COURSE?

You will want to double-check your first week that you've been correctly placed in courses that have different levels, like math and science classes, writing classes, and classes with prerequisites. A **prerequisite** is a requirement for a class that must be completed before a course is taken. For example, an Intermediate Algebra class may have as a prerequisite a course in Elementary Algebra or a score of 85 or better on the math placement test. If you don't have either prerequisite, your chances of doing well in that course are poor. The college catalog and the current course listings will list course prerequisites. If you find yourself registered in a class for which you don't have the proper prerequisites, discuss with the instructor or your advisor whether you should drop the class.

If you've been placed in a course as a result of your scores on a basic skills placement test, you want to be sure that you've been directed to the right class. When you get a sense of what material is covered in the course, form your own opinion as to whether the work is too difficult or too easy for you. Your test score may not have been an accurate reflection of your actual ability, or you might feel more comfortable taking a lower level course. If you believe that you may have been misplaced in a course, bring your case to the instructor's attention.

IS THIS COURSE RIGHT FOR YOU?

The kind of information gathering you did in Exercise 1 will enable you to decide if a course you registered for is one you should take. One of the advantages of college is that you have some say in what courses you take. Often, even if a course if required, you have a choice of different instructors and different sections. Use the first few days of each semester to exercise your options. If you feel more comfortable in small discussion classes, but find that you registered for a section of Psychology 101 that is a large lecture class, see if you can locate a smaller section. If your humanities instructor announces that he will not be discussing the history of film and you are a serious film buff, scout around for other instructors who include film on their syllabus. If the book for your biology class looks dull while your roommate's text looks exciting, see if you can get into your roommate's section. If you picked art over music when you registered, but have recently developed a burning interest in music, try to drop your art class and pick up a music class.

If you are considering switching classes or sections, discuss the move with your advisor first. Then make your move as soon as possible. The first sessions of a class are important for learning the basic principles of a subject. If you add a class a week after it's begun, you're decreasing your own chances of success in that class—and you'll have to work double time the first week to catch up on what you missed.

COURSES AND YOUR COLLEGE PROGRAM

Finally, evaluate the way each course you are taking fits into your college program as a whole. Each college course you take should move you toward your long-term goals—of fulfilling requirements for graduation, of preparing you for work in your major field, and of giving you opportunities to learn about subjects that interest you. You can expect to spend a lot of time and effort on each course that you're enrolled in, and taking a course that doesn't fit your goals is a waste of your energies.

Probably most of the courses you take in your first year or so will be courses that fulfill the general education or core curriculum requirements of your college, courses that prepare you for work in your major, or courses that provide you with essential basic skills in reading, writing, and math. Your top priority should be to take any basic skills courses that are recommended for you as soon as possible, as you will need good reading, writing, and math skills immediately to do well in any of your other courses. If you postpone taking a recommended writing course until late in your college career, you may struggle needlessly through many writing assignments because of your neglect.

■ _____

EXERCISE 2

Write an initial evaluation of each of the courses you are taking this term. For each course, give the following information:

> Your academic reasons for taking the course
> Your opinion as to whether your placement in the course is correct
> What the course is about and if it matches your preconceptions as to what material would be covered
> Your initial reaction to the instructor and to the instructor's approach
> Your initial impression of the textbook
> Your evaluation of whether this course will be difficult or easy for you

ADDING AND DROPPING CLASSES

If you need to switch sections or classes for some reason, visit the new class (with the professor's permission), so that you can see if it suits your needs. However, continue to attend the class you registered for until you make a decision and until you actually add the new class and drop the old one. That way, whichever class you stay in, you'll have gotten the important information presented in early class meetings. It's not always possible to switch sections, of course, but many professors are receptive to a direct and reasoned plea from a prospective student, particularly if you explain your reasons for wanting to switch. Persistence works also—if you show up for the first two or three sessions of a class you're hoping to get into, the instructor may allow you to take the place of another student who was a "no-show."

Be sure that you officially change your registration if you decide to add or drop a class.

MAKING A STRONG START

In addition to sizing up your classes, there are several things you can do in the first weeks of class to get yourself off to a good start. Here are ten recommendations for you:

1. *Speak out in class the first week.*   In many classes, it's important to participate by answering questions, asking questions, or making comments in a discussion. Many students find it difficult to speak out in class. If you make it a point to say something—anything—in class the first week, you'll have broken the sound barrier in that class. Try answering a simple question, or asking a question about classroom procedures. (See Chapter 6 for more help on how to participate actively in class discussions.)

2. *Practice listening in each of your classes.*   You may be surprised to find that listening in your classes requires an intensive effort on your part. Go to each class session prepared to work hard at listening for the entire period. (See Chapter 4 for advice on listening in classes.)

3. *Find places to study.*   As you explore the campus, scout out some places where you can study between classes—the library, an empty classroom, a study carrel in the student center, or a quiet corner in the cafeteria, for example. If you are able to use breaks between classes for short study sessions, you can make more efficient use of your time. (For more advice on managing your time, see Chapter 3.)

4. *Start taking notes the first day.*   You may not have had to take notes in class at your last school, but you need to take notes in every session of every college class. Begin at the first class meeting when the professor is giving you an overview of the course. Write down anything that strikes you as important, striving for a page of notes for each class meeting. (You'll learn more about notetaking in Chapter 5.)

5. *Set up a system for notes and handouts.*   For each class you take, you can expect to accumulate a lot of material—your notes from each class meeting, as well as handouts, charts, or copies of articles that the professor distributes. You need to keep all these materials together and organized for studying. Spend some time in the college bookstore looking at the different folders, binders, and notebooks that are available and choose items that will work for you. Also, buy a **college organizer**—a daily assignment book to use for keeping track of your assignments, writing down your schedule, and recording your test grades.

6. *Survey each of your textbooks.*   Buy your textbooks as soon as you can, and take the time to preview each one, paying attention to what material the book covers, how it is organized, the audience it is intended for, and what features and study aids it has. The preface to the textbook may have helpful advice on reading and studying from the text. (See Chapter 7 for more advice on learning from textbooks.)

7. *Meet another student in each class.*   Remember the buddy system from swimming? The same system is useful to keep you from drowning in college. Meet another student in each of your classes, and make an agreement to call each other if either one of you doesn't understand an assignment or misses a class.

8. *Stop by the instructor's office.*   One difference between college professors and high school teachers is that professors have office hours when they are available to talk to students individually. During the first few weeks of the term, make it a point to locate your professors' offices. Stop in for a few minutes to introduce yourself to each one and to ask any questions you have about the class. If you've been to your professor's office once, you're more likely to stop by later when you're in need of help.

9. *Go to all class sessions.*   Many students are overwhelmed by the comparative freedom of college compared to high school. In high school, whether it was last year or twenty years ago, you had a rigid schedule of classes to follow, and if you cut class, everyone knew about it—your teacher, your division teacher, your advisor, and your parents. In college, if you decide to skip a class, it's likely that no one will even notice. That's because the instructors make you responsible for deciding whether you want to learn or not. If you don't attend class, you won't.

10. *Get in the habit of doing all assignments on time.*   A student once pointed out that homework takes just as long whether you do it on time or late, so you might as well do it on time. Her point is a good one. Use the early weeks of the term to get in the habit of being prepared for each class. In fact, usually the assignments in the first weeks of a term are relatively light, so you might use those weeks to get a bit ahead in each class.

SUMMARY

The first class sessions of each term provide an opportunity for you to get an overview of the course and find out what your responsibilities are for the class. Use this information to make sure that you've been correctly placed in your classes and that each of your classes fits your needs. Also, take steps to get yourself off to a strong start the first weeks of the term. Make a point to start actively participating in each of your classes by attending all class sessions, speaking out in each class, starting to take notes from the first day, working on listening actively, and doing all assignments. Also, take time to familiarize yourself with your textbooks, to set up a system for organizing your materials, and to locate places on campus to study. Start to build a system of support for each of your classes by getting to know a student in each class and by visiting the instructor in his or her office. Taking active charge of your academic progress right at the beginning of the term is a safeguard against the kind of "first term floundering" that many beginning college students experience.

■
JOURNAL WRITING

1. Write up your personal strategy for succeeding in each of the classes you have enrolled in.
2. Explain the system you plan to use for your notes and handouts for your classes and why you prefer that system.
3. To monitor your use of time, keep a diary of your time use for the first weeks of the semester. At the end of each day, summarize the time you spent going to class, studying, relaxing, working, or on maintenance activities (activities like eating, traveling, getting dressed, and so on).

■
ACADEMIC WRITING

Using Exercise 1 as a draft, write a report on the class that you feel will be the most difficult this term. Use the following outline:

Title of the class: _____

Instructor's name: _____

I   Overview of the class:
II Materials for the class:
III Requirements for the class:
IV Evaluation policy:

2

ORIENTING YOURSELF TO COLLEGE

In this chapter you will

▲ explore the services and resources available at your college
▲ learn the academic requirements for graduation
▲ work on designing your academic program
▲ learn about the grading system at your college

The idea of orientation originated with explorers investigating a new territory. It was necessary for them to survey the land, investigate how they needed to adapt to survive in that environment, and chart a course for their travels. Likewise, when you orient yourself to college, you learn the information you need in order to survive and thrive in college.

This chapter is an opportunity for you to begin. In working through the exercises in this chapter, you will need your own copy of your college catalog, a copy of the current term schedule, and any information that was handed out to you during registration or orientation, such as a list of student services or college organizations. Any information that is not available in these sources you can find out with some leg-work—by asking someone, or by calling the appropriate campus office.

SURVIVAL INFORMATION

Begin by learning information that may help you survive the first few weeks of college.

■
E X E R C I S E   1

Between now and the next class session, locate the answers to as many of the following questions as you can. Use the sources of information suggested above.

1. What is the deadline for paying your tuition for this term?
2. What happens if tuition isn't paid on time?
3. Where is the financial aid office?
4. Are there any regulations governing students' use of cars?
5. Do students need a parking sticker? If so, where can you get one, and how much does it cost?
6. Where on campus can you cash a check?
7. Where can you go to watch your favorite soap opera between classes?
8. Where can you go for help if you're looking for a part-time job?
9. What buses or trains are located near campus? Where can you get schedules for them?
10. Where's a good place to get a quick lunch?
11. Is there a swimming pool on campus? If so, where is it located and what are its hours?
12. Does the campus have a child care center? If so, what age range does it accommodate and what are the hours?
13. Is there anywhere on campus you can play a video game? If so, name one game located there.
14. What hours is the library open?
15. Where do you go to get your I.D. picture taken and/or validated?
16. Name all bookstores that service your campus.
17. When is the last day this term you can add a course? When is the last day you can drop a course and get a full refund on tuition?
18. Name an off-campus restaurant you can walk to.
19. Where on campus can you get a refund if you lose money in a vending machine?
20. Does the library have a record collection and a listening booth?
21. Are lockers available on campus? If so, where do you go to rent one?
22. How could you find someone to type a paper for you? How much would you expect it to cost? Are typewriters available anywhere on campus for student use?
23. Are there computers on campus available for student use? If so, where and what kind?
24. Where could you go to get something notarized?
25. Where is the lost-and-found office?
26. Where do students go to socialize off campus?

27. Name a campus club that you might be interested in joining.
28. Name a student event that is coming up this month or next.
29. What is the name of one student athletic team?
30. Does any group show movies on campus? If so, name one movie that's coming up and where it will be shown.
31. Where could you go for medical help if you injured yourself while exercising on campus?
32. What holidays are there this term?
33. Is there anywhere on campus that you can get an ice cream cone?

COLLEGE SERVICES

A college or university is more than just a place where classes are held. Most colleges offer a wide range of services for students, from career counseling to health services. Often colleges provide services to students for free or at minimal cost. For example, personal counseling through a campus counseling center is usually much more affordable than private counseling off campus. You will probably not use all the services provided by your college, but if you know about them, you will have the option of using them when you need to.

■
E X E R C I S E   2

Use your college catalog, student handbook, and other sources of information available to you (such as bulletin boards) to investigate which of the following services are available at your college. If a service is available, attach a comment explaining what you learned about it, such as location and hours.

Service	Available on your campus?	Comment
Academic advising	_____	_____
Counseling for students on academic probation	_____	_____
Math tutoring	_____	_____
Reading tutoring	_____	_____
Writing tutoring	_____	_____
Supplemental instruction	_____	_____

Support groups for:
    Minority students   _____   _____

    Transfer students   _____   _____

    Returning adults/
    nontraditional students   _____   _____

    Women   _____   _____

    International students   _____   _____

    Handicapped students   _____   _____

Health services   _____   _____

Student job placement   _____   _____

Medical insurance   _____   _____

Life insurance   _____   _____

Exercise facilities/programs   _____   _____

Personal counseling   _____   _____

Career counseling   _____   _____

Financial aid counseling   _____   _____

Child care   _____   _____

Self-development classes
and workshops   _____   _____

National student
exchange program   _____   _____

International student
exchange program   _____   _____

One resource that you are certain to need your first term is the college library. Information on orienting yourself to your college library and on using the library to do assignments is found in Chapter 16 in this textbook.

MEETING ACADEMIC REQUIREMENTS

The material in the front of your college catalog spells out the requirements that you have to fulfill in order to be awarded a degree by the college you are attending. You are responsible for knowing what these requirements are and for making sure you fulfill them. In fact, even if some requirements are changed in the future, you will still be bound by the requirements that are listed in the college catalog for the year you were admitted. So it makes sense to know these requirements thoroughly.

Your college may provide academic advising services for you, but even if you have an excellent advisor, you are ultimately responsible for ensuring that you meet the requirements of your college. No one else is as intensely interested in your college career as you are, so it is in your self-interest to actively seek out information about college requirements, double-check any advice you are given, and frequently monitor your progress toward graduation.

■
—————————————
E X E R C I S E 3

Read the material in your college catalog that explains the requirements for a degree at your college. As you read, highlight the information that is relevant for you. (When you highlight, you use a watercolor pen to make important information in a book stand out.) Based on your reading of the college catalog and on any other sources of information available to you, answer the following questions:

1. What general education or core curriculum courses are you required to take?
2. How many credits are required for graduation? How should these credits be distributed?
3. What are the minimum and maximum number of credits you can register for as a full-time student?
4. Is there a minimum grade that you need to get in certain courses in order for them to count toward graduation?
5. What grade average must you have to qualify for graduation?
6. Are there any competency tests you must pass as a requirement at your college? What are the deadlines by which you must have passed them?
7. Are you required to have a minor as well as a major?

INVESTIGATING A MAJOR

At some point in your college career, you will need to select a major field of study. One purpose of general education or core curriculum courses is to expose students to a broad range of fields before they decide upon a major course of study. So even if you think you know what you want your major to be, you should be open to the possibility that you might change your mind. A college career counseling office can often help you if you're undecided about a major by providing information about career options for different majors or by administering an interest inventory to you.

Each major field has its own set of requirements, and these are also contained in the college catalog. You need to become familiar with the requirements for the majors you're considering so that you can make an intelligent decision as to which field you prefer and so that you can select courses that will prepare you for majoring in that field. The undergraduate advisor for majors in that department can often advise you about the courses that will help prepare you for that major.

■
_____

EXERCISE 4

Select one area of study that you are considering as a major. In your college catalog, read the information about the requirements for majoring in that field. Summarize the information, including:

Required courses
Any prerequisites for required courses
Any criteria you have to meet before declaring your
   major
Total number of credits required in the field
Distribution of credits
Grade or grade-point average requirements
Any non-course requirements for the major, such as an
   internship, a comprehensive exam, or a major paper

SELECTING COURSES

Your college career consists of a series of educational experiences, most of them organized around classes. Teach yourself to be an intelligent consumer of college classes—to shop around for the best value, just as you shop for clothes. Such care in selecting your classes often means the difference between a good education and a mediocre one.

The time to begin selecting your courses for next term is at the beginning of the previous term. Begin with a worksheet like that in Figure 2.1, including academic needs, possibilities, and preferences. If you have a college advisor, your next step should be a conference with him or her. Right around preregistration time, students are lining up in the halls to see their advisors, and the advisors are often too rushed to take the time they'd like to with each student. If you see your advisor early in the term, you will get better attention. Bring your worksheet with you—both of you can use that as a starting point for your conference. In addition to a general advisor, you might also wish to talk to a departmental advisor, the person who advises students who are majoring in a certain field.

Figure 2.1   **SAMPLE PLANNING SHEET FOR COURSES**

Need:	Possibilities for Fall Term
Basic Skills Courses English 100, then English 101 & 102 Math 099 then College Algebra	* English 100 (try for Robinet's section) * Math 099 *= have to take these
General Education Courses 3 humanities classes 4 science classes 3 social science classes	{ History of Modern Europe or Colonial Times pick one! { Geology 101 Physics for Practical People Our Changing Environment
Prerequisites for Major English 101 College Algebra Introduction to Scientific Methodology	Introduction to Scientific Methodology (ask advisor if I should take this now)
Interests / other History of Film Weight Training	Weight Training (if I can fit it in!)

You can also investigate different courses and instructors in a variety of ways: by noticing the textbooks the bookstore has stocked for different instructors, by listening to friends' comments about their classes, and even by visiting a class, with the instructor's permission.

Finally, remember that the earlier you register, the more likely you are to get your first choices.

MAKING THE GRADE

How important are grades? A brief answer to that question is that grades are to be valued to the extent that they enhance learning and criticized to the extent that they hurt learning. For example, wanting to get a good grade in a course can make you work harder. In that case, grades are playing a positive role. On the other hand, sometimes you might avoid taking a course only because you're afraid of getting a poor grade in it. In that case, grades are playing a negative role.

Grades provide feedback on your progress in courses and in college. A low grade at midterm time is a message that you should change your learning strategy in that course or seek extra help. Your **grade-point average** (GPA) indicates whether you are making satisfactory progress toward completing the college's requirements.

At most colleges, letter grades (A,B,C,D,F) are used instead of numerical grades (87, 64, 93, and so on). Each letter grade has a point value attached to it. Some colleges use plus and minus grades, like B + or C −, while at other schools the same value is attached to a B + and a B.

Your grade-point average or GPA is calculated by dividing the point equivalent of your grade in a course by the credit value of the course. (See Figure 2.2 for an example.) In a semester system, for example, most courses that meet three times a week are three-credit courses, but a biology course with lab might be worth four credits.

At most schools, students must maintain a certain grade-point average or else they are placed on **academic probation**. Students on academic probation have to meet certain requirements, such as bringing up their average within a prescribed time, working with an academic advisor, or taking academic support courses. Students who do not meet these requirements are eventually dropped. Of course, you hope that you will never be placed on academic probation. But you need to know what rules govern students in this situation.

Colleges also have other, alternate grades that students can receive. An I (incomplete) grade may be an option for students who have not completed course requirements during the term. A W (withdraw) or R (registered) grade may be offered for students who elect to drop a class after registration. Pass–fail grades may be an option for students in some courses. Under a pass–fail option, there are

Figure 2.2

CALCULATING
YOUR GRADE-POINT AVERAGE

Here are the steps to take in calculating your grade-point average.

1. List your courses, the grade you got in each course, and the credits for each course. Then multiply the course credits by the grade value for each course.

COURSE	CREDITS	GRADE	GRADE VALUE	GRADE POINTS
Psych 101	3	B	3.00	9.00
Humanities 201	3	C	2.00	6.00
Biology 101	4	B	3.00	12.00
Intermediate Algebra	4	A	4.00	16.00
Writing	2	D	1.00	2.00
	16			45.00

2. Total the number of credits you completed and the number of grade points and divide the total number of grade points you earned by the total number of credits:

TOTAL NUMBER OF CREDITS	TOTAL GRADE POINTS	AVERAGE
16	45.00	$45.00 \div 16 = 2.815$

This student's average for the term would be 2.815, or a high C.

only two possible grades for a course: a P for passing work or an F for failing work. Most of these alternate grades have rules that govern the conditions under which they might be used.

Students can use these alternate grades to their advantage. At some colleges, if you are in clear danger of failing a course, you can drop the class, although you probably will have to pay for the class. You can request an I grade from an instructor if you suddenly find out that you have more work than you can possibly complete that term, or if illness or another unanticipated crisis prevents you from completing a course. Incomplete courses should be made up as soon as possible, and preferably before the next term begins. Opt to take a course on a pass–fail basis when you want to take a challenging course but don't want to be penalized for your lack of background or talent in the area. For example, a business major interested in photography might want to pursue that interest by taking a course in photography intended for art majors. Taking the course on a pass–fail basis would allow her to pursue her interest without worrying about the grade she might get.

■
EXERCISE 5

Write a report on the grade system used by your college, including:

Point value for different grades
Minimum grade-point average requirements
Alternate grades and rules attached to their use
Academic probation

SUMMARY

The information that you learn from orienting yourself to college is the basis for your taking an active role in planning your college career. As a student, it's useful to know about the range of services and resources available at your college, so that you can make informed decisions as to what services to take advantage of. Also, since you are the one most directly interested in your academic progress, it makes sense for you to develop a long-range perspective on your college career by familiarizing yourself with the academic requirements for a degree and by beginning to think about the areas you will select as your major. This information will help you plot out a course of study for the upcoming terms. Finally, knowing your college grading system will allow you to monitor your academic progress.

■
JOURNAL WRITING

1. What major or majors are you considering? What attracts you to these areas of study?
2. Talk to another student majoring in this field about his or her experiences as a major, and write up a report of what you learn from this interview.
3. Reflect on your own experience with grades and write about times when you think grades helped you learn and times when you feel that they interfered with your learning.

■
ACADEMIC WRITING

Imagine that you were your own advisor and write yourself a letter listing the courses that you think you should take during the next three terms and the reasons for your suggestions. As you make up your list, keep in mind:

> Courses you need to improve your basic skills (reading, writing, math)
> Required core curriculum courses
> Courses that are prerequisites for courses in your preferred major
> Courses that will help you investigate a major you're considering
> Courses that will allow you to pursue a personal interest
> Alternate courses in the above categories

Check the course descriptions provided in the catalog for further information and general descriptions of the courses you list.

3

MANAGING YOUR TIME

In this chapter you will learn:

▲ to work up a plan to manage your study time
▲ to use a daily list to remind you of your obligations
▲ to use a calendar to keep on schedule for long-term assignments

When you were in high school, whether is was last year or twenty years ago, your time was managed for you. The greater part of your day in school was spent in classes, with perhaps one period a day set aside for study hall. Most homework was due the next day. Teachers may have reminded you frequently when assignments were due or overdue. Perhaps when you got home, your parents reminded you to do your homework at a certain time. In college, the situation is very different. Your total amount of time spent in class is probably much lower, perhaps between twelve and twenty hours a week. You might have large blocks of time when you have no classes scheduled. Also, there are probably fewer checks on your use of your time by your parents or your professors. You are in charge of how you use your time.

Different college students often face two very different sets of problems with time. One group, used to the more structured time of earlier high school days, is overwhelmed with the amount of free time available and, perhaps, tempted by all the ways time can be enjoyably spent on a college campus—in the cafeteria, in the game room, playing cards, making new friends, watching television. Another group has the opposite problem—too little time left for studying, because work or family responsibilities take up much of their out-of-class time. Both groups will profit from learning the three techniques of time management presented in this chapter: designing a study plan as a tool for planning a study strategy, using a Things to Do or TTD, list to keep track of daily obligations, and using a calendar to schedule work on long-term assignments.

MAKING A STUDY PLAN

One of the most effective time management techniques is the **study plan**. A study plan is simply a systematic way of approaching your present time structure and needs. Half the value of a study plan comes from what you learn during the process of constructing one, because it makes you take a realistic look at your use of time. The rest of the value lies in the finished product, which becomes a useful guide to organizing your days. Some people dislike the idea of a study plan or schedule because they feel it's too rigid. But remember, the

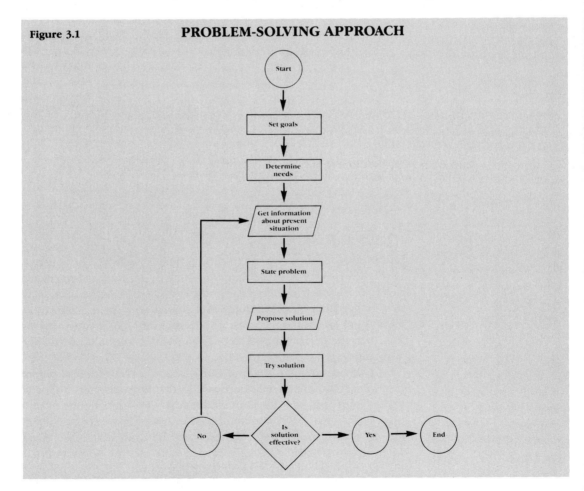

Figure 3.1   **PROBLEM-SOLVING APPROACH**

study plan you come up with is your own creation; if you decide that it's too rigid, then you can revise it to make it more flexible.

One way to approach the question of your use of time is to use a procedure adapted from business management techniques called a problem-solving approach (see Figure 3.1). A problem-solving approach is a systematic procedure for analyzing a problem, proposing a solution, and evaluating it. Since this technique can be used to tackle many problems, it's useful to learn in itself. The steps in the problem-solving approach are as follows:

1. Define your goals.
2. Determine your needs.
3. Analyze the problems.
4. Work out a plan for solving the problems.
5. Try out the solution and evaluate its effectiveness.

In applying a problem-solving approach to managing your time, you would follow these five steps. The next few pages provide step-by-step instructions and exercises to teach you this technique.

1. Define your goals. Decide on what your goals are for the current term. This task requires some thought on your part, as the

Reprinted by permission: Tribune Media Services

setting of goals involves self-examination. Try to make your goals realistic—for instance, if you are taking a difficult course in advanced algebra, a goal of getting an A in that course may be unrealistic. Include at least one goal for each course you are taking, as well as any personal goals that will take up your time. In listing your goals, consider what you'd like to learn this term and how you'd like to change your behavior this term, as well as the grades you'd like to get. Here are some examples:

> Learn enough about word processing to write my paper using a computer
> Decide whether I'm more suited for a major in accounting or art
> Survive my Western Civ course
> Maintain a B average
> Finish work on paper for art course I got an I (incomplete) in
> Become good enough on drums to try out for band
> Exercise more frequently

EXERCISE 1

Make a list of your goals for the present term.

_____

_____

_____

_____

_____

_____

_____

_____

2. Determine your needs. Analyze how much time per week you need to study for each of your courses. Use the information you have about reading assignments and other required work to estimate the amount of time you need to spend on each course per week. As a general rule, figure an average of two hours of study time for each hour of class time. In addition to the average amount of study time

Figure 3.2   **SAMPLE ANALYSIS OF STUDY REQUIREMENTS**

Course	Tasks	Time
Psychology	Reading, reviewing notes, studying for tests	*6 hrs
Biology	Reading, reviewing notes, working problems, lab reports, studying for weekly tests	8 hrs
Humanities	Reading, reviewing notes, doing journal assignments, going to exhibits	4–6 hrs
English	Writing, doing textbook exercises, reading	4–6 hrs
Academic Skills	Reading, doing journal assignments, doing projects	4–5 hrs

*10 hours during exam weeks

per week, list the types of studying you need to do for each course, and any comments about special time requirements, such as time needed for a special project. Figure 3.2 is a sample analysis of study needs.

■

E X E R C I S E   2   List your courses. For each course, name the types of work required, and estimate the amount of time you need to spend studying each week for that course.

Course	Tasks	Amount of time per week

Another type of need is the kind of atmosphere in which you study best. Some people are night owls, preferring to work when everyone else has gone to sleep, while others concentrate best in the morning. Some people like to work in a quiet corner of the library, while others find quiet corners too conducive to napping, and prefer to work where there's some nondistracting noise. For some, home is a good place to study, while for others the distractions (and temptations) of home force a retreat to another environment. Answer the following questionnaire to give yourself a better sense of your study needs.

■
E X E R C I S E   3

1. During what period or periods of the day are you best able to concentrate? _____

   _____

2. What kinds of studying do you do that require a lot of concentration? _____

   _____

3. What kinds of studying require less intense concentration? _____

   _____

4. How much quiet do you need while studying? _____

   _____

5. Do you need the same level of quiet for different types of studying? _____

   _____

6. For what kinds of studying do you need large blocks of time?

   _____

   _____

7. What kinds of studying can you do in shorter study periods? _____

   _____

8. What places are available to you for studying? _____

   _____

9. What kinds of distractions do you need to remove yourself from when you study? _____

   _____

10. Where on campus is a good place for you to study? _____

_____

11. Where at home is a good place for you to study? _____

_____

PROCRASTINATION

Things that lead to procrastination	. . . and how to deal with them
Magnification: You make an assignment so large that you intimidate yourself.	Break the assignment down into a list of smaller, more manageable jobs and set up a work schedule.
Lack of Motivation: You avoid the assignment because it doesn't interest you.	Get started. It's easier to get interested once you prime the pump. Once you do a little, you'll feel like doing a little more.
Fear of Success or Failure: You wait until the last minute to begin because you then have a wonderful excuse for not having done well.	(a) Have a stern talk with yourself. (b) Talk with another student who's already working on the same assignment to remind you that real people can do this task.
Too Many Pulls on Your Time: You have a lot of obligations that are necessary to survival, like a job or children.	(a) Be realistic as to how many obligations you can handle at one time. (b) Give the people that you're supporting a chance to support you in return by sharing some of the work.

3. Analyze what the problems are. The next step is to identify the difficulties you're having with your use of time now. You can use observation and reflection to do so. For example, consider doing a time analysis by writing down how you spend your time each day for a week and then totalling how much time you spend on each type of activity when the week is over. (This kind of record keeping was suggested in Journal 3 in Chapter 1.) Students who do a time analysis are often surprised by their observations—for example, sometimes the number of hours they spend watching TV are much greater than their original estimate, while the number of hours they spend studying are fewer than they thought.

You can also get a deeper sense of the problems you have with your present use of time by reflecting on them, as the next exercise directs you to do.

EXERCISE 4

Use writing as a tool to reflect on your present use of time. Comment on the following areas:

Activities that you don't spend enough time on
Activities that you spend too much time on
Things that distract you from studying
Problems you have with using your time now

When you've finished, make a list that summarizes the main problems your reflections have uncovered.

*4.   **Work out a plan for solving the problems.***   A study plan is your attempt at a solution to your time problems. It is a useful tool for making decisions about how you want to use your time. Here's an example: One student, who played in a band, began his plan by blocking out time for practicing and performing each week. He had also registered for a heavy load of courses. In making out his plan, he realized that there were not enough hours in the week for him to practice and study for all his courses as well. Something had to go. (He decided to drop one of his courses.)

Your completed plan will also be a guide for you. It probably won't predict how you will spend every day—you know that things will come up that will cause a change in schedule. But, just as a financial budget reminds you of your money needs, a study plan will remind you of your time needs. So, if you decide to go out for pizza one night instead of studying, you will remember that you're "borrowing" three hours of study time, hours that you need to pay back.

Figure 3.3 shows a sample study plan for a student who is taking five classes and working part-time. Study it as a model before you begin to construct your own plan.

To make out your study plan, use the grid that follows on page 30 (Figure 3.4). Work in pencil, so you can make changes as needed. Follow these steps:

a. In the first column, fill in the hours in your day, beginning with the earliest you get up, and ending with your typical bedtime.

Figure 3.3   **SAMPLE STUDY PLAN**

DAY / HOUR	MON	TUES	WED	THURS	FRI	SAT	SUN
8:00	✕	French	✕	French	✕	W	Free Time
9:00	Biology	coffee	Biology	coffee (prep for psych disc)	Biology	O	
10:00	Read - Hum (library)	Psych	Read - Hum (library)	Psych	Read - Hum (library)	R	
11:00	Hum I	Lunch	Hum I	Lunch	Hum I	K	
12:00	English	Biology -	English	Biology -	English		
1:00	Lunch	read, review	Lunch	study	Lunch		
2:00	Bio	notes	Hum writing	for quiz	Review notes - Hum		
3:00	Lab	✕	asgt	✕	Swimming		Library - reading or
4:00	Bio - write up lab report	W	Psych - homework	W			work on long - term
5:00	Begin read asgt for week	O R	asgt and review notes	O R	✕		projects
6:00	Dinner	K	Dinner	K	Free		Dinner
7:00	Psych - reading	✕	French - reading,	✕	Time		Free (or
8:00		Psych - reading	exercises, flashcards	English - read, write			make up studying)
9:00	French exercises	Psych - review notes	TV time	essay			
10:00	TV time	English - reading		Bio - review study notes			English - journal
11:00				for quiz			work, essay writing
12:00							

Subject	Hours of Study Per Week
French	3 hrs
English	5 hrs.
Biology	9 hrs.
Hum	6 hrs.
Psych	7 hrs.

Figure 3.4   STUDY PLAN GRID

DAY / HOUR	MON	TUES	WED	THURS	FRI	SAT	SUN

Subject   Hours of Study Per Week

_____   _____

_____   _____

_____   _____

_____   _____

_____   _____

b. Next fill in your fixed obligations—scheduled class time, work time, regularly scheduled meetings, and so on. If your work schedule or work hours vary from week to week, chart in a typical week, and note at the bottom the kinds of variations you can expect.

c. Put X's in time slots for "maintenance activities"—travel time, meal time, and so on.

d. The time you have left is the time you have available for studying and relaxing.

Now the real planning begins. Look for a balance between study time and play time. Also, as you plan, consider your preferences and habits—don't plan a heavy dose of studying late at night if you've tried studying at night in the past and know that you're not very alert then. On the other hand, do some experimenting—maybe a certain time might be very good for studying, even though you've never tried it. This is the step at which you will be using the eraser on your pencil, as you try out alternate ideas and decide which ones you prefer. In periods that you schedule for studying, be specific. Name the subject you'll be studying, the type of study, and, if necessary, the place. Use the sample plan (Figure 3.3) as a guide.

As you work, refer back to your planning work on earlier exercises to remind you of your goals for the term, the time you estimate to be needed for studying each course, the activities you felt you were spending too little or too much time on, and the problems you want this plan to resolve. Continue to work and make changes until you are satisfied that you've created a workable plan.

When you are finished, use the space provided at the bottom of the page, note down any expected variations in your planned schedule from week to week. Also write down any steps you need to take to implement this plan.

5. Give that solution a trial and evaluate its effectiveness. The next step is to use your plan as a guide to your daily activities. Take one day at a time. Since following your new plan will involve a change in some of your old habits, don't expect instant success. Consider rewarding yourself each day you follow it closely. Consult your plan once in the morning, and mentally make any adjustments in it to fit in an errand you have to run or a lunch date you made. See if you can trade off so that each day you end up with the same amount of study time that you had planned. A reasonable period to try out your plan would be for two to three weeks.

At the end of your trial period, ask yourself how effective your schedule was. Was your plan realistic, or was it too ambitious? Did it provide enough time for studying? for relaxing? Did you try to study at any of the times you had planned and find yourself too sleepy or too distracted? Are there any improvements you could make in the plan? Do you need to make any radical changes, such as cutting back on work hours, dropping an activity, or withdrawing from a class? Did making the plan enable you to solve some of your problems with time? Did trying to follow the plan help you use your time more effectively? Asking yourself these questions will help you evaluate the effectiveness of your solutions. Your answers may lead you to revise your plan, coming up with a new plan to try out, or going further back in the problem-solving process to reconsider your goals and problems before working forward to a revised study plan.

You may also find that you need to revise your study plan even if it is a good one for now. For instance, in the weeks around midterm and final exams, you will probably want to devote more time to studying and less to relaxing. Also, any time there is a change in your fixed obligations, such as when your job hours change, you quit a job, start a new job, change your course load, or start a new term, you'll need to work out a new study plan.

USING A THINGS TO DO (TTD) LIST

While a study plan is a plan of attack for a semester, a Things to Do or **TTD list** is a tool for making the most effective use of your day. It is a list of tasks you want to accomplish that day. Just as with a study plan, the process of making a TTD list is as valuable as the product. Making a TTD list causes you to concentrate on your obligations and consider which jobs are most pressing. Referring to the list during the day reminds you of what you want to accomplish that day. Crossing out the items you have taken care of can be a very satisfying testament to your productivity.

To make a TTD list, first list the tasks you need to do that day. Don't include routine activities that you're not likely to forget, like attending class or eating breakfast. Then label items according to their priority. Use the following system of labels:

A—for tasks that must be done that day
B—for tasks that should be done soon, but not necessarily that day
C—for tasks you need to remember but which aren't that pressing
Z—for tasks you need to remember, but which can be postponed indefinitely

Figure 3.5 is a sample TTD list using priority labels. To make the best use of your time, concentrate on the A-priority items first, and then the B-priority items. Turn to the C and Z items only after you have attended to those top priority tasks.

You'll probably be able to use your TTD list most effectively if

Figure 3.5

SAMPLE TTD LIST

Tuesday, November 26th

A   Study for Humanities quiz

B   Make appointment for haircut

A   Call Marla about Saturday

A   Read Ch. 8, Biology

B   Get copy of next assignment
     from Prof. Bowler

Z   Clean desk

C   Get car washed

B   Pick topic for psychology paper

Z   Write Uncle Martin

you make it out in the evening or early in the morning. Carry it around with you in a convenient place so that you can refer back to it—there's nothing more frustrating than making a TTD list and then being unable to locate it. Some suggestions:

Buy a **college organizer**—a daily assignment book designed especially for students—from your school bookstore and use it for your TTD list as well as for your daily assignments and appointments.

Use paper or large (5 x 8) index cards for your list and clip them to the front of your notebook.

At the end of the day, cross out the tasks you've completed, and edit your list or make a new one for the next day, including tasks you didn't get to and new obligations that have cropped up.

■
E X E R C I S E 5

Make a TTD list for tomorrow. Label tasks on it A, B, C, or Z according to their priority. Carry a copy of the list with you tomorrow and refer to it often. Try to complete all the tasks that you labeled A.

USING A CALENDAR

The third tool important to your success in managing your academic time is a **term calendar**. Your calendar will serve two functions. You can use it to keep track of important dates such as preregistration, the dates of your exams, and your brother's anniversary. You can also use it to help you approach long-term assignments in a manageable way. Any assignments requiring preparation over longer than a week's period of time are long-term assignments. Examples would be term papers, many reports, and most midterm and final exams.

If it's two days before your ten-page report on the differences between Piaget and Vygotsky is due, and you haven't begun working on it, you have a problem. Likewise, if you spend weeks worrying about writing a paper of that length but getting little work done on it, you have a problem. Many students are intimidated by large projects. But every new challenge you face in life, whether it's choosing a college, fixing up a house, learning a new job, or writing a ten-page report, is made up of a series of smaller tasks. And when you break a major assignment down into a series of smaller steps, it becomes less intimidating.

For example, imagine that you had been assigned the following report for your psychology class:

How does an individual's point of view affect the way he or she remembers an event? In order to examine this question, I want you to collect accounts of a memorable event in your family's

Reprinted by permission of UFS, Inc.

history from several members of your family. Try to choose an event that you know everyone will remember—like the time your brother drove the car into the side of a building, for example, or the time the neighborhood bully stuffed dirt into your sister's mouth. Ask each person to tell you his or her account of the story separately, and tape each of their responses. Then analyze the differences in remembering that you found. Look for differences that may show the processes of long-term memory distortion that we discussed in class. Also look for ways in which each individual's role in the event may have distorted his or her memory of it. (Length 4–10 pages typed. Due Oct. 16th.)

A breakdown of this assignment might look like this:

1. Select event and get hold of tape recorder.
2. Tape my own recollection of event and transcribe it.
3. Tape my mother's and brother's accounts of it and transcribe them.
4. Make table of differences: Mother vs. Brother, Brother vs. Me, Mother vs. Me.
5. Write up Part One of paper—the event, and the differences in the three accounts of it.
6. Review notes on long-term memory distortion.
7. Write up Part Two—types of distortion that occurred and possible reasons for distortions.
8. Revise draft.
9. Type up paper and proofread it.

The process of breaking a task down like this is useful in itself, as the individual steps seem manageable even if the paper as a whole doesn't. You can also use a breakdown like this to help you plan enough time to do the paper, by estimating how many days it will take you to complete each step.

Figure 3.6 shows a student's estimate of how long the paper on memory would take. Once he had figured this out, he began with the due date, October 16th, and, counting backward, figured that he needed to start work on September 30th, and to begin his first draft on October 8th. These dates on his calendar act as memory joggers, to make sure that the work isn't delayed so long that success is impossible.

EXERCISE 6

Imagine that you had been given the following assignment in a biology class. Break the assignment down into a series of subtasks and estimate how long each step would take you.

Find a textbook in the library dated prior to 1960 and read the information in it about genes and chromosomes. Write a one-page summary of it. Next, compare that information to the

Figure 3.6　　　**USING A CALENDAR TO BREAK DOWN**
AN ASSIGNMENT

1. Choose event & get tape recorder
2. Tape & transcribe my account } 3 days
3. Tape Mom & Allen's accounts　　1 day - on weekend
4. Make table of differences } 2 days
5. Write Part One
6. Review notes on long-term memory } 2 days on weekend
7. Write Part Two
8. Revise　　1 day
9. Type & proofread　　1 day

SUNDAY	MONDAY	TUESDAY	WEDNESDAY	THURSDAY	FRIDAY	SATURDAY
SEPTEMBER		1	2	3	4	5
6	7	8	Alexis's 9 birthday	10	11	12
13	14	15	16	17	quiz 18 biology	19
20	21	22	23	24	25	26
27	Dentist 28 2:00	29	Start 30 paper: Memory			
OCTOBER				Payday! 1	2	Tape Mom 3 & Allen →
analyze 4 →	5	appointment 6 with advisor 11:00	7	Pt 1 - Memory paper 8	quiz 9 biology	Write 10 Pt 2 - Memory paper
11 →	Revise 12 Memory paper	Type & 13 proofread	14	15	Memory 16 Paper Due	17

information in our textbook. Using the library, research the scientific discoveries that explain the differences in information about genes between 1960 and 1980. Find out what discoveries were made by scientists, when they were made, and who made them. (Your paper should have three parts, and should be three to six pages long.)

Subtasks	Time for each task
_____	_____
_____	_____
_____	_____
_____	_____
_____	_____
_____	_____
_____	_____
_____	_____
_____	_____
_____	_____

Now make up a due date for the assignment and enter it on the calendar (Figure 3.7). Working backward from this date, also enter a date to start work on the paper and a date to start writing.

SUMMARY

Scheduling your time as a college student requires a good deal of maturity, as your study time in college is not structured for you. One approach to managing your time is to use a study plan to make decisions about your use of time. In making up a study plan, you define your goals for the term, determine your study needs, analyze the problems that you're battling now, work out a schedule in light of the information you've gathered, and test it out. Another useful time management technique is the TTD list, used to keep track of daily obligations. Finally, a term calendar is a tool for keeping your work on long-term assignments on a schedule and for keeping track of important academic dates.

Figure 3.7   **CALENDAR GRID**

MONTH: _____

SUNDAY	MONDAY	TUESDAY	WEDNESDAY	THURSDAY	FRIDAY	SATURDAY

MONTH: _____

SUNDAY	MONDAY	TUESDAY	WEDNESDAY	THURSDAY	FRIDAY	SATURDAY

■
JOURNAL WRITING

1. Think of a problem that you are currently grappling with that is not related to time. Following the steps in the problem-solving approach outlined in this chapter, work through an analysis of the problem and propose a solution.
2. Interview someone you know who seems to handle a heavy load of work easily. Ask that person to discuss with you how he or she manages time. Specifically ask if he or she uses any of the time management techniques presented in this chapter, and ask about any other ways the person manages to be so efficient.
3. Use your journal to explore your feelings about time, and the demands it makes on you. Write a dialog between yourself and time.

■
ACADEMIC WRITING

When you evaluate something, you judge its value or usefulness. In this chapter, you have tried three time management techniques. Evaluate each technique. For each of the techniques, discuss specific ways in which it helped or did not help you to manage your time. Attach to your evaluations a copy of your study plan, term calendar, and a TTD list for one day.

GOING TO CLASSES

ACTIVE LISTENING

In this chapter you will learn:

▲ how to motivate yourself to listen
▲ how to focus your attention
▲ how to analyze an instructor's lecture style
▲ how to prepare yourself to listen
▲ how to listen actively

A major portion of the time that you spend learning in college is the time that you spend in class listening to the instructor. Yet, of all the communication skills (speaking, listening, reading, and writing), listening is the most neglected. Few students even think of listening as a skill or are aware that it's possible to improve their listening abilities. It's more common to blame the instructor if they don't understand a lecture—"That Mr. Devlin talks too fast, and I can't follow what he's saying," or "Dr. Parroge talks way above the students' heads." If you have trouble following an instructor when he or she lectures, you need to work to improve your listening skills so that you can get the information that you need from the class. Moreover, you need to take notes in your classes, a skill that depends on your ability to listen well. In this chapter, you will learn to improve your listening skills so that you can get the most out of your classes. Then in the next chapter you will work on improving your notetaking skills.

LISTENING: AN ACTIVE PROCESS

The popular view is that listening is a passive activity, that in an oral speech situation in which one person is talking and one person is listening, the speaker is doing all the work and the listener is simply receiving the signal. In order to refute this concept, it's necessary to make a distinction between hearing and listening. **Hearing** is a passive physical activity, the reception of sound waves by the ear and their conduction to the brain. **Listening**, on the other hand, is an active cognitive activity, involving the decoding of a spoken message, the comprehension of the meaning of the message, and an understanding of the message's implications. For instance, if you turn on a radio broadcast in a foreign language, you will hear it, but you will be unable to understand it, because you cannot perform the first step in the listening process, decoding.

Since listening is an active cognitive process, it is something that can be done poorly or well. Also, different types of speech situations require different levels of listening. If you have difficulty following lectures in college classes, you need to teach yourself how to listen actively in this environment. The first task is to motivate yourself.

MOTIVATING YOURSELF TO LISTEN

Listening to a lecture is hard work. We listen without any effort when the message is clearly important to us. If you're listening to a friend who's passing on some hot gossip, you probably have no trouble paying attention. It's much more difficult to pay attention to a lecture on cell structure in your Biology class at 8:00 on a Monday morning. In this situation, you have to make a conscious effort to listen. This fact is an important piece of knowledge in adapting your listening skills to a college classroom. If you had expected that you could just sit in your seat and learn, you were wrong. Instead, you have to work at listening.

How do you get yourself to listen? The first step is to resolve to do so. Convince yourself that paying attention in class is in your self-interest. For example, think about the class in which you have the most difficulty keeping your attention focused. Check off any of the items below that you could use to motivate yourself to listen in that class.

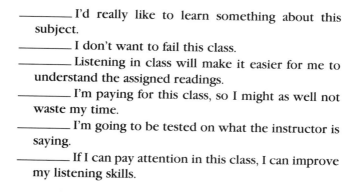

—————— I'd really like to learn something about this subject.

—————— I don't want to fail this class.

—————— Listening in class will make it easier for me to understand the assigned readings.

—————— I'm paying for this class, so I might as well not waste my time.

—————— I'm going to be tested on what the instructor is saying.

—————— If I can pay attention in this class, I can improve my listening skills.

_____ Listening in this class will be good mental exercise.

_____ If I listen, I'll be prepared to contribute to class discussions or to answer questions.

_____ It will be easier to do the homework if I pay attention in class.

_____ I'll try listening for a week to see if paying attention gets easier.

_____ If I listen attentively during class, then after class I'll give myself a small reward.

The next step in motivating yourself to listen is to promise yourself that you will do so. Think about a time in the past when you resolved to change your behavior in some way. Maybe you began an exercise program, decided to stop being late for work, went on a diet, stopped smoking, decided to spend more time reading, or resolved to stop spending too much money on clothes. Probably you had to remind yourself consciously of your resolution and of your reasons for making it. The same process will be at work as you strive to improve your listening—you'll have to remind yourself every day before class and several times during class to pay attention, and you'll have to discipline yourself to listen.

FOCUSING YOUR ATTENTION

If you've begun to monitor, or consciously watch, your listening processes in class, you may have been surprised at the number of times you were distracted. Most common is daydreaming. If your mind is not engaged with the material at hand, it wanders off into more interesting directions. Your job is to bring your mind back to the present before it wanders off too far. Other times, you're distracted by thinking or worrying about things you have to do. If you're keeping a TTD list as suggested in Chapter 3, you can write down errands or tasks that occur to you on your list and quickly return your attention to the lecture. If hunger or thirst or fatigue distract you during classes, take common-sense measures to eliminate these problems. If other students distract you, try moving your seat.

A simple trick that will help you to concentrate on listening is to adapt your body stance. If you sit up in an alert pose and try to maintain eye contact with the instructor, you will find that your concentration is easier to maintain.

Perhaps the best way to focus your attention during a lecture is by giving yourself a task to do—challenging yourself to work at really understanding the instructor's point and getting a good set of notes from that class session.

Remember that concentrating on listening is difficult. Expect to have to actively work at listening—to constantly monitor your attention and to frequently have to bring your mind back from its many attempts to wander. At the end of a class, don't be surprised if you feel tired just from the effort of focusing your attention.

■
EXERCISE 1

Try an experiment. In the next meeting of the class in which you have the most difficulty listening, monitor the number of times you are distracted. Place a check in the margin of your notebook each time you notice yourself thinking about something else. After class, make a list of the different types of distractions that occurred. Finally, discuss ways that you dealt with the different types of distractions, or could deal with them in the future.

ANALYZING AN INSTRUCTOR'S LECTURING STYLE

What about the instructor? All of the emphasis so far in this chapter has been on ways for you to change your behavior. Many students complain that they have difficulty listening because the instructor is a poor lecturer. Some lecturers have a monotonous tone of voice; some speak too fast or too slow, too loudly or too softly, or have an accent that makes them difficult to understand. Some lectures may seem disorganized or rambling. One instructor may have a distracting nervous habit or may use too many words you don't understand. While any of these conditions may make it more difficult for you to listen in that instructor's class, *they do not relieve you of the obligation of listening in that class.* You're still responsible for learning the material.

There are some strategies you can use to change the instructor's behavior. You can ask him or her to speak more slowly or ask that an explanation be repeated. But you also have to acknowledge the fact that not every instructor you have in college is going to be witty, entertaining, or talented as a speaker. You have to learn to adapt your listening to many different styles of delivery and to expect to work harder at listening in some classes than in others.

In fact, one of the ways that you can improve your listening comprehension is by being aware of an instructor's style of delivery. Take the following questionnaire to one of your lecture classes and use the questions as a guide to analyzing how the instructor organizes information and delivers his or her lecture.

■
EXERCISE 2

Answer the following questions after class, after observing an instructor's lecture:

1. Does the instructor usually review the material from the last class? If so, at what point does he/she do so?
2. Does the instructor follow the syllabus?
3. Does the instructor present an overview or an outline of the day's lecture?

4. Does the instructor stop to summarize the points that have been made? If so, at what point or points are summaries made?
5. Does the instructor review material in the text page by page?
6. Does the instructor lecture on the material in the text?
7. Does the instructor lecture primarily on topics not covered in the text?
8. Does the instructor define technical terms during lectures?
9. Does the instructor give signals that indicate the organization of the lecture?
10. Does the instructor give signals that indicate which ideas are main ideas?
11. Does the instructor use visual aids, such as the blackboard or overhead transparencies? If so, what kinds of information are visual aids used to convey?
12. Does the instructor provide examples to illustrate main points?
13. Does the instructor provide any verbal or nonverbal cues as to what is important or what students should take notes on?
14. Does the instructor digress frequently?
15. Is there anything about the instructor's style of speech that is different from what you're used to?

PREPARING FOR LISTENING

A critical factor in how much you comprehend when you listen or read is how much background knowledge about the subject you have before you begin. For instance, someone who had never used a computer would have great difficulty following an article reviewing a new computer graphics program, while someone who routinely used such programs at work would have a much higher comprehension rate. When you listen to a college lecture, the more knowledge about the subject you have at the beginning of class, the more you will get out of the lecture. Taking some time to introduce yourself to the topic of a lecture beforehand is the most efficient way to increase your listening comprehension. Take the following steps to prepare for a college lecture:

1. Check the syllabus to see what the present topic is and how it fits into the overall outline of the course.
2. Do the assigned readings. If you don't have time to do the assigned reading in depth, at least **skim** the chapter. To skim the chapter, read the chapter objectives, the headings and subheadings, look at all illustrations and charts, and read any chapter summaries. This kind of survey will orient you to

the subject matter before the lecture. Make sure that you read the chapter in depth as soon as you can.

3. Make a list of new technical vocabulary from the readings. Your listening comprehension will be slowed down by words you are unfamiliar with. To eliminate this problem, part of your preparation should be to list any technical vocabulary that might be included in the lecture. List the words and a brief definition for each in your notebook on the page opposite the one on which you will begin your notes. Then you can refer to them easily during the lecture.

4. Read the notes over from your last class. This review will help you establish continuity from one lecture to the next. As you review your notes, write down any questions you have for the instructor.

5. Have your notetaking materials ready.

■
EXERCISE 3

Prepare for the next lecture in one of your lecture classes by making up a *listening worksheet* (see Figure 4.1 for an example). On a sheet of paper write down:

1. What the topic of the lecture will be
2. A summary of the assigned reading for that day's class based on your reading or skimming of that material
3. A list of specialized vocabulary words and brief definitions of them
4. A one-paragraph summary of your notes from the last class

Bring this sheet to class and use it as a reference during the lecture. Finally, report the extent to which your preparation helped you to comprehend the instructor's lecture.

While the listening worksheet you prepared in Exercise 3 is probably more extensive preparation than you will take to prepare for every class, it reflects the steps that you can do orally and mentally to prepare for listening: noting the topic and how it fits into the overall plan of the course, skimming or reading the chapter, listing the technical vocabulary, and reviewing your notes from the previous class.

LISTENING ACTIVELY

Actually, listening actively includes all of the topics discussed in the chapter so far: motivating yourself to listen, monitoring your attention, having a sense of the instructor's lecturing style, and being prepared to listen. In addition, there are specific ways that you can work at listening to learn during a lecture.

*1.   **Get a sense of the organizational pattern of the lecture.***
When you listen, you listen to hear information. In addition, when listening to a lecture, you should work to get a sense of how the instructor is organizing the information he or she presents to you. For example, in a lecture in a biology class on the human respiratory system, the instructor may announce that she will first explain the parts of the respiratory system and then discuss how they interact. This information about the organization of her lecture will help you listen and comprehend, for you will know what the parts of the lecture are and how they are related to each other.

*2.   **Work to discriminate between main ideas and supporting information.***   In presenting information orally, speakers usually put forth a main idea, explain it, give examples and illustrations, and then repeat the main idea. For instance, in a psychology lecture, the lecturer might explain conditioned responses in the following way:

main idea { Conditioning can be defined as an association between stimulus inputs. For instance, you might demonstrate conditioning when
first example { you wake up in the morning to the smell of coffee and feel hungry for breakfast. The stimulus of the smell of coffee is triggering
second example { a hunger response in you, because you associate the smell of coffee with breakfast. Likewise, in Pavlov's experiments with dogs, the dogs learned to associate the sound of a bell with eating.
restatement of main idea { ing. So, conditioning occurs when a subject learns to associate two stimuli with each other because they often occur together.

Understanding this typical pattern of oral presentation will help your listening comprehension, as you can hold the main idea in mind while you listen to the explanatory material that will help you understand its meaning.

*3.   **Use questions as listening goals.***   You can use questions as a way to increase your comprehension of a lecture. As you hear a statement the instructor makes, turn it into a question, and then listen to construct an answer to the question. For example, if you hear an instructor in your humanities class say "The origins of both dance and drama are tied to early agricultural and religious rituals," you can ask yourself "How far back do these art forms go? What kinds of rituals were they? How did these early forms become drama and dance as we know them today?" These questions will give you listening goals as the instructor continues her lecture; in other words, as you continue to pay attention, you will listen for the information that answers these questions.

In fact, often lecturers themselves will provide questions that you can use as listening goals. They will say "What are the origins of

Figure 4.1   **EXAMPLE OF LISTENING WORKSHEET**

Psych 101

Topic: Altered States of Consciousness
Reading: pp 68-82 in Understanding Human Behavior

In an altered state of consciousness, a change occurs in the speed at which we take in & process information in our brain. Examples are falling asleep, dreaming & drug-induced altered states. Most drugs affect neural transmitters by increasing or slowing down neural firing. Some drugs like "uppers" & "downers" affect general activity level. Others affect the input from your senses, while others affect how your brain perceives that input. Drugs also affect your muscles.

Vocabulary:

  autonomic nervous system — controls involuntary actions
      (like breathing)
  endorphins — natural painkillers that are produced inside
      the brain.
  analgesics — painkillers
  hallucinogen — drugs that affect the central processing
      area of the brain, making you sense things that
      aren't there.

Last Class: On Dreams. Everyone dreams several times a night, mostly during REM sleep (stage 1 sleep). Most dreams about things you find interesting / important. Dreams in other stages of sleep are more fragmented than Stage 1 / REM dreams. Dreaming seems to be a mostly right hemisphere function.

the arts of dance and drama?" and then proceed to answer their own question. Questions like these—questions a speaker poses and then proceeds to answer—are called **rhetorical questions**. If you hear a lecturer use a rhetorical question in introducing a topic, jot it down and adopt it as a listening goal for yourself.

Questions can also be incorporated into your notes. In fact, you may want to organize your notes in a question–answer format, as this format makes study and review wonderfully easy. To do so, make a wide left margin of about 2½ inches on each page. Write your notes on the right side, and use the left margin for writing down questions that point to the central ideas in each part of the notes. Figure 4.2 is an example of notes in this format, called the **Cornell System** of notetaking. In the next chapter, you'll get practice in taking notes on college lectures.

■
EXERCISE 4

In one of your lecture classes, draw a wide left-hand margin on the pages on which you will be taking notes. During the lecture, try to make up questions based on what the instructor is saying and write them in the left margin. As you listen, note the answers to your questions in your notes in the right-hand column. After the class, fill in any questions or notes that you didn't have time to record.

SUMMARY

Listening is an active process, and listening in college classes requires conscious effort on your part. To keep your attention focused, you might have to increase your motivation by reminding yourself about your reasons for listening. No matter how high your motivation, you'll still have to devise individual techniques for dealing with distractions. One way to focus your attention and keep from being distracted is by taking notes.

Preparing for listening is the single most effective strategy for improving your listening. Prepare for each class session by noting what the topic is and how it relates to the course syllabus, by getting an overview of the assigned readings, by noting technical terms that the lecturer might use, and by reviewing the notes from the previous class. During the class, work to get a sense of the organizational pattern of the lecture and listen for main ideas and supporting information. As you listen, pose questions or listen for rhetorical questions posed by the lecturer, and use these questions as listening goals. Consider incorporating these questions into your notes.

■
JOURNAL WRITING

1. For one week, keep a listening journal in your classes. Write about what was easy or difficult about listening in each class, what steps you tried to improve your listening in that class, and how useful they were.
2. Write down your favorite daydream. Perhaps getting it on

Figure 4.2   **EXAMPLE OF NOTES IN CORNELL SYSTEM**
USING QUESTIONS

	May 17, 1989 Psych 101
	Altered States of Consciousness
How do <u>uppers</u> affect people?	<u>Uppers</u> - speed up your involuntary activities (autonomic nervous system) - speed up mental function NOTE: "speed up" doesn't necessarily mean "improve" → you might have trouble concentrating Examples of uppers: caffeine (common) amphetamines (prescription drug)
What are downers?	<u>Downers</u> — drugs that slow down neural activity Ex: barbiturates & tranquilizers
How do they work?	They depress neural activity in some way. Effects: slow down heart rate & breathing slow down mental & physical reactions

paper will keep it from distracting you when you're trying to concentrate in class.

ACADEMIC WRITING

1. Write a report on the lecturing style of one of your instructors, basing your work on the worksheet you did in Exercise 2.
2. In one of your classes use the active listening techniques suggested in this chapter for a week, including using a listening worksheet. At the end of the week, report on the results.

5

TAKING NOTES

In this chapter you will learn:

▲ why it's important to take notes
▲ how to improve your notetaking skills
▲ how to edit your notes so that they are complete, accurate, and easy to study from

Taking notes is a vital skill in college. Here's why:

1. Taking notes helps you concentrate during lectures. When you set yourself a goal of getting a good set of notes from each class, you challenge yourself to actively engage your mind in listening in order to produce a complete and accurate set of notes. In fact, taking notes often offers a quick fix for your concentration if you ever find your attention wandering or your eyes starting to close during a class.

2. The activity of writing down notes helps you to learn. Have you ever made out a shopping list and then left it at home when you went shopping? Chances are you still remembered most of the items when you went shopping. That's because the activity of writing down the items reinforced them in your memory. Likewise, taking notes in your classes will reinforce the material being presented.

3. You will need your notes to study from. Without notes, your recall of what was said in class fades sharply after 24 hours. Your notes provide a permanent record of what was said in class, a record that you can review to prepare you for the next class, and that you can study to prepare for a test. In fact, in most courses, your notes are a more important source of exam questions than your textbook. Think about it—instructors select for their lectures the ideas they consider the most important. These ideas are also the ones most likely to be stressed on an exam.

ORGANIZING YOUR NOTES

At the end of the term, you want to be able to sit down to study and find all your notes from a course in order. That means you need to pay attention to how you're going to organize your notes right from the beginning of the term. If you tour your college bookstore or a good stationery store, you can survey the possibilities for notebooks and folders for your notes. Each system for keeping notes has advantages and disadvantages. Notebooks keep pages in order but make it harder to rearrange notes, while looseleaf binders and file folders are more flexible and better for filing handouts, but create chaos when dropped. Whichever system you choose, keep in mind the following:

All notes should be dated and labeled with the day's topic.

You'll need a way to keep up with handouts as well as class notes. Date and label all handouts and keep all the handouts from each class together.

Once a week, do an inventory of your notes from each of your classes. If you missed a day's notes or accidentally put them in the wrong notebook, skip pages for adding them later. Get the missed notes by the end of the week.

LISTENING AND NOTETAKING

"Garbage in, garbage out." That's the way that people who work with computers characterize the relation between input and output. Your notes are the output of your classroom listening, so a good set of notes rests on a foundation of good listening—the skills stressed in the previous chapter. As your skills of focusing your attention, preparing yourself to listen, and listening actively improve, the quality of your notes will improve also. In fact, it's important to have a long-range view of notetaking as a skill that will improve steadily during your college career. Like most skills, your notetaking ability will grow as you practice taking notes and learn from your experience.

To get you started taking good notes, this chapter presents a series of notetaking labs. Each lab concentrates on one skill of good notetaking, and includes a discussion of the skill and exercises for practice. You may do these labs in your study skills classes, working with practice lectures given by the instructor. Or, you can practice in one of your other academic classes, doing one practice per day following the directions in the exercises.

WORK ON COMPREHENSION

Taking notes on a lecture is a different activity from taking dictation. Your aim is not to get down every word that's spoken as it's spoken, but to make a record of your comprehension of the lecture. In fact, it's better to have fewer, more accurate notes than to have a whole jumble of notes that you don't understand. So your first goal when you're taking notes is to understand the point the lecturer is making. Once you understand it, you write down a phrase reflecting what you learned.

If you wait until you understand before you write a note down, you'll always be a step behind the lecturer in your notetaking. Students often worry about this time lag, because they recognize that it's hard to listen to a new point and write down the last point at the same time. However, you'll soon learn that there's quite a bit of repetition of main ideas and use of multiple examples in most instructors' oral presentations. So if you wait to write a note down until you understand the instructor's point, you'll have time to write while he or she is elaborating on that point.

■
EXERCISE 1

A. ***Warm-up #1.*** Here is a transcript of a lecturer's explanation of how desensitization therapy is used to teach patients to overcome phobias. To practice waiting for comprehension before you take notes, read it with the goal of understanding what desensitization therapy is. Keep reading until you understand. When you reach that point, stop and write down your explanation.

Some therapists have found an approach called desensitization therapy useful when dealing with patients who have a certain phobia. The idea behind desensitization therapy is to get the patient used to whatever he or she is frightened of in stages. For instance, take the example of a child who is afraid of dogs. The first step a therapist might take would be to get the child to relax and visualize a dog in his mind. The therapist will stop any time this exercise becomes uncomfortable for the child. Next, the therapist might show the child pictures of dogs. Again, the therapist will stop the exercise if the child becomes tense, but will return to this exercise at the next session. Once the child had become comfortable with looking at pictures of dogs, the next step would be observing dogs from a distance. From there, the therapy might progress to briefly touching a very quiet dog and so on. The idea is the therapist would start with a very remote stimulus and not move on to the next step until the child was comfortable with that level of encounter. So desensitization therapy is based on the idea of introducing a subject to a feared object gradually, in small steps, and waiting for the patient to be comfortable with that level of encounter before proceeding to the next.

Notes: Desensitization therapy:

_____

_____

_____

_____

B.   Practice #1.   Now practice listening for understanding in an actual lecture, either a practice lecture by your academic skills instructor, or a portion of a lecture in one of your other classes.

Directions: Listen to the lecture, working at understanding what the instructor is saying. Don't begin to write until you have a clear idea of what the instructor's point is. When you do, write down some notes that reflect your understanding. You don't have to write in sentences; you can write in phrases—remember that your notes are written for you to read. Just make sure that you write enough so that you will be able to understand what you wrote. See if you can time your writing so that you're writing while the instructor is elaborating on his or her point. Work at this skill for ten minutes.

CONCENTRATE ON THE MAIN IDEAS

One skill that you need to have as a notetaker is the ability to discriminate between main ideas and supporting material—a skill that was mentioned as an important listening skill also (see Chapter 4). You can identify main ideas in several ways. In an oral presentation, the lecturer may highlight the main idea by mentioning it first and then elaborating on it through examples and further explanation. He or she might also repeat a main idea several times or state it more slowly, so students can get it down in their notes.

You can also often identify main ideas in lectures by listening for *verbal cues* that signal that a point is a main idea—words like "My point is . . . ," or "An important concept in art is. . . ." Another type of verbal cue indicates that a series of main ideas will be presented. For instance, the lecturer might say "There are three main types of stages in theaters." These words alert you to listen for three main ideas, main ideas that often will be introduced with signal words like "First . . . ," "The second type . . ." and so on. Also, if the instructor begins a section of a presentation with a question, the main idea will most likely be the answer to that question.

Some instructors make notetaking easy by writing main ideas on the board—a nonverbal cue to an idea's importance. Other instructors might indicate main ideas nonverbally by glancing at their notes, waving their glasses, pausing dramatically, or speaking with greater emphasis.

Why is listening to the main idea important in notetaking? As you work on your notetaking skills, your first goal should be to produce a set of notes that accurately outlines the main ideas presented in a lecture. Only after you have achieved this level of competence should you work toward fleshing out your notes with explanatory materials and examples. If your notes accurately record the main ideas of a lecture, then you can always add explanatory material later when you edit your notes.

Concentrating on the main idea is an especially good idea in situations where it's hard to keep up with the professor for one reason or another, perhaps because the instructor goes quickly or because the material is difficult or because the instructor's speaking style is hard for you to follow. In these cases, work to produce an outline of the main ideas of the lecture, writing down what you perceive to be the main ideas and leaving lots of space for filling in explanations and examples later.

■
────────────
E X E R C I S E   2

A. Warm-up #2.   Practice concentrating on the main idea by taking notes on this transcript of a lecture on stage settings from a humanities class. Aim for a bare-bones set of notes—notes that concentrate on the main ideas (the three different types of stage settings). For this warm-up, don't try to include any supporting material.

One aspect of a play is the space in which it takes place—the stage setting. I'd like to look at the different types of stages used in plays from the point of view of the playgoer. One type of stage setting can be characterized as highly realistic. In a highly realistic stage setting, it's as if you were looking into someone's living room, except that one wall of the room has been removed so that you can see in and observe what's going on. This type of setting is called a box set. In this kind of set, there are lots of props provided—pictures on the wall, a cup and saucer on the table. The setting provides the illusion that you're looking at a real place reproduced on the stage. Stage settings like this are typical of Victorian plays—and you're also familiar with sets like these from television and movies. At the other extreme is a highly unrealistic stage setting—one in which there may be almost no props and no attempt to create an illusion of a realistic setting. The entire set could consist of two chairs and a table, and the same set could be used for a scene in someone's kitchen and one outside in the park. This kind of set demands that you mentally create much of the scene in your mind—often the words of the play will refer to physical details that you can't see, and that's the playwright's way of helping you to use your imagination to mentally create the scene. You might think of stage settings like this as being typical of modern plays, but they're also the kinds of setting that were used in the very earliest Greek plays, like *Oedipus Rex*. So you can see that highly unrealistic sets are both a very ancient and a very modern idea in theater. A third type of setting lies in between these two extremes—let's call it a semirealistic stage setting. In this type of stage setting, there is some scenery and some attempt to be realistic, but there are also some demands placed on the playgoer's imagination. For instance, in a Shakespearean play, the stage setting might include two doors at center stage, with two sets of stairs leading up from them to a balcony above the doors. In one scene, the doors will be opened and the king will be sitting on a throne inside the doors addressing his court. In the next scene, the doors will be closed and the scene played in front of the doors will be taking place outside the palace. The balcony above the doors can be a balcony in one scene and the hill above a battlefield in the next scene.

Main ideas:

_____

_____

_____

_____

_____

B. *Practice #2.*   For your second lab, you are going to concentrate on listening for the main ideas in a lecture, again either a lecture by your study skills instructor or a portion of a lecture in one of your other classes.

Directions: Time yourself so that you're working at this skill for about ten minutes. This time, in addition to listening to understand, as you did in the first lab, focus on identifying the main points the lecturer is making and on getting them down in your notes. Put down the general topic that the instructor is talking about at the top of your page. Then, begin to listen for and write down the main ideas the instructor develops. Remember to use verbal and nonverbal cues as an aid to identifying the main ideas. Skip several lines after each main idea so that your notes are well spaced out. Again, you don't have to write your notes in sentence form—phrases are fine.

ADDING SUPPORTING INFORMATION

As mentioned above, a basic set of notes will include the main ideas from a lecture. A more complete set of notes will include the main ideas and some supporting information for each idea. The supporting information will help you to clarify the main ideas when you study your notes. Once you find yourself getting the main ideas of a lecture down with ease, try to make your notes more complete by adding at least one piece of supporting information to back up each main idea.

The main types of supporting information are examples, details, and reasons. The kind of supporting information an instructor uses will vary according to the main idea. Often, lecturers will give several types of supporting information or a series of the same type—like three examples. As with main ideas, you can use verbal cues to identify supporting information. *For instance,* and *for example* are verbal cues that can introduce supporting examples or details. Words like *Evidence for this idea ...* might signal a supporting reason.

In the next lab, you will work on including at least one bit of supporting information to explain each main idea.

■
_____
E X E R C I S E   3

A.   *Warm-up #3.* For this warm-up, revise your notes on the different types of stage settings. This time, in addition to noting the three different types of stage settings the lecturer describes, include one piece of supporting information for each type—an example or some supporting detail.

Notes:

_____

_____

_____

_____

_____

_____

_____

_____

B.   *Practice #3.* In this practice, in addition to writing down the main ideas, try to get down one bit of information in explanation for each main idea—something that clarifies the main idea for you. Take notes on a classroom lecture for around fifteen minutes for this lab. Remember to listen for verbal and nonverbal cues that identify ideas as main ideas or as supporting information. As you take notes, space your notes out—write the supporting information under the main idea, and then skip several lines before the next main point.

USING AN INFORMAL OUTLINE FORMAT

The best format for your notes is an informal outline format, one in which main ideas are well spaced out, supporting information is indented under main ideas, lines are skipped between each main idea, and there are wide margins on either side of the page. This format is easy to produce and allows enough room for later editing. Also, notes taken in this form are easy to study from. Figure 5.1 is an example of notes using an informal outline format.

■──────────────
E X E R C I S E   4

A.   *Warm-up #4.* Take notes on the following transcript of a lecture introducing Mendel's four laws of inheritance of genetic information. Your main ideas will be his four laws. In addition to recording the main ideas, write down at least one piece of supporting information for each law. Use an informal outline format for your notes, with supporting information indented under main ideas, skipped lines between each main idea, and wide left and right margins.

Gregor Mendel, an Austrian monk, laid the foundation for modern work in genetics. His monastery was an active farm and he was involved in working on techniques for improved agriculture. Mendel became interested in how traits in plants were passed from parent plants to their offspring, and he experimented extensively to discover the patterns. He was an active member of the local natural history society—a kind of pre-biology forum—and reported most of his work in papers published in their journal. The principles he discovered are called Mendel's laws of inheritance. There are four of them. The first states that heredity is transmitted by units that exist in pairs—units that we now call genes. A gene, you will recall, is a region of DNA containing the information that governs a certain trait. Examples of human traits that are genetically determined are height, skin color, and eye color. These traits are governed by genes. The information governing these traits is contained in paired genes located in chromosomes. His second law is the law of segregation. It states that sex cells receive only one gene from each pair of genes. For instance, a woman with brown eyes might have a paired set of genes—a gene for brown eyes and a gene for blue eyes that isn't expressed. An egg produced by her

Figure 5.1

SAMPLE NOTES IN INFORMAL OUTLINE FORMAT

3/17/89
Humanities 1

Ancient Egyptian Art

Cultural principles that affected art:
- king most powerful figure, next to a god
- polytheism
    (except under Amenhotep IV)
- belief in life after death
    Central concept in art
    Ex. mummy cases
        death masks
        portraits
        tomb paintings
- originality and naturalism discouraged

Figures in Egyptian paintings
- heads always in profile
    (like Picasso today)
- eyes face forward / so does body
- see side of arms & legs
    often figures have 2 left feet. Look for both
    big toes on the same side
- impt figures are larger
    Children are small but have same body proportions
    as adults
- women are colored white, men are colored red

body will contain only one set of chromosomes, and thus only one of the two genes, either the gene for brown eyes or the one for blue eyes. His third law is the law of dominance, which states that in cases where paired genes carry different genetic information, one trait may dominate the other. For instance, in the example I just mentioned, a person with a gene for blue eyes and a gene for brown eyes will have brown eyes, since brown is dominant over blue. Mendel's fourth law is the law of independent assortment, which states that most heritable traits are independent of each other. In other words, you can inherit your mother's brown eyes without necessarily inheriting her brown hair.

Notes:

_____

_____

_____

_____

_____

_____

_____

_____

_____

_____

B. Practice #4.   Take notes for twenty minutes either on a lecture given in your academic skills class or in one of your other classes. For this practice, continue to concentrate on getting down the main ideas and at least one bit of supporting information for each main idea. Skip several lines before each main idea. Indent supporting information under the main idea it explains so that your notes look more like a list with two levels. Keep your left and right margins fairly wide—at least an inch on either side. Use the model informal outline format (Figure 5.1) as a guide to the layout of your notes.

USING GRAPHICS

Another way to improve your notes visually is to add graphics to your notes. Here are some examples of graphics to use in note-taking:

Headings and subheadings to indicate the topics of notes
Diagrams to visually show ideas
Underlining for emphasis
Boxes around key terms to highlight them
Stars to mark key concepts
Question marks next to information you want to check after class or ask the instructor about
Tables to organize information for comparison and contrast

■
EXERCISE 5

For this practice, do the following:

1. Take notes for fifteen to twenty minutes.
2. Continue to listen for the main idea and at least one bit of supporting information, and to use an informal outline format.
3. Head your notes with a heading indicating the general topic of the lecture and the date.
4. Use subheadings in your notes.
5. Box any technical terms that are introduced and draw a line from the term to its definition.
6. Use any of the other graphics that are appropriate—diagrams, underlining, question marks, tables, or stars.

PRACTICE INCREASING YOUR EFFICIENCY

If you feel comfortable with the notetaking skills presented so far, you can turn now to working on increasing your speed without sacrificing accuracy. Notice that some of the skills introduced so far have helped you to take notes more quickly. Notetaking is faster when you use phrases instead of complete sentences, when you use an informal outline format, and when you use graphics. In addition, you can practice using a more rapid handwriting style and abbreviations to improve your notetaking speed.

Just as your reading speed should vary with the purpose for reading, so your writing speed should vary depending on the purpose for writing. You'll probably use a careful handwriting style when addressing a letter, but in notetaking you can use a style of handwriting that is less careful—as long as it's legible (you do want to be able to reread your notes a few months later). Practice with several handwriting styles, including printing and a mix of printing and cursive writing, to find a style that is rapid but legible.

WHAT ABOUT USING
A TAPE RECORDER?

It may seem easier to simply bring a tape recorder to class and tape the lecture, instead of trying to keep up with the instructor. (In fact, the thought may have occurred to you that notetaking would be easier if instructors came equipped with a pause button just as tape recorders do.) The problem with relying on a tape recorder instead of on your own listening abilities is that you have to set aside time to listen to the tape later and take notes on it—it will take one and a half hours to listen to a tape of a one-hour lecture and take notes on it. So a tape recorder is really not a very efficient alternative to notetaking.

There are some situations where a tape recorder is a very useful tool for learning. If you're going to miss a class, you can have a friend tape the lecture (with the professor's permission, of course), and use his or her notes and the tape to learn the information you missed. In language classes, a tape recorder is a great way to review pronunciation. You can even make up self-study tapes before a test and study while you jog around campus. But in general, don't rely on a tape recorder as an alternative to taking notes.

You can also increase your notetaking speed by using abbreviations. Figure 5.2 lists some common abbreviations used by students in their notes. In addition, you can coin your own abbreviations. Just be sure that you'll be able to recall what they mean. For instance, if you use the abbreviation *con* for conclusion, you may well forget in a few weeks whether you meant *conference, condition, connecting,* or some other word. *Cnclsn* would be a better abbreviation.

When an instructor is lecturing on a certain topic, you can be certain that that phrase will be mentioned again and again. That's a situation when an invented abbreviation will help your notetaking speed greatly. For instance, if your humanities professor is lecturing this week on the Neoclassical Style in art and architecture, you can use the abbreviation NCS for Neoclassical Style, write a reminder to yourself by writing NCS = Neoclassical Style in the margin, and avoid the problem of having to write out the whole phrase every few minutes.

Figure 5.2

ABBREVIATIONS FOR LECTURE NOTES

¢	and	↗	increases
e.g. Ex. }	for example	↘	decreases
		=	equals
w/	with	≠	does not equal
w/out	without	// c.f. }	compare
∴	therefore	#	number
>	is greater than		
<	is less than		

A simple way to recall your abbreviations is to make up a list of the abbreviations you use and the terms they stand for, and to write the list in your notes, either in your left margin or on a separate page at the back of your notebook.

Even using a rapid style handwriting and abbreviations won't help you keep up with every idea in a class where a lot of information is presented quickly. Here are some additional pointers:

> If the instructor is already going on to the next point before you have finished your notes on the last one, write down some key words, leave space for adding notes later, and go on.
> If the instructor uses a word you don't know and you can't ask for a definition, spell it the way it sounds, and check it later.

■
─────────────
E X E R C I S E   6

In one of your classes, practice taking notes for around twenty-five minutes using a rapid handwriting style and abbreviations. You may want to bring this textbook with you so you can use Figure 5.2 as a reference. Make up at least one abbreviation for a term the instructor is using repeatedly in the lecture. Note the abbreviation and what it stands for in the margin of your notes, and use the abbreviation in your notes.

ADAPTING NOTETAKING TECHNIQUES

There are some classroom situations in which you need special techniques for taking notes. One situation is in a math class. Another is a discussion class, where ideas are brought out in a dialog between the instructor and students or among students. Another situation that calls for adaptation is a skills class: a science lab, a dance class, a music class, an art class, or a gym class in which it may be physically impossible to take notes.

In a *math class,* you need to record sample problems, explanations of the steps in the problems, technical terms, and concepts. Try using a regular format for concepts, but switching to a two-column format for sample problems. Use the left column for the sample problem, and the right column for explanation of the steps. Number the steps. If the instructor works a sample problem too quickly for you, get the sample down in the left column and fill the right column in later.

Be aware that you'll have two types of technical terms in math and science classes: vocabulary items, and symbols like $<$ for "is less than." Record definitions of both vocabulary items and symbols in your notes. In fact, you might want to make up a chart of symbols for reference in the back of your notebook.

In a *discussion class,* the problem is that the ideas are unordered. (The same problem exists with an instructor with a rambling style of presentation.) In a class of this type, keep a running list of ideas that are mentioned that strike you as important and skip lines between unrelated ideas. When the class is finished, take ten minutes to review your notes and write a summary of the main ideas. You can use a simple organizing principle such as summarizing two opposing positions that emerged or enumerating four or five key principles that were brought out.

In a *skills class,* you'll need to take notes if you're to be tested on the content of the course as well as on your level of achievement. Many students also find that notes in a skills class help them learn and practice the skill, so they write down the tips that the instructor has given them during class. For instance, many dance students write down the routines they're practicing so they can rehearse at home. Since you can't take notes during classes like these, you want to reserve ten minutes after class to write down what you learned and what you practiced that day—a running log of what went on in the class.

Figure 5.3 shows examples of student notes from a math class, a swimming class, and from a stress discussion in a psychology class.

EDITING YOUR NOTES FOR COMPLETENESS

As long as you can take a minimal set of notes—a list of the main ideas—during class, you can have a good set of notes for the class if you follow through on your notes and edit them. Editing gives

Figure 5.3

NOTES FROM A SKILLS CLASS

Class: June 17th / Breast Stroke

Tips: The Stretch
      Keep arms about 8" underwater
      arms & legs extended

The Pull
      pull up palms outward
      keep elbow high for more strength
      Don't lift shoulders out of water!

The Recovery
      Move hands back in; don't touch chest
      Practice: 14 lengths for next class

NOTES ON DISCUSSION OF STRESS

Psych 102
April 13

Main Ideas
{ Some stress is good.
Different people tolerate different levels of stress
    and cope with stress differently.
Some coping mechanisms are good; some are negative.

Questions
- What's the relation between stress & motivation?
- What are the effects of living with high stress
    for a long period of time?
- Is there really a Type A personality? [Prof. G says no.]

NOTES FROM A MATH CLASS

3/7 Math

Solving
a
ratio

① $6 : 36 :: 102 : X$

② $(36 \cdot 102) = 6X$

③ $\dfrac{3672}{6} = \dfrac{6X}{6}$ 612

④ $612 = X$

① Inside terms are <u>means</u>
  Outside terms are <u>extremes</u>

② The product of the <u>means</u> equals
  the product of the <u>extremes</u>, so
  set up an equation and multiply

③ Now divide both sides by 6 to
  solve for X

④ Answer is 612. Means 6 relates to
  36 the same way 102 relates to 612.
  First # is 1/6 of second.

you a second chance at having a good set of notes. But in order to have this chance, you must edit your notes soon after class, before your memory of what was said begins to fade. That means you must edit your notes within a day of taking them.

The first step in editing your notes is to read over your notes with pen in hand. Fill in any gaps that you can—that's why you left lots of space and wide margins in your notes. Add missing information, add any supporting details or examples that you couldn't get down during class. At the same time, box definitions and add other graphics that will improve your notes.

Once you've done all the filling in you can based on memory, you want to turn to other sources. Use your textbook to double-check any information you weren't sure of. You'll especially want to check the spelling and definition of any technical words that you're not sure you got down accurately.

Another possibility, particularly in a class where notetaking is difficult, is to work with a partner. Some students team up and regularly meet after class to edit their notes. Offer to buy a student a cup of coffee and go over your notes together—the price is low and the process will benefit both of you.

When you've finished editing your notes, there still may be points you need cleared up. As a last step, write down any questions you have so you'll be prepared to ask them in the next class session.

■
_____

E X E R C I S E   7

Take notes on a lecture given by your study skills instructor or in one of your other classes. Then, to practice editing, take the following steps:

1. Edit your notes as soon as possible after class.
2. First, reread them and add missed material or additional supporting information.
3. Also add graphics wherever it's appropriate.
4. Next refer to your textbook to check the accuracy of your notes. Check the spelling and definition of any technical vocabulary words.
5. Next, go over your notes with a partner and add further information or revise to make your notes more accurate.
6. Finally, write down any questions you have for the next class.

EDITING YOUR NOTES FOR STUDYING

An additional step you can take is to edit your notes to make them easier to study. One way to do this is to use the left-hand margin to write down either a series of phrases or short questions that you can use to test yourself. This notetaking format, called the Cornell System, was introduced in the previous chapter. Figure 5.4 shows two samples of notes edited for studying in this way, one with

Figure 5.4   **EXAMPLES OF NOTES EDITED FOR STUDYING**

whole blood (structure)	whole blood consists of · plasma - watery substance containing cellular material cellular material { red blood cells / white blood cells / platelets
Plasma (structure)	Plasma - 92% water + some proteins and salts + some materials being transported Plasma like body's pipeline → EX: | fibrinogen | plays a role in blood clotting
How is an opera different from a play?	Opera: a play set to music all lines are sung generally, music more impt than drama in opera often in a different language than one of the audience often written by several people - EX, a writer might help the musician with the | libretto | — the words of the opera
What are the characteristics of opera?	Characteristics: highly stylized music more impt than drama (designed to show off singing voices) elaborate staging attracts wealthy - often in lg. cities

key phrases written in the margin, the other with short questions in the margin.

You can readily see why this format makes it easy to study your notes. When you review, you can cover up your notes and use the words in the left-hand margin to test your recall. Then you reread your notes to check if you knew the answer.

A second way to edit your notes for studying is to write a summary of your notes after each class or periodically, perhaps once a week. The process of writing these summaries is valuable in itself, as it forces you to synthesize the ideas of each class. Then, when you review, you can study by rereading your summaries.

SUMMARY

You need to take notes in all your college classes because your notes record the ideas presented in class, ideas you'll need to learn for exams. Not only that, the activity of taking notes helps you to concentrate during class and actually helps you retain the material. You need to keep your notes organized: that involves having a system for both your notes and class handouts, labeling and dating all notes, and getting missed notes right away.

Your notes should be the product of your comprehension, so you need to understand an idea before you try to paraphrase it. At first, concentrate on the main ideas of a lecture, often identified by the instructor's verbal and nonverbal cues. Once you're comfortable at that level, aim for more complete notes, with supporting information for each main idea. Use an informal outline format in your notes, and enhance your notes with graphics. Work on improving your speed by using abbreviations and a quick style handwriting. Also, expect to adapt basic notetaking techniques for different classes, such as math classes, discussion classes, and skills classes.

Edit your notes for completeness soon after the class, adding missed information, checking for accuracy, and adding graphics. You may also edit them for studying by writing key phrases or questions in the left margin as study prompts, and by writing short summaries of each lecture.

■ ────────────
JOURNAL WRITING

1. Practice taking notes by taking notes on a television show such as a news broadcast or an informational program for half an hour. (If you want to practice taking notes for discussion or skills classes, look for a talk show or a skills demonstration instead.)
2. Compare your notes before you did the labs in this chapter with the notes you're taking now. How have they changed? What skills did you pick up easily and which ones do you still need to practice?
3. Describe the particular notetaking problems posed by each of your classes. Plan a strategy for notetaking in each class.

4. If you can, ask one of your instructors to look at your notes from one day's lecture and to comment on their completeness and accuracy.
5. Edit your notes from one class session for studying by adding study questions in the left margin and by preparing a summary.

■
ACADEMIC WRITING

1. Apply the notetaking and editing skills to one of your classes for a week. After the week is over, select one page of your notes for evaluation.
2. Take notes on a lecture given in your study skills class by your instructor or by a visiting lecturer. After the lecture, edit your notes and hand them in to be evaluated.

6

Speaking Out In Classes

In this chapter you will learn how to participate in your classes by:

▲ asking and answering questions
▲ participating in small group discussions
▲ participating in class-wide discussions

Perhaps the most visible way to distinguish between an active and a passive student is by observing his or her behavior during a class. A passive student does not speak out in class, while an active student will use a class session to seek out information and to test ideas. This chapter presents tips and techniques for participating actively in your classes, through answering and asking questions, and through participating in small and large group discussions. The types of participation are arranged progressively, so if you are not used to participating in class, begin by working on answering questions and go on from there.

ANSWERING QUESTIONS

The easiest way to begin participating in class is by answering questions. In many of your classes, you will not have a choice, as instructors will routinely call on students to answer questions. In other classes, instructors will only call on students who volunteer. If you volunteer, the instructor will get to know you, you'll get an informal chance to test your understanding, and you may boost your grade (since some instructors grade for participation).

Instructors vary in the types of questions they ask. Some instructors call on students for answers to homework problems or exercises done in class. Others review by asking students to recall information from earlier lectures or from assigned readings. Sometimes an instructor will ask students to relate relevant personal experiences or to apply knowledge from other areas. Other questions challenge the students to reason and draw inferences.

Part of your preparation for class should be preparing to answer these types of questions. If the instructor calls on people to give responses from the homework assignment, do the assignment and bring it with you. If the instructor asks review questions, skim over the notes from the last few classes before class. If the instructor asks questions related to that day's topic, think about the major ideas in the chapter when you do the reading assignment and anticipate questions that might be asked.

■
E X E R C I S E   1

For each of the classes you are taking, list the types of questions the instructor asks in class and collect a sample question of each type.

Class	Types of questions asked	Sample questions
_____	_____	_____
_____	_____	_____
_____	_____	_____
_____	_____	_____
_____	_____	_____
_____	_____	_____
_____	_____	_____
_____	_____	_____
_____	_____	_____
_____	_____	_____

ASKING QUESTIONS

The instructor strides into the room and puts her books on the desk and her notes on the lectern. She says, "Today's lecture is on the late nineteenth-century movement in art called Impressionism. Before I begin, are there any questions on last week's lectures on Romanticism?" She waits a few seconds, and no hands appear, so she begins her lecture. One student, sitting in the second row, remembers that there was some point he didn't understand when he was reading the textbook, but by the time he has opened his text to the chapter on Romanticism, the instructor has already begun lecturing. Another student has a question she'd like to ask, but she's never asked a question in the class before, and she's afraid of looking like a fool. The instructor meanwhile assumes that everything she has said about Romanticism is perfectly clear.

Both students have missed an important opportunity to customize their college education. When you ask questions in class, you invite the instructor to respond to your individual learning needs. Your ability to ask questions is one of the most important tools you possess as a learner.

The first key to asking questions is to be prepared for them. For each of your instructors, you need to be aware of when questions from students are invited: whether it's at the beginning of class, at a logical breaking point in the lecture, or at the end of class. In a large lecture class, there may be no opportunity for asking questions during lectures, but you may be able to do so during a discussion section later in the week, immediately before or after class, or during the instructor's office hours. In an informal class, you may be able to ask questions related to what the instructor is saying at any time.

Next, you need to have your questions ready when the opportunity presents itself. Often there are only seconds for you to get your hand in the air. To prepare your questions for a class, review your notes from the last class and skim through the assigned readings you've done. In your notebook, right on the page where you'll begin taking notes, write down any questions you have. Note that the practice of listing questions before a class will also help direct your listening, by defining the types of information you want to listen for. You might also have questions on assignments that have been given. List them also.

FRAMING YOUR QUESTIONS

The next task is to ask the question. In your question, aim to be *specific, to the point,* and *polite.* Figure 6.1 gives some examples of questions that, because they follow these guidelines, are likely to get a positive response. On the other hand, questions that are unfocused, too vague or broad, or downright rude will probably get a negative response.

Figure 6.1

SAMPLE CLASSROOM QUESTIONS

Questions that are specific, to the point, and polite:

- ▲ Could you review the explanation of . . . . . ?
- ▲ On page 64 of the text, it says ". . . . ." Can you explain what that means?
- ▲ About how many sources should we use for the report on . . . . ?
- ▲ My notes say that . . . . . . Is that correct?

Questions that are either too broad, too indirect, irresponsible, or rude:

- ▲ I didn't understand last week's lecture on Romanticism. *(Too broad)*
- ▲ Your explanation of . . . . . was confusing. *(Rude)*
- ▲ I was absent on Wednesday. Did I miss anything important? *(Rude. Most instructors think they say important things in every class. Find out what you missed from another student.)*
- ▲ I lost my copy of the . . . . . . assignment. *(Get it from the instructor before or after class or during office hours.)*
- ▲ I was talking to my friend last week and he said . . . . and I said . . . . . But he thought . . . . . So I said . . . . . And that made me wonder . . . *(Too long-winded)*

You may feel self-conscious about asking questions in class, but that's a hurdle you can (and should) overcome. First, asking questions is the only way to get answers. A question represents a bit of knowledge that you are seeking and, as a student, your job is to seek knowledge. Second, in whatever career you're preparing for, you can expect that there will be meetings in which you'll need to participate. Speaking out in your classes is good training for your future career.

If you never speak out in any of your classes, try the following strategy. Select the class that you feel most comfortable in and set a goal of making one comment a day in it. Keep it up for two to three weeks, or until you feel comfortable with speaking there. Then try the same approach in your other classes, one at a time, until you're participating in all of your classes at some level.

USING QUESTIONS TO IMPROVE INSTRUCTION

Sometimes students report good results when they team up to ask questions. For instance, one professor in an anthropology class consistently used class time to talk about the research he was do-ing—very interesting, but he wasn't helping students deal with the very difficult material that they needed to learn. Four of the students began to meet in the cafeteria before class to discuss the problem. They decided to draw up a list of questions for the professor on the chapter they had been assigned to read. Then they divided the ques-tions among themselves, so that one student wouldn't seem to be making a pest out of herself. The next day, at the beginning of the class, they took turns asking their questions. To their surprise, the professor was very receptive to their questions and his answers were clear and illuminating. Soon other students chimed in with questions of their own. By the time the professor had finished answering their questions, he had covered all the material in the chapter. The stu-dents used this strategy for the entire term, and what had initially looked like a wasted class turned into a valuable learning experience.

What do you do, however, with professors who give confusing answers to student questions, or respond hostilely to them? First, be sure that the fault is not with you, the questioner, and when or how you ask questions. If it isn't, then realize that professors have differ-ent styles, just as students do. In an occasional class, asking questions will not be productive. But on the whole, professors complain that their students ask too few questions, not that they ask too many.

■
EXERCISE 2

Choose one of your classes and review your notes and the readings for the next class. Write down a list of the questions you have on the material. Edit them if necessary to make sure that they are specific, polite, and to the point. Ask one of your prepared ques-tions during the next class session.

PARTICIPATING IN SMALL GROUP DISCUSSIONS

In some classes, instructors will divide the class into groups to discuss a point and work on a problem. For example, in a psychology class, the instructor may divide the class into groups of five students, ask each student to recall a recent dream, and have the group analyze the content of the dreams and determine what themes predominate in dreams.

You may be asked to take on a certain role in a small group, such as discussion leader, recorder, or reporter. The **discussion leader** conducts the discussion, the **recorder** takes notes on the group's work, and the **reporter** summarizes the group's findings to the class as a whole. Often the recorder and reporter jobs are combined.

The first goal of the group should be to be sure that it under-stands the task at hand. Then, the discussion leader needs to keep the group on track and to make sure that every group member has an opportunity to contribute. The recorder either writes down the main ideas presented by the group, or, if a specific task has been set, the group consensus on the output. The reporter can use these notes to prepare a summary. If time allows, the reporter should rehearse his or her report to the group and get feedback on it before the group session ends.

PARTICIPATING IN CLASS DISCUSSIONS

In some classes, instructors will routinely conduct class by leading discussions on topics rather than lecturing. Instructors who use this approach hope to actively engage students in thinking about the subject matter. Often discussions are based on assigned readings.

The key to participating in class discussions based on readings is preparation. To prepare for a class discussion, take notes as you read, preferably in the notebook you will have in class. Your notes should be your reactions to whatever you're reading—more commentary than summary. Include in your notes the following:

> Points you agree with
> Points you disagree with
> Questions you have
> Personal connections or associations with the reading
> Connections with other material you have read
> A list of main ideas in the reading

During the discussion, there are several different types of contributions you can make:

> You can answer a question.
> You can state an opinion.
> You can agree or disagree with what another person has
>   said.
> You can ask a question, either to a person who has spoken
>   recently, to the class as a whole, or to the instructor.
> You can summarize the discussion to that point.
> You can relate a relevant experience or give an example.

There are also some unspoken rules that govern classroom discussions:

1.   Be polite.   You can disagree with another person's opinion strongly without resorting to name-calling.

2.   Be relevant.   A classroom discussion on animal patterns of communication is not the place for your amusing story about how your dog loves to chase your mechanical robot.

3.   Be concise.   In a lively discussion, many students will want an opportunity to speak. You should make your point briefly and then yield the floor to the next speaker. Students who are long-winded or who insist on taking every other turn will be resented by their classmates and the instructor.

4.   Listen.   If, as your hand is in the air, you are mentally rehearsing what you will say and ignoring what the present speaker is saying, you may repeat the same idea or say something irrelevant. Many students find it useful to jot down key words related to what they want to say, so that they can free their mind for listening. If the discussion progresses to another point before you get a chance to have your say, abandon that point and listen for a new opportunity to contribute.

If you find it difficult to participate in class discussions, resolve to make one contribution to each class discussion, even if it's just answering a yes-or-no question.

TAKING NOTES ON CLASS DISCUSSIONS

Class discussions are less formal and less organized than lectures; consequently, they are more difficult to take notes on. During the discussion, you want to make an unordered list of the main points that are brought up and the major questions that are raised. After the class, when editing your notes, write a summary of the discussion. Your summary might include, for example, a summary of two opposing positions presented during the discussion, or a statement of the major theoretical questions raised during the discussion.

SUMMARY

The simplest level of participation in classes is answering an instructor's questions. To prepare to answer questions, notice the types of questions a particular instructor asks and, as part of your preparations for class, prepare to answer questions of that type. Asking questions is an important tool in students' hands, and students can learn to ask questions designed to get positive responses: questions that are specific, to the point, and polite.

More is asked of you in small group discussions and whole class discussions. In a small group discussion, you may be asked to perform the role of discussion leader, of recorder, or of reporter. In a classwide discussion, you can play many roles, such as answering a question, stating your opinion, agreeing or disagreeing with another person's opinion, raising a question, summarizing the discussion as you see it, or relating relevant examples. In your contributions, be polite, be relevant to the topic under discussion, and keep your contribution brief. As you listen, write down the main points being made. Later, synthesize the notes into a summary.

■
JOURNAL EXERCISES

1. Is there any relation between where a student typically sits in class and whether he or she participates in class discussions? Write your observations on this topic, based on what you've observed about yourself and also about your fellow students.
2. All of us participate in many speech situations: dinnertime conversations, phone conversations, verbal interactions on the job, meetings, and so on. Describe the speech situations in which you feel most comfortable speaking and those which make you nervous.
3. Summarize the ways that writing can be used to prepare yourself for each of the four different speaking situations in classes: answering questions, asking questions, small groups, and class discussions.

■
ACADEMIC WRITING

Four types of academic speech situations have been discussed in this chapter: answering questions, asking questions, participating in group discussions, and participating in class discussions. Write a report about each class that you are currently taking discussing:

The type or types of participation needed in that class (including specific examples)

The extent to which you presently speak out in that class

Steps you could take to improve your participation in that class

P A R T

THREE

Doing College Reading Assignments

7

AN INTRODUCTION TO COLLEGE TEXTBOOKS

In this chapter, you will learn:

▲ how surveying a textbook can help you in doing reading assignments
▲ how to discover a textbook's organizational plan
▲ how to identify and use a textbook's study aids
▲ what the parts of a typical textbook are

Much of the learning that occurs in college occurs on your own—in the interaction between you and a textbook. In fact, you can consider your textbook's author as the second instructor in a class. This chapter and the following two present strategies to help you learn from textbooks. In this chapter, you will learn how to survey a textbook so you can use its features to help you do reading assignments. A **textbook** is a book written for use by students in a classroom. It differs from a **trade book** (a book written for the general public) in several ways: it is written specifically for students; its content corresponds to the content of a college course; and it contains features designed to make learning easier, such as study questions and glossaries.

Recent research in reading has emphasized that knowing how a book is organized and what its unique features are increases your ability to understand what you're reading. So, the more you understand about the design of your textbooks, the more you will get from reading them. In this chapter you will learn how to survey a textbook to discover its organization and features.

SURVEYING A TEXTBOOK

When you **survey a textbook,** you read the preface, study the table of contents, and look at the appendixes, glossary, and index to get an understanding of the book's contents, its features, and how it is organized. You survey a textbook when you begin using it to gain important background information so you can relate each reading assignment to the overall plan of the book.

STUDYING THE TABLE OF CONTENTS

A valuable tool for getting an overview of a textbook is the **table of contents.** Typically a table of contents lists the topics and subtopics for each chapter in the book, along with the pages on which they appear. Readers most frequently use tables of contents to locate the part of a book to read next. However, you can also study a textbook's table of contents to see how the book is organized, what topics are covered, where they are covered, what study aids are provided, and where they are placed. This information will help you construct a mental overview of your textbook. Then when you do a reading assignment, you will be able to see how the information in the individual chapter you are reading fits into the overall framework of the book.

In order to see how this process works, let's examine the tables of contents from two humanities textbooks. Figure 7.1 is the first page of the table of contents from a humanities textbook, *Arts and Ideas*. The first chapter, "Genesis of the Arts," both acts as an introduction to the humanities and presents information about ancient art of the Stone Age, Mesopotamia, and Egypt. The next three chapters present the Classical period of art, including the Hellenic period, the later Greek Hellenistic period, and the Roman period. This textbook is organized *chronologically,* or in time order, with each chapter covering a different period in art. Chronological order is a common organizing principle in textbooks, particularly those that present a subject from a historical perspective.

If you look at the outline of Chapter 2, "The Hellenic Style," you'll see that in this text different forms of art are discussed in the same order within each chapter, beginning with architecture and then sculpture.

As a quick glance at the table of contents for *Explorations in the Arts* (Figure 7.2) reveals, this textbook, although also an introductory humanities text, is organized quite differently. The principle of organization is not chronological but *topical.* The arts are organized into three categories: the arts of space, the arts of time, and the composite arts (arts that combine space and time). You can examine the table of contents to see which art form belongs to what category. The first three chapters discuss the three categories of arts, the

Figure 7.1   **TABLE OF CONTENTS FROM *ARTS & IDEAS***

fourth chapter discusses point of view in all of the forms of art, and the fifth chapter presents the principles of performance of art forms such as music and drama.

As these examples show, studying the table of contents can give you a quick overview of how chapters are organized and how information within chapters has been ordered. In addition, you can find information about how the book has been organized that will help you devise reading strategies. For instance, if you look at the outline of Chapter 2 in *Arts and Ideas,* you'll see that the chapter ends with the topic "The Hellenic Heritage," which is likely to be a summary of the chapter or a transition to the next chapter. Other chapters have a similar section. Once you note this kind of summary as a feature of the text, you can plan to use it as a check on your comprehension when reading.

■
_____

E X E R C I S E   1

Study the table of contents of one of the textbooks you are using this term and answer the following questions:

What are the major divisions of the material in the text?
What organizing principle does the author use?
What study aids are listed in the table of contents?
What is the typical chapter length?
Is there a pattern to the presentation of topics within a chapter?
Does it seem necessary to read the chapters in order? Explain.

READING A PREFACE

A **preface** (pronounced pref'iss) is an introductory overview of a book, usually written by the author. The preface and the table of contents make up the **front matter** of a textbook, the material that appears in a textbook before the first page of the first chapter. The preface is a direct source of information about how a book has been structured. Typically a preface will include information about:

The audience for whom the book was written
The scope of the book (what topics it includes and which it does not include)
The organization of material in the book (the way topics have been arranged and the reasons for choosing that arrangement)
Features of the book (aids to learning included in the book, and characteristics that make this book unique)
Changes made in this edition, if the book is a second or later edition
The theoretical approach of the author (the author's phi-

Figure 7.2   TABLE OF CONTENTS FROM *EXPLORATIONS IN THE ARTS*

losophy as to what concepts are important in a subject area or about how a subject is best learned)

Suggestions for teachers and students on how to use the book

A list of supplemental material available (such as a teacher's guide or student's study guide)

Acknowledgments (recognition of people who helped the author in developing the textbook)

Students often neglect to read the preface in their textbooks, thinking that the information it contains is irrelevant. In fact, the more you understand about the author's perspective, the more you will comprehend what you read. Reading a textbook without first having read the preface is like trying to operate a new appliance without first having read the instruction manual.

EXERCISE 2

At the end of this chapter on page 94 is a preface from the humanities textbook *Explorations in the Arts*. Read it and mark the information that's mentioned on the list above. Then answer the following questions.

1. For what type of course is this textbook intended?
2. What forms of art are presented in the text?
3. What is the principle of organization used in this book? Why isn't a chronological order used? What does this principle of organization allow the authors to show?
4. For what audience is this text intended?
5. What are some of the concepts related to art that are discussed throughout the text?
6. Where in the text would you find works of art discussed briefly? Where would you find them discussed in more depth?
7. What features in each chapter would help a student read the text?
8. What material at the end of the book would be useful to students?

After reading this preface, you now know why the authors chose to treat the arts in three broad categories as they did. You also have some idea of the basic concepts of the book and what study aids are provided. Information like this is the basis for your reading comprehension.

EXERCISE 3

Read the outline below for a summary of a preface. Then read the preface from one of your own textbooks, underlining the information on the topics in the outline. Finally, follow the outline and write a report on the preface by summarizing the information you found.

Title:
Author:
Copyright date:
Number of this edition:
Publisher:
Audience for whom the book is intended:
Scope of the text:
Organizational principle used:
The author's theoretical perspective on the subject:
Changes made in this edition (if the book is a second or
    later edition):
Student study aids included in the text as a whole:
Student study aids included in chapters:
Supplemental material available:
Appendixes included in the text:

PREVIEWING A CHAPTER

When you survey a textbook, in addition to studying the table of contents and reading the preface, you should preview a chapter to see what features are included to make studying and learning easier. To preview a chapter, pick a chapter from the center of the book that looks interesting. Turn to it and look through it, looking at (but not necessarily reading) every page. Look for:

A set of learning objectives or chapter goals at the begin-
    ning of the chapter
A preview of the chapter at the beginning
Subheadings, graphs, charts, and illustrations within the
    chapter
A list of concepts you should have learned, placed at the
    end of the chapter
Study or review questions, usually found at the end of the
    chapter
A summary at the end of the chapter

All of these textbook features can be used to help you tackle reading assignments. Use objectives or previews at the beginning of the chapter to give you an overview of the content and organization of the chapter. Use the graphs and charts within the chapter to help you visualize concepts. Use any of the features listed above to set **reading goals** for yourself, lists of topics about which you want to get information as you read. (See the following chapter for more about using reading goals when tackling reading assignments.) Use material at the end of the chapter like summaries and review questions to test your comprehension and to reinforce your learning.

APPENDIXES, GLOSSARIES, AND INDEXES

As you have seen, the front matter in a book is useful for getting a sense of the topics covered in a textbook and the overall organizational framework in which they are discussed. The **back matter** in a textbook is more frequently used for reference. Back matter in a textbook might include:

A **glossary:** a list of technical terms used in the textbook and their definitions

A **bibliography:** a list of books referred to in the text that may provide a basis for suggested further readings

An **appendix:** a collection of information a student might need to refer to frequently, such as tables, charts, and lists

An **index:** a list of people and topics discussed in the book, arranged alphabetically with page numbers for each item

Different textbooks will have different combinations of these features and will handle them differently. Familiarizing yourself with the back matter your textbooks have will allow you to take advantage of them as you work with the textbook.

The glossary is one of the most important study aids a textbook can have, as it provides an easy reference to the technical or specialized vocabulary terms a student needs to know. Different textbooks present glossary terms and definitions in different ways. The most common way (used in this text) is to highlight a term the first time it appears in the text by printing it in boldface print, and then to include the term and its definition in an alphabetically arranged list in the back of the text. Take a minute to glance at the glossary in this textbook as an example.

In other textbooks, glossary definitions for each chapter may be included at the end of the chapter instead of at the end of the text, or they might be highlighted at the top of the page or in the margins of the page on which the terms appear. Some authors combine the index and glossary, presenting the definition of a term along with the page references to the parts of the book where that topic is discussed. Figure 7.3 illustrates different methods for presenting the glossary in three different textbooks. Since learning technical vocabulary is such an important part of your coursework, a separate chapter is devoted to this topic (see Chapter 11).

A bibliography or list of books in a textbook is an excellent source of selected further readings for you on a topic that interests

Figure 7.3a   **THREE GLOSSARY METHODS**

DICTIONARY-STYLE GLOSSARY FROM *EXPLORATIONS IN THE ARTS*

cadenza A musical passage intended for ornament or *virtuoso* display, at one time improvised by the performer at the moment of performance but now usually written out in advance. Most often heard near the close of the first movement of a *concerto* before the full orchestra plays for the final time.

caesura A pause within a line of poetry.

cantilever In architecture, a horizontal projection, such as a balcony, that extends beyond its vertical supports and appears to be self-supporting.

capital The decorated top of a column [see Figure 45, page 51].

cella The windowless inner shrine of a Greek temple that housed the statue of a god.

chamber music An intimate form of music performed by few players, each taking a separate part.

choir In architecture, the part of a church beyond the *transept* that may include an *apse* and chapels.

chord A group of three or more pitches that sound together as a unit; an element of *harmony.*

classicism The style of classical Greece and Rome. In music, the dominant style of the late eighteenth century. See *neoclassicism.*

coda The closing section of a piece of music.

Figure 7.3b

GLOSSARY AS PART OF AN INDEX FROM *WORLD OF BIOLOGY*

Absorption (ab-**sorp**-shun) Passage of material into or through a cell or tissue
  of nutrients, 559, 571
  by plant roots, 403il

Abyssal zone, 794

Acetabularia, 202f–203f

Acetylcholine (**ass**-ee-tel-**ko**-leen) A compound of choline and acetic acid. The transmitter substance employed by cholinergic nerves
  in muscle movement, 443, 444il
  in nervous systems, 463, 465t

Acetyl Co A A key intermediate compound in metabolism; consists of an acetyl group covalently bonded to coenzyme A, 140

Acid (**ass**-id) A compound that dissociates in solution to produce hydrogen ions and some type of anion, **38–40**

Acoelomate organisms (a-**seel**-o-mate) Organisms that lack a body cavity (coelom), **303–305**

Acquired immunodeficiency syndrome, 539f

Acrosome, 170, **652f**

Figure 7.3c

GLOSSARY RUN-IN WITH TEXT FROM *UNDERSTANDING HUMAN BEHAVIOR*

you pleasure by feeding you and caring for you. But your *love* for your mother exists in the *combination* of your conscious associations with your unconscious feelings.

Freud's view of the emotions has often been called an *energy theory.* He believed your body continually creates "psychic energy" much as a dynamo continually produces electrical power. Freud called this psychic energy **libido**. According to Freud, *libido* is the motivating force that "powers" all your thoughts, feelings, and behaviors. *Expending* libidinal energy is associated with sensory pleasure. *Repressing* libidinal energy almost always leads to unpleasant tension, anxiety, and other negative emotional states.

Whenever you suppress an unpleasant thought or emotion, Freud said, you *block the release of libidinal energy.* Psychic tension builds up in your unconscious mind in much the same way that physical pressure builds up in an overheated steam boiler. Some of the repressed energy will "leak out" in variety of ways—through unusual dreams, fantasies, "slips of the tongue," and feelings of anxiety. However,

> **Libido** (lib-BEE-doh). The psychic energy created by your innate instincts. According to Freud, all behavior is "energized" by libido.
>
> **Catharsis** (kah-THAR-sis). From the Greek word meaning "to purge, or to clean out." If you are constipated and take a laxative to "clean out" your digestive system, you have undergone a physical catharsis. Freud believed psychotherapy could act as a psychological catharsis to cleanse the mind of bottled-up libidinal energy.

according to Freud, the best way to discharge the pent-up tension is through **catharsis**, which involves the open expression of your feelings.

Because Freudian theory is so rich and detailed, we will postpone a fuller discussion of his views until later. We should note, though, that one emotion frequently repressed is that of *anger.* From a Freudian point of view, releasing pent-up anger—particularly through *aggressive acts*—should always reduce stress through catharsis.

you or on a topic that you are thinking of writing a paper about. Some authors list related books and articles at the end of each chapter. Other authors, however, include one lengthier bibliography at the end of the text. By scanning the titles you can select books that are likely to contain information on topics you're interested in.

A textbook's appendix usually includes tables, charts, and lists that the authors feel will be useful reference information for you while you are doing assignments or reviewing for a test. For example, you might find a summary of symbols used in statistical formulas, a chart explaining the metric system, a brief summary of musical notation, or a review of the parts of a laboratory report. In some textbooks, answers to selected study questions in the text will be provided in an answer key in the appendix.

An index lists the topics that appear in a textbook alphabetically, with page references to the pages on which those topics are discussed. It is more detailed than a table of contents. For example, if you wanted to read about the sculpture *David* by the Renaissance sculptor and painter Michelangelo, you would not find it listed in the table of contents for either of the humanities texts discussed ear-

Figure 7.4

INDEX EXAMPLES FROM *UNDERSTANDING HUMAN BEHAVIOR*

SUBJECT INDEX

Abnormal psychology, 568–595
  holistic approach to, 594–595
Abstinence, *383*
Academic psychology, 19
Accommodation, 492–*493*, 693
Achievement tests, 562
Acne, 447
Acoustical coding, 396–*397*
Acquired Immune Deficiency syndrome, *see* AIDS
ACTH, 320, *321*
Action potentials, 33, 35, 69
Action research, 637
Activity pattern, *see* Beta waves
Acuity, *157*
  sensory, hormones and, 155–156
  visual, 180, 181
Adaptation, 492
  dark, 181–182
  receptor, 150–151
  visual, 181–182
Adaptation-level theory, 668, *669*, 671
Adaptive response, 58, *59*
Addicted, 75
Addiction, opiate, 75
Adjustment disorders, 588
Adrenal glands, *297,* 319
Adrenalin, 56, *57,* 319
Advertising, 688
  subliminal, 238–239
Aerial perspective, 206, *207*
Affect, 227, *229,* 317
Affective disorders
  causes of, 584–585
  types of, 585
Age regression, hypnosis and, 427
Aggression, 532
  pain and, 104–105
  Type A behavior and, 323
  violence and, 101, 103
Aging, model for, 538
AIDS, *39*
Alarm reaction, 320
Albinism, 186, *187*
Alcohol, 79–81
  pregnancy and, 450
  taking other drugs in combination with, 76
Alcoholism, 79, 382–385
Algorithm, *247*

NAME INDEX

Adams, Henry, 253–254
Adler, Alfred, 506, 510, 522, 523–524, 525, 530, 535, 572
Akil, H., 81
Albritten, Bill, 102
Alderfer, Clayton, 722
Allport, Gordon, 549–550
Ambron, Sueann, 473, 478, 479, 495, 504
Ames, Adelbert, 211
Amoore, John, 155
Amundsen, Jack, 139–141, 160
Anastasi, Anne, 548, 560–561
Andersen, E. S., 485
Andrasik, Frank, 379–380
Angell, James, 129, 130
Angst, Jules, 606, 628
Anne M., case of, 353–355
Aristotle, 90, 499
Arnold, Magda, 324, 325, 338
Aronson, E., 665
Asch, Solomon, 641, 666–667, 669, 691
Aserinsky, Eugene, 66
Ash, Philip, 592
Atkinson, R. L., 274
Axelrod, Julius, 320
Azrin, Nathan, 104–105, 106

Bakan, David, 524
Baker, Robert, 427
Baldwin, James Mark, 497
Bales, Robert, 649–650
Baltes, Paul, 535
Bandura, Albert, 533, 703, 707
Barber, Theodore X., 426, 427, 429, 433
Barclay, A., 720
Bard, P., 321, 326
Baribeau-Braun, Jacinthe, 582

Barnhart, C. L., 367
Barrios, Billy, 283
Bateson, Gregory, 582
Baum, A., 338
Beach, Frank, 156
Bean, P., 587
Bell, Alan, 301, 302
Bell, Alexander Graham, 151
Bell, A. P., 311
Belson, William, 100–101, 113
Bem, Daryl, 702
Benbow, C. P., 311
Bennett, W., 277, 278, 289
Berger, H., 65
Bergum, Bruce, 199–200
Bergum, Judith, 199–200
Bernard, Russell, 403
Berne, Eric, 619
Berscheid, Ellen, 642
Berwick, Robert, 246
Bexton, W. H., 251
Binet, Alfred, 552–*553*, 558
Bini, L., 604
Biron, Colette, 158, 159
Black, Stephen, 158, 161
Blake, Robert R., 667–668, 669, 670
Blau, Zena, 555–556, 567
Bloom, Benjamin, 556, 558
Blum, J. D., 597
Bogal-Albritten, Rosemarie, 102
Bograd, Michele, 102
Bolles, R. C., 271, 272, 286–287
Bond, Jennifer, 479
Bond, Lloyd, 560
Bonica, John, 420
Boring, E. G., 161
Bowlby, J. A., 462, 463
Braginsky, B. J., 189
Braginsky, D. D., 189
Brazelton, T. Barry, 448, 466
Braid, James, 425
Breger, Louis, 524

lier in this chapter, but you would find it in the indexes to both books.

Indexes contain references to people, topics, and terms discussed in a book. In many books, all references are combined into a master index, while in others there may be more than one index. For instance, the psychology text *Understanding Human Behavior* has separate indexes, a name index listing the names of psychologists and other individuals mentioned in the text, and a subject index listing topics and terms. Figure 7.4 shows part of the name index and the subject index from *Understanding Human Behavior.* In the subject index, a term which is defined in the text is printed in boldface, and the page number on which the definition appears is in italics. Items which are indented under a central heading are subtopics for that heading. For instance, general information on alcohol appears on pages 79–81, but information on pregnancy and alcohol will be found on page 450.

SUMMARY

Familiarizing yourself with your textbooks is an important step to enable you to get the most from reading assignments. Studying a table of contents can give you an overview, not only of the topics the book contains, but also of how the book has been organized. The preface provides direct information about the organizing principles at work in a text, about study aids provided, and about what makes a book unique. A preview of a typical chapter will reveal study aids such as chapter objectives and study questions. You can use these study aids to get an overview of the chapter, to set goals, to direct comprehension while reading, and to review and reinforce learning after reading. In the back of textbooks, useful reference sections are found such as glossaries, indexes, and other appendixes.

■
JOURNAL WRITING

What features attract you to a textbook? Do these features also help you to learn from that book?

■
ACADEMIC WRITING

1. Report on the textbook you are currently using that is most difficult for you. Include in your report the following information:

   I. Title, author(s), date and place of publication, edition number
   II. The text's subject matter, organizing principle, scope, intended audience, level of difficulty and format
   III. Study aids found in the book as a whole and in individual chapters
   IV. Your evaluation of the strengths and weaknesses of the book. A good point of view is to consider what makes

the textbook easy to learn from and what makes it difficult to learn from.

2. Use the above outline to compare and contrast two textbooks for the same course—one you are currently using
   and another that is used in other sections or that is in the
   college library.

READING FOR EXERCISE 2, PAGE 87: PREFACE FROM *EXPLORATIONS IN THE ARTS*

Explorations in the Arts is intended for introductory, interdisciplinary
Humanities courses that integrate the study of the various visual, verbal,
and performing arts. This broad perspective fosters awareness of the elements common to all the arts as well as of the distinctive characteristics
of each art form.

Rather than presenting a chronological survey of the arts or discussing each art form separately, *Explorations in the Arts* groups the arts into
three broad categories: the spatial (painting, sculpture, architecture, photography), the temporal (music, poetry, prose narrative), and the composite (theater, film, dance, opera). This organization enables us both to introduce the basic elements of each art form and to show what the arts
within each group have in common. Furthermore, we have linked the
well-known concepts of perspective and point of view to demonstrate
how artists shape their material, and we have used comparable terms in
discussing how performers reshape a work as they interpret it. We have,
moreover, considered works of art in several broader contexts: in relation
to certain major cultural traditions, to genres, and to several historical
periods. Finally, we take up the knotty problem of evaluation, giving attention to a number of criteria for judging works of art and suggesting to
what degree these are useful. Here, as elsewhere in the text, we test
these theoretical principles by applying them to specific works.

Explorations in the Arts is basically a self-sufficient text that includes
over 200 illustrations, two short stories, a number of poems, and two reviews of actual performances. In the earlier chapters we discuss a variety
of works rather briefly; later, we consider a few works in depth. Throughout, we offer vivid examples—some well-known and some unusual—to
illustrate basic concepts.

We have tried to make *Explorations in the Arts* as understandable
and useful as possible. We have adopted a level of writing and chosen
examples that are, we hope, appropriate for students whether they come
with traditional preparation or with more limited experience and whether
they are enrolled in two- or four-year colleges. Although our text is written for students of widely varying backgrounds, it has several distinctive
features that will be of benefit to all. The "Questions for Study and Discussion" at the end of each chapter encourage students to consolidate

their understanding of the material and to apply what they have learned to new situations. Occasional bars of music are reproduced in the text as visual guides and require no ability to read notes. Technical terms are identified by bold-faced lettering and carefully defined in the chapters in which they first appear; they are, moreover, redefined in the Glossary. An appendix offers a brief review of musical notation for those students who are asked to deal with this more technical material. In addition, the specially prepared cassette (available for student purchase) allows students to hear some of the music they are reading about; it also describes and demonstrates the key musical terms.

8

TACKLING READING ASSIGNMENTS

In this chapter you will learn:

▲ to set up a time strategy for completing reading assignments
▲ to get an overview of a reading assignment
▲ to set reading goals to guide your comprehension of textbook reading

Reading for a class is different from other kinds of reading you do because of your purpose. When you read a mystery novel, your aim is to entertain yourself. When you read a newspaper, your aim is to keep informed on current events and topics that interest you. When you do a reading assignment for a class, your purpose is to learn the material. Therefore, textbook reading requires a different approach from other kinds of reading. So as a student, you need to develop a specific set of strategies for academic reading, especially since, as you've probably already discovered, the greatest part of your studying for college classes consists of reading. This chapter and the following ones will teach you strategies for tackling academic reading assignments that will make your reading effective and efficient. Specifically, in this chapter you will learn how to tackle a reading assignment and how to construct reading goals to guide your comprehension. The next chapter, Chapter 9, will present strategies to use while reading to increase your comprehension and retention, including strategies for marking textbooks and strategies for reviewing.

PACING YOURSELF

How much time do you need to do a reading assignment for one of your classes? The answer may be different for different classes. For example, it's not unusual for a student to need just an hour to read thirty pages in one textbook, but to need three hours to read the same number of pages in a second textbook. In fact, no one has a single reading rate. The rate at which we read different material varies according to:

Our background in the subject

Our motivation for reading (such as reading to learn versus reading to entertain ourselves or reading to pass the time)

The level at which the material is written (difficulty of vocabulary, density of ideas)

In other words, you will read material more quickly if you're familiar with the subject, if you're highly motivated to read it, if you know you don't need to retain what you're reading, and/or if it's fairly readable. However, your reading rate will be much slower if you're not familiar with the subject, if your level of interest is low or if you are reading to learn the material, and/or if the material is written in a difficult manner. See Figure 8.1 for a guide to selecting the reading rate to use for a reading task.

In tackling college reading assignments, then, you need to allow different amounts of time for doing reading assignments in different courses. Find out about how long it takes you to do a typical reading assignment in each of your textbooks simply by timing yourself during one reading session. As you read, also notice how long you read productively before you begin to suffer from information overload.

Use these observations to set up strategies for doing your reading assignments in each of your textbooks. You should be able to answer these questions.

How long will it take you to read a typical chapter?

Should you do the assignment in one sitting or in several sittings?

At the beginning of each week, plot out how you will break up each reading assignment and write your plan in your college organizer or assignment book, as in this example:

Mon.:   Bio, Ch 4, pp. 77–87
        Hum, Ch 3 (read 1/2)

Figure 8.1

VARYING YOUR READING RATE

Background:
How much background information do you have on this topic?

Quite a bit (1 point)   _____
A fair amount (2 points)   _____
Some but not much (3 points)   _____
None (4 points)   _____

Purpose:
Why are you reading this material?

No particular reason (1 point)   _____
To get an overview (2 points)   _____
To get a thorough understanding (3 points)   _____
To both understand and learn (4 points)   _____

Difficulty:
How hard is this material?

Easy (1 point)   _____
Average (2 points)   _____
Challenging (3 points)   _____
Demanding (4 points)   _____

Total number of points   _____

Rating

3 to 4 points	Use a rapid reading rate
5 to 6 points	Use an average reading rate
7 to 9 points	Use a slow reading rate
10 to 12 points	Use a very slow reading rate, with very frequent rereadings or pauses to think

Note: Reading rates vary from individual to individual, with a typical college student's reading rate for average material ranging from 200 to 350 words per minute. Expect that your slow reading rate will be 1/2 of your average reading rate, and your very slow reading rate will be even less.

Tues.:   Psych, Ch 7, pp. 163–175
           Bio, pp. 87–93 (next section)

Wed.:   Finish Hum ch.
           About 10 more pages in Bio

Thurs.:   Psych, Ch 7, pp. 175–187
           Bio, p. 103 to end

■
——————————————
EXERCISE 1

List five types of reading material that you typically read during a week. (Some examples might be a weekly news magazine or a hobby magazine, a textbook assignment, a letter from a friend, a mystery novel, a movie review, or memos at work.) Use the questionnaire in Figure 8.1 to determine the reading rate you should use for each type of material.

GETTING AN OVERVIEW

When you are given a reading assignment in class, you will be tempted to open the book and begin reading on that page immediately. If you take a few steps before you begin to read, however, your reading will be more efficient—it will take less time and you will learn more from it.

Many of the strategies presented in this chapter and the next are adapted from a reading approach called SQ3R, an acronym for the key words *Survey, Question, Read, Recite,* and *Review* (see Box). Many people complain that when they read something for a class they understand it, but the next day they realize that they have retained little of what they read. SQ3R was designed to improve your comprehension and retention of reading material.

Your first step in tackling a reading assignment should be to look back at the table of contents. Study the table of contents for a few moments to observe how the chapter you are about to read fits into the overall organizational plan of the book and how it relates to the chapters before and after it.

For example, if you were assigned to read a chapter entitled "Hearing and Seeing" in the psychology textbook *Understanding Human Behavior,* a glance at the table of contents (Figure 8.2) would show that the chapter was placed in Part II of the textbook, in the section entitled "Sensation and Perception." The chapter before it is called "Introduction to Sensory Psychology: 'Touch,' Taste, and Smell." The following chapter is "Visual Perception and Speech Perception." This quick survey tells you that you will be reading a chapter about a subfield of psychology called sensory psychology, and that the discussions of hearing and seeing follow the discussions in the previous chapter on touching, tasting, and smelling.

SQ3R: A SYSTEMATIC APPROACH TO TEXTBOOK READING

The material in this chapter and the next breaks down the process of reading a textbook into a series of stages and strategies within each stage. These stages and strategies are based on a famous study–reading system developed in the 1940s called SQ3R (for Survey, Question, Read, Recite, and Review). The steps in SQ3R are:

Survey: Look over the chapter, paying attention to the chapter heading, chapter subheadings, any learning objectives for the chapter, charts, illustrations, and diagrams, the chapter summary, and any study or review questions.

Question: Create some overall reading goals for the chapter—questions that you expect to find the answers to as you read. As you read each section, create more specific reading goals for that section.

Read: Read section by section. As you read, look for the answer to the reading question you posed for that section. When you find it, mark it by underlining or by writing in the margin.

Recite: When you have read a section and found the answer to your question, fix the material in your mind by reciting it. Look away from the book and try to answer your question in your own words. If you can't, look over the section again.

Review: When you have finished reading the chapter, review it as a whole in order to see how the separate sections of the chapter relate to each other.

(This method is adapted from Francis P. Robinson, Effective Study, 4th ed. New York: Harper & Row, 1970.)

Once you've studied the table of contents, you're ready for the second step in getting an overview: **surveying a chapter**. Surveying a chapter is a highly recommended textbook reading strategy. It is an application of a partial reading technique called skimming. **Skimming** involves looking over a text rapidly, reading only whatever

Figure 8.2

TABLE OF CONTENTS FROM *UNDERSTANDING HUMAN BEHAVIOR*

provides an overview of the material. For example, you use skimming when you look through a page of the newspaper and read only the headlines. Another example of skimming is when you look through a magazine without stopping to read more than the first lines of any article.

When you survey a chapter, you skim the chapter from beginning to end, reading chapter objectives or previews, headings and subheadings, glancing at charts, noting glossary terms, and reading end-of-chapter summaries. The purpose is to get an overview: to give you a sense of the topics covered, to introduce you to how material in the chapter is organized, and to remind you of the study aids provided in the chapter.

Note that the technique of surveying a chapter is the same technique used in the last chapter as a step in surveying a book. However, when you survey a chapter as part of tackling a reading assignment, your goal is not just to note the study aids provided. It is to construct a framework for your comprehension when you read the chapter in its entirety.

As you will learn when you survey a chapter, skimming is not very time-consuming. It is a surprisingly efficient technique to give you a cognitive map of the chapter before you tackle reading it.

To summarize, to get an overview of a chapter:

1. Look at the table of contents to see how the chapter you are going to read fits into the overall organizational plan of the book.
2. Survey the chapter:
   Read chapter objectives or previews
   Read all the headings and subheadings
   Note any charts, diagrams, tables, or figures
   Notice new glossary terms
   Read any summaries at the end of the chapter

■
_____

E X E R C I S E   2

Answer the following questions about a reading assignment from one of your other classes:

1. What is the assignment?
2. Would you get more out of your reading if you did this assignment all at once or in several parts?
3. If it would be better to divide the reading into parts, how could you divide it?
4. What reading rate would be best suited for this assignment? Why?
5. How does this chapter fit into the overall organizational plan of the textbook? How does it relate to the chapter before it and the chapter after it?
6. Which of the following study aids are provided in the chapter: a list of learning objectives, an introduction, subheadings, glossary terms, study or review questions, or a summary?
7. What information did you learn from surveying the chapter about the topics covered and the organization of the chapter?
8. How much time did it take you to get an overview of the chapter and to decide how to pace yourself to read it?

DIRECTED READING: SETTING READING GOALS

How do you read to learn? One way is to use a strategy called **directed reading**. In directed reading, you set specific reading goals for yourself before you begin to read. Then, as you read, you read with these goals in mind.

Here's a demonstration that will show you how directed reading can help you learn from your textbooks. Read the following passage from *Explorations in the Arts:*

Symphony

Characteristic of a *symphony* is its use of a large number of musicians, generally between thirty and one hundred, playing a variety of instruments that make up the symphony orchestra (see Chapter 2). Today, major symphony orchestras generally comprise nearly one hundred players, although before the middle of the 19th century, composers had a smaller group at their disposal. Another characteristic of a symphony is that it is a long work. Haydn's and Mozart's last about twenty minutes; but the *Third Symphony,* known as the *Eroica* (1806), by Ludwig van Beethoven (1770–1827) takes about forty-five minutes to perform, and some symphonies are longer. Moreover, a symphony is divided into contrasting parts, called **movements**. These are often virtually complete pieces in themselves, coming to a clear final cadence. In performance, each movement usually is separated from the next by a substantial pause. The division into movements separated by a pause is one of the conventions of the symphony as well as of other long works.

The basic pattern of a symphony can be clearly seen in Beethoven's *Eroica.* Like the majority of symphonies, this has four movements, each designated by its principal tempo marks:

1. *Allegro con brio*
2. *Marcia funebre: Adagio assai*
3. *Scherzo e Trio: Allegro vivace*
4. *Allegro molto: Poco andante: Presto*

The key words for an understanding of the symphonic structure here are: *allegro,* "fast"; *adagio,* "quite slow"; *scherzo,* "joke," and *allegro vivace,* "fast and lively"; *allegro molto,* "very fast." In other words, the overall scheme follows the conventional pattern of fast, slow, fast, fast. In the *Eroica,* however, we will hear many changes in emotional character and many different melodic ideas (themes), without which we would scarcely want to keep listening for five minutes—let alone forty-five minutes.

In general terms, the first movement can be characterized as heroic, epic, noble, and grand. The second movement, as the heading *Marcia funebre* indicates, is a funeral march, slow and somber, with a contrasting major key section that suggests consolation for the tragedy expressed in the opening and closing sections of the movement. The "joking" character of the third movement is vigorous and humorous in a down-to-earth, hearty way, and the music has an infectious swing, partly as a result of its rapid ¾ meter. The last movement varies widely in mood, but ultimately expresses a feeling of heroic triumph. Here Beethoven uses the theme and variations form, in which a basic melodic idea is stated as a whole and then repeated with increasing elaboration and embellishment. Thus, the *Eroica,* like most symphonies, embraces a wide range of musical themes, fully developed in varying tempi in the course of four separate movements.

Because you read the passage without any goal in mind, your reading was not directed—that is, you had no specific aim in reading it. Now read the passage a second time. This time read it with the goal of finding the answer to this question: *"What are the characteristics of a symphony?"*

If the demonstration worked, your first reading yielded a general impression of what the passage was about, much like the general impression you have after reading a newspaper article. And, like your comprehension of a newspaper article, that general information will not be retained unless it is of high interest to you. However, your second reading should have produced a specific bit of information: the answer to the question posed above. You are probably able to recall the characteristics of the symphony after your second, directed reading of the passage—in other words, you have retained the information.

In the demonstration you just completed, you used a question to direct your reading. Questions that you ask yourself before you begin to read are called **reading goals**. They represent your learning goals for a reading assignment. If you set reading goals for yourself before you begin a reading assignment, you will be more likely to learn as you read.

USING TEXTBOOK FEATURES TO SET READING GOALS

How do you develop a set of reading goals for yourself before you read? The answer is in your textbook. Since textbooks are designed for student reading, their authors almost always provide some feature in each chapter that can be used to generate reading goals. Any of the following can be used to generate reading goals:

A set of learning objectives or chapter goals found at the beginning of the chapter

A preview that is part of the introduction to the chapter

The subheadings in the chapter

A summary or a list of key concepts placed at the end of the chapter

Study or review questions (usually found at the end of the chapter or in a student study guide that accompanies the textbook)

If the textbook authors have provided learning objectives for the chapter, then the work of setting reading goals has been done for you. Here, for example, are the learning objectives for Chapter 6 of *The World of Biology,* "The Energy of Life."

Learning Objectives

After you have finished studying this chapter you should be able to:

1. Define the term *energy* and contrast potential and kinetic energy.
2. State the first and second laws of thermodynamics and discuss their applications to living organisms and to the ecosphere.
3. Distinguish between endergonic and exergonic reactions and explain how they may be coupled so that the second law of thermodynamics is not violated.
4. Describe the energy dynamics of a reaction that is in equilibrium.
5. Explain the function of enzymes and describe how they work.
6. Describe factors, such as pH and temperature, that influence enzymatic activity.
7. Compare the action and effects of the various types of enzyme inhibitors (e.g., competitive and noncompetitive inhibitors).
8. Describe the chemical structure of ATP and its role in cellular metabolism.
9. Describe the role in metabolism of hydrogen and electron acceptors, such as NAD.

In naming these objectives for you, the authors are specifying what the most important concepts in this chapter are. If you read the chapter with the aim of fulfilling these objectives, your reading will be more efficient, as you will be concentrating on the chapter's key ideas.

Study questions found at the end of a chapter or in a student study guide also set learning goals for you. The trick is to read them *first,* before you read the material on which the question is based. Here are some examples of study questions, also based on the chapter "The Energy of Life."

1. Trace the various forms that energy takes from sunlight to the heat released during muscle contractions.
2. Imagine that you could redesign your body so that you

Figure 8.3   **SUB-HEADS FOR CHAPTER 8, GENRES OF THE ARTS OF TIME, FROM *EXPLORATIONS IN THE ARTS***

MUSIC
> **Symphony**
> **Concerto**
> **Sonata**
> **Song**
>> **Art song**
>> **Folk songs**
> **Chamber Music**

POETRY
> **Epic**
> **Lyric**
> **Ballad**
> **Sonnet**

PROSE NARRATIVE
> **Short Story, Novella, Novel**

could create all the energy you require. What advantages would this ability confer on you?

3. What is activation energy? How does an enzyme affect activation energy?

CREATING READING GOALS

In textbooks where reading goals in the form of learning objectives or study questions have not been provided, you need to create your own. One way to do this is by using the subheadings in the chapter as the basis for your own questions. For example, Figure 8.3 lists the subheadings from Chapter 8 of the humanities text *Explorations in the Arts*. As you look them over, notice that the typefaces used for each heading signal the level of the heading. The three main headings are in large boldface print and written all in capitals. Second-level headings under the main headings are written with capital and small letters and in a slightly smaller boldface print. Headings on the lowest level are written in print that is the same size as the print used in paragraphs and appear on the first line of a paragraph instead of on a separate line.

Reading these subheadings by themselves gives you an overview of the information contained in these pages. It can also be the basis for setting up a series of questions to use as reading goals for your reading. Here is an example of the questions that could be generated from these subheadings:

Figure 8.4

SOURCES OF READING GOALS

Source	Example
1. A learning objective	
Explain the function of enzymes and describe how they work.	What does an enzyme do? How does it work?
2. A chapter goal	
In this chapter you will learn: • to get an overview of a reading assignment.	How do you get an overview of a reading assignment?
3. Subheadings	
Memory Systems Sensory Information Stage	What different memory systems are there? What is the Sensory Information Stage?
4. Statements from a chapter summary	
(a) **Arousal Theory** was developed by Elizabeth Duffy to counter the criticisms of Hull's drive theory.	What is arousal theory? What is Hull's drive theory? What criticisms of Hull's drive theory were there?
(b) Another important pre-reading strategy is the setting of reading goals, question based on your overview of the chapter that will direct your attention to the main ideas in the chapter as you read.	Why are reading goals useful? How are they based on a chapter overview? How do they work?
5. Study questions	
What are the differences between the art song and the folk song?	What is an art song? What is a folk song? How do they differ?

What are the characteristics of a symphony?

How is a concerto different from a symphony?

What is a sonata?

What is the distinction between folk songs and art songs?

What is chamber music?

What are the characteristics of epic poems?

Is there any relation between a lyric poem and song lyrics?

Is a ballad a song or a type of poem or both?

Is a sonnet a type of love poem?

What is the difference between a short story, a novella, and a novel?

As these examples indicate, the questions you ask can be very simple—in fact, often a reading goal is a straightforward *who, what, when, where, why,* or *how* question. Note that your questions should reflect what you want to know about the subject. A student who already knew what chamber music was might ask a different question from one who didn't, for example.

Figure 8.4 summarizes the different sources in a textbook you can use for creating reading goals, along with examples of reading goals. The next exercise gives you an opportunity to apply this skill to your own textbook.

■ _____

EXERCISE 2

Select a current reading assignment for one of your other classes.

1. Survey the chapter, and note what textbook features are available to base reading goals on (chapter objectives or a chapter preview, subheadings, a chapter summary, or study questions).
2. Based on these sources, write a set of questions that you can use as reading goals for that chapter.

SUMMARY

Strategies for reading textbooks are different from the ones you use for more general reading tasks. You should expect that your reading rate will vary according to your background information on the subject, your reason for reading, and the level of difficulty of the material. Before tackling a reading assignment, estimate how long it will take and decide how to break your time up. Before you read, get an overview of the chapter. First, refer to the table of contents to note how the chapter relates to other chapters. Next, survey the chapter, reading chapter objectives, previews, headings and subheadings, and end-of-chapter summaries, to provide a framework for your comprehension. Use the information from surveying the chapter to generate reading goals, questions based on your overview of the chapter that will direct your attention to main ideas as you read.

■
JOURNAL WRITING

1. Give examples of things you read at a rapid reading rate, at an average reading rate, at a slow reading rate, and at a very slow reading rate. Time yourself reading some of these materials and figure out what your range of reading rates is.

2. Use the table in Figure 8.1 to assess the best reading rate for each of your current textbooks. Explain your reasons for rating each textbook the way you did.

3. Practice using reading goals when you read the newspaper. Choose an article that interests you and use the headline to generate a question to guide your reading. Then read with that question in mind. Write down what you learned from the article and how this reading experience differed from your usual experience in reading the newspaper.

■
ACADEMIC WRITING

In the appendix to this text on page 276, you'll find a sample chapter from a textbook—Chapter 3, "Components of the Composite Arts," from *Explorations in the Arts.*

1. Read a short sample section and estimate what level of difficulty the material poses for you. Work out a strategy for reading it in its entirety.

2. Survey the chapter.

3. Use the subheadings in the chapter to write a set of reading goals for the chapter.

CHAPTER

9

ACTIVE READING

In this chapter, you will learn:

▲ to use underlining to mark main ideas in textbooks
▲ strategies to use when reading difficult sections in textbooks
▲ to use margin notes to make your reading more active
▲ techniques for reviewing what you have read

What does it mean to be an active reader? It means that you approach reading as an active process of searching for meaning and that you use active means of learning as you read. This chapter will teach you techniques to become a more active reader. You will find that these techniques will greatly increase the amount of information you learn and remember from reading assignments.

Whether you are taking notes on a classroom lecture or reading your textbook in your room, the presence of a pen in your hand marks you as a student actively engaged in learning. Just like taking notes, marking textbooks helps you learn by increasing your concentration while you are reading, by reinforcing the material, and by providing a useful reference when you review the material. In this chapter, you will learn to mark your textbook in two ways: by underlining and by writing notes in the margin. Additionally, you'll learn a cluster of strategies for dealing with difficult reading material, along with the situations in which to apply each one. Finally, you'll learn some techniques for reviewing reading.

UNDERLINING

In the last chapter, you learned to use textbook features like learning objectives or subheadings to create reading goals: questions about each section of a chapter that guide your reading of the chapter. In addition to guiding your comprehension, reading goals are useful guides to what to underline. You will find reading goals make it easier to locate the main ideas in your textbooks.

For example, in the last chapter, you read a section from the humanities textbook *Explorations in the Arts,* using as your reading goal the question: "What are the characteristics of a symphony?" If, as you read, you underlined the material that answered this question, your work might have looked like Figure 9.1.

The central idea of this passage is that symphonies characteristically involve a large number of musicians, are relatively long, are divided into movements, and have a range of themes and a variety of tempi which are developed in the movements. The underlined words highlight these central ideas.

To use reading goals to underline, do the reading assignment section by section. For example, in a textbook that uses subheadings, read and mark the material under one subheading before going on to the next section. If there are no subheadings, you'll need to survey the chapter and use the overview you get from surveying to divide the chapter into sections yourself.

As you read each section, identify a reading goal for that section. Read the section once at a fairly rapid pace, aiming for an overall understanding of it. As you read, note any new terms that are used. If you don't understand the meaning of a new term after your first rapid reading, look up its meaning in the textbook glossary before your second, more careful reading.

Now reread the passage, reading more slowly. This time look specifically for the information that is a response to your reading goal. When you locate this information, underline it. As Figure 9.1 illustrates, you do not have to underline complete sentences— phrases and partial sentences are fine.

At the same time, if new technical vocabulary in the section is not highlighted already, circle new technical terms and underline their definitions. Draw a line from the term to the words that define it. This technique will make it easy to review vocabulary when studying.

Before you go on to the next section, check your understanding by reading what you underlined. The words you highlighted should provide a brief answer to the question that your reading goal posed.

In summary, take the following steps to outline a reading assignment:

1. Skim the passage to get an overview and to create a reading goal.
2. Read the passage once quickly.

Figure 9.1

EXAMPLE OF UNDERLINING

Reading Goal: What are the characteristics of a symphony?

Symphony

Characteristic of a *symphony* is its use of a large number of musicians, generally between thirty and one hundred, playing a variety of instruments that make up the symphony orchestra (see Chapter 2). Today major symphony orchestras generally comprise nearly one hundred players, although before the middle of the 19th century, composers had a smaller group at their disposal. Another characteristic of a symphony is that it is a long work. Haydn's and Mozart's last about twenty minutes; but the *Third Symphony*, known as the *Eroica* (1806), by Ludwig van Beethoven (1770-1827) takes about forty-five minutes to perform, and some symphonies are longer. Moreover, a symphony is divided into contrasting parts, called movements. These are often virtually complete pieces in themselves, coming to a clear final cadence. In performance, each movement usually is separated from the next by a substantial pause. The division into movements separated by a pause is one of the conventions of the symphony as well as of other long works.

The basic pattern of a symphony can be clearly seen in Beethoven's *Eroica*. Like the majority of symphonies, this has four movements, each designated by its principal tempo marks:

1. *Allergro con brio*
2. *Marcia funebre: Adagio assai*
3. *Scherzo e Trio: Allegro vivace*
4. *Allegro molto: Poco andante: Presto*

The key words for an understanding of the symphonic structure here are: *allegro*, "fast"; *adagio*, "quite slow"; *scherzo*, "joke," and *allegro vivace*, "fast and lively"; *allegro molto*, "very fast." In other words, the overall scheme follows the conventional pattern of fast, slow, fast, fast. In the *Eroica*, however, we will hear many changes in emotional characters and many different melodic ideas (themes), without which we would scarcely want to keep listening for five minutes — let alone forty-five minutes.

In general terms, the first movement can be characterized as heroic, epic, noble, and grand. The second movement, as the heading *Marcia funebre* indicates, is a funeral march, slow somber, with a contrasting major key section that suggests consolation for the tragedy expressed in the opening and closing sections of the movement. The "joking" character of the third movement is vigorous and humorous in a down-to-earth, hearty way, and the music has an infectious swing, partly as a result of its rapid ¾ meter. The last movement varies widely in mood, but ultimately expresses a feeling of heroic triumph. Here Beethoven uses the theme and variations form, in which a basic melodic idea is stated as a whole and then repeated with increasing elaboration and embellishment. Thus, the *Eroica*, like most symphonies, embraces a wide range of musical themes, fully developed in varying tempi in the course of four separate movements.

**WRITE IN YOUR TEXTBOOKS?
DEFINITELY!**

Years of habit may have convinced you that you shouldn't write in your textbooks, particularly if you went to schools where your books were lent to you for the year and had to be returned in good condition after you had finished using them. But in college, you'll be buying your own books, and they are yours to write in. You'll find that if you get in the habit of doing your reading assignments with pen in hand and using that pen to underline and write comments in your textbooks, you'll be learning more while you read. As a bonus, your markings will make it easier to review material for a test. Buying a textbook and not marking it up is like buying a new pair of shoes and refusing to wear them.

---

3. Read it a second time, looking for the information that answers the question you posed, and underline it.
4. Circle any new technical terms and mark their definitions.
5. Check your underlining by reading what you underlined. Make any additions or deletions needed.

EXERCISE 1

At the end of this chapter on page 122 are three sections from textbooks. Practice reading and underlining them using the steps outlined above.

HOW NOT TO UNDERLINE

The main mistakes students make in underlining are underlining too much material or underlining minor points instead of major points. Figure 9.2 illustrates these errors.

In the first example, more than 50 percent of the material has been underlined, including sentences that state the main idea, sentences that restate the main idea, and supporting information and examples. The fact that the student underlined so much suggests that he didn't have a goal in mind when reading this passage. With no reading goal, he had difficulty separating the main ideas from the supporting material. Dense underlining like this is almost useless when the student returns to review. In going over what he has underlined, he will be forced to reread almost the whole passage. A good level of underlining is to mark between 10 percent and 20 percent of a passage.

Figure 9.2

EXAMPLES OF POOR UNDERLINING

A. Too much is underlined — No evidence of reading goal.

Symphony

Characteristic of a *symphony* is its use of a large number of musicians, generally between thirty and one hundred, playing a variety of instruments that make up the symphony orchestra (see Chapter 2). Today major symphony orchestras generally comprise nearly one hundred players, although before the middle of the 19th century, composers had a smaller group at their disposal. Another characteristic of a symphony is that it is a long work. Haydn's and Mozart's last about twenty minutes; but the *Third Symphony*, known as the *Eroica* (1806), by Ludwig van Beethoven (1770-1827) takes about forty-five minutes to perform, and some symphonies are longer. Moreover, a symphony is divided into contrasting parts, called movements. These are often virtually complete pieces in themselves, coming to a clear final cadence. In performance, each movement usually is separated from the next by a substantial pause. The division into movements separated by a pause is one of the conventions of the symphony as well as of other long works.

B. Level of underlining is acceptable, but main ideas aren't marked.

Symphony

Characteristic of a *symphony* is its use of a large number of musicians, generally between thirty and one hundred, playing a variety of instruments that make up the symphony orchestra (see Chapter 2). Today major symphony orchestras generally comprise nearly one hundred players, although before the middle of the 19th century, composers had a smaller group at their disposal. Another characteristic of a symphony is that it is a long work. Haydn's and Mozart's last about twenty minutes; but the *Third Symphony*, known as the *Eroica* (1806), by Ludwig van Beethoven (1770-1827) takes about forty-five minutes to perform, and some symphonies are longer. Moreover, a symphony is divided into contrasting parts, called movements. These are often virtually complete pieces in themselves, coming to a clear final cadence. In performance, each movement usually is separated from the next by a substantial pause. The division into movements separated by a pause is one of the conventions of the symphony as well as of other long works.

In the second example, the amount of material underlined is acceptable, but the student hasn't underlined any words that express the passage's main idea. The student in this case had trouble discriminating between the central idea and the supporting material. For instance, the information that Haydn's and Mozart's symphonies were shorter than Beethoven's is supporting information and should not have been underlined.

■
_____

EXERCISE 2

Select a section from one of your textbooks (2 to 4 pages). Read the section and underline it, following the steps suggested above.

WORKING TO COMPREHEND

What can you do if you read a section in one of your textbooks and don't understand it? There are a variety of strategies to use when you can't seem to get at the meaning of something you're reading. What strategy you use will depend on where the knot occurs: on what's keeping you from understanding what the author is saying.

The first step is to read the entire section through once quickly to identify where your comprehension is breaking down. Place a checkmark at this point, and then try one of the following strategies.

If the problem is that the material is very dense, with a lot of ideas packed into the section, read it very slowly, sentence by sentence. Check your comprehension of each sentence by paraphrasing (putting the idea into your own words) each sentence.

If there is an idea that you don't understand, even after a slow and careful reading, capture what you don't understand in a question. Write the question in the margin of your text. Verbalizing what you don't understand may direct you to the answer on your own. If not, you'll have a specific question prepared for your instructor.

If there is a key word in the passage that you don't understand, use the glossary or a dictionary to find the word's meaning. Come up with a paraphrase for the word—a phrase that states the word's meaning in other words. Now reread the passage and mentally substitute the paraphrase for the word that is giving you difficulty.

If you understand the separate ideas in the section but have difficulty seeing how they relate to each other, first look for any kind of visual aid that accompanies the section, like a diagram, a map, a table, or a chart. As you reread the section, keep looking from the text to the visual and back again to increase your sense of how the ideas are represented graphically in relation to each other.

If ideas haven't been visualized for you, you can construct a visual aid yourself. For example, if the section of the text is outlining a series of steps or stages, you can make a flow chart to visualize them. If you are trying to figure out how ideas are logically related, you can try **mapping** the ideas—making a simple visual to represent the re-

Figure 9.3

EXAMPLE OF MAPPING

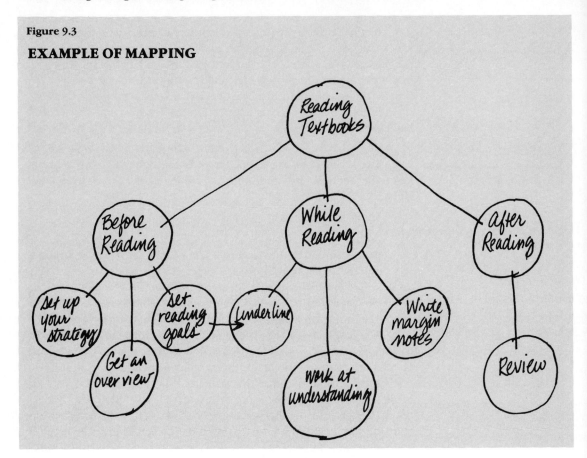

lationships between ideas. Figure 9.3 is an example of a map of ideas. It shows the relationship between the main ideas about the reading process in this chapter and the preceding one.

■
E X E R C I S E   3

Beginning on page 122 at the end of this chapter, you will find three passages from textbooks to use for practicing these comprehension strategies.

1. Begin by generating a reading goal based on the subheading.
2. Next, read the passage at a fairly rapid rate both to get an overview and to identify spots that are difficult to comprehend.
3. Now read the passage again, reading the parts that were difficult to understand at a slow to very slow rate.
4. Capture what you don't understand in the form of a question. Write your question in the margin.
5. Try each of the following strategies in one place where it's appropriate:

Use a paraphrase for a new term (try this in the "Eu-stress" passage on page 125).

Read while referring to a visual (apply this strategy while reading the "Harmony" passage and the "Muscle Tissue" passage on page 124).

Map out the ideas (try this strategy in the "Muscle Tissue" passage).

RESPONDING AS YOU READ

In a classroom lecture, even when most of the lecture is mono-log, you have chances to interact with the instructor—to stop to ask questions or answer them, to make comments, to ask for clarification of a certain point, and so on. All of these activities engage you more actively in the learning process.

Just as you can participate more actively in a classroom lecture by speaking, you can engage yourself more actively in the reading process by writing margin notes as you read. **Margin notes** are comments in the margins of your textbook that record your reactions to the ideas you're encountering. When you write margin notes as you read, you will find it easier to concentrate, and you will also find that you will learn and recall more from what you read.

To write margin notes, imagine that the author is actually your classroom teacher, speaking to you through the pages of the book. As you read what he or she has to say, you can respond to the message, just as you might do in class. Since the author is communicating to you through the medium of writing, your responses will also be in writing. If what you read raises a question in your mind, you can write that question in the margin of the book. If you disagree with what's being said, you can record your opinion. If something you read recalls a personal experience, you can write a comment in the margin to remind you of this tie-in.

Figure 9.4 is an example showing one student's responses to a section from a text.

The comments the student wrote are evidence that she was thinking about the material as she read and struggling to make it her own. Through the process of responding to what she read, she became a participant in the reading process instead of an observer. It's not surprising that she will remember what she read more easily than another student who read the same passage passively.

Figure 9.5 lists the types of margin comments written by readers. Study it before you practice writing margin notes yourself.

■

EXERCISE 4   Read the passage at the end of the chapter on page 126 about an experiment in training army recruits, " 'Sink or Swim' Learning." As you read, write margin notes of the types suggested in Figure 9.5.

Figure 9.4

RESPONSES TO A TEXT

Type A Personalities

In 1973, Meyer Friedman and Ray Rosenman published a book entitled *Type A Behavior and Your Heart.* After years of studying heart patients, these two physicians concluded that many types of heart failure are due to "a particular complex of personality traits including excessive competitive drive, aggressiveness, impatience, and a harrying sense of time urgency." They named this behavioral syndrome "Type A Behavior." The opposite sort of behavior pattern—relaxed awareness, patience, and a lack of excessive aggression—they call "Type B Behavior."

According to Friedman and Rosenman, the hallmark of Type A Behavior is *aggressiveness.* Type A people are highly concerned with proving themselves to others. Therefore, they try to complete as many tasks as possible in the shortest possible amount of time. Their pursuit of "measurable excellence" is so extreme, they leave themselves no time for leisure. They usually ignore or neglect their families. They have few close friends because most others interpret their aggressiveness as hostility or lack of trust. *Suppressing* aggressive instincts merely makes things worse, Friedman and Rosenman say, because "repression always leads to increased stress and tension."

Type A individuals also have many bad health habits. They skip meals, then "pig out" on rich, fatty foods. They often smoke too much and drink too much. They have no time for exercise, and their sleep habits are poor. All these behaviors put them "at risk" for a variety of stress-related illnesses.

Friedman and Rosenman believe that the major *physical* factors leading to heart failure are high blood sugar, high blood pressure, and high cholesterol intake. All these physical factors are, of course, made much worse by Type A Behavior. So it is the *personality pattern* that kills Type A people. Thus, therapy must be *psychological,* not *medical.* Friedman and Rosenman recommend that anyone who recognizes him- or herself as a Type A person should immediately change to a more healthy way of life or the person is likely to suffer a stress-related heart attack early in life. And, following the Freudian model, Friedman and Rosenman suggest that "cathartic discharge" of the emotions will be followed by a healthy decrease in blood pressure and other physical signs of tension.

Handwritten margin notes:

Their distinction might be too sharp — a lot of people are part Type A, part Type B.

Ex: John can't wait on line.

See notes on Freud May 3rd Class.

Type A = competition aggression impatience

Are Type A's basically insecure?

But suppression is necessary sometimes (see Tarvis).

Does the behavior cause the bad habits or vice-versa?

Do doctors still believe this? Possibly a Type A can't change without outside help.

Figure 9.5

TYPES OF MARGIN COMMENTS

Type	Example
1. **Summary comments**—phrases highlighting central ideas in the text. Summary comments are a useful alternative to underlining.	Type A = competition, aggression, impatience.
2. **Questions**—including questions about points you don't understand and questions that aren't answered in the text.	Does the behavior cause the bad health habits or vice-versa? Are Type A's basically insecure? Do doctors still believe this?
3. **Opinions**—comments agreeing or disagreeing with ideas presented in the text.	Their distinction may be too sharp—a lot of people are part Type A, part Type B.
4. **Personal associations**—individual tie-ins with your life.	Ex: John—can't wait on line.
5. **Cross-references**—reminders of other places in the book or in another book where related ideas are discussed.	See notes on Freud, May 3rd class.
6. **Contrasts**—similar to cross-references, but references to another idea that is different.	But suppression is necessary sometimes (see Tavris).
7. **General comments**—ideas that occur to you as you read.	Possibly a Type A can't change without outside help.

REVIEWING

Remember when you were a child and you were sent to the store to buy some things for dinner. On the way, you kept reciting the list of things you had to buy over and over: "Milk, bread, tuna fish ... milk, bread, tuna fish." Even at that early age, you instinctively knew something important about learning: that the more often you review ideas, the more likely you are to recall them.

You may choose to review reading assignments only right before a test, but you'll learn the material better and more efficiently if you review it more often. In fact, the best time to review a reading assignment is soon after you've finished reading it, because then the material is still fresh. Even ten minutes of review will fix the material in your mind. When you go over the material again before a test, you'll find that you have retained much of it. There are many ways to review a chapter that you've read.

1.   Review by testing yourself.   If you've used the directed reading approach recommended in this chapter and the last, you've directed your reading by asking yourself a series of questions. To review, ask yourself the same series of questions and try to answer them mentally. If you can, fine. If you can't, scan to find the part of the chapter that has that information and reread that part. (**Scanning** is looking through a text to find where a certain piece of information is located. For example, when you look through the telephone listings for a person named Rogers who lives on Sutton Street, you're scanning.)

2.   Review by rereading chapter objectives and summaries.   When you read chapter objectives and summaries after you've read the textbook chapter, try to mentally summarize the information they refer to. This mental exercise is a good way to synthesize the material in the chapter—to see how the ideas in the separate sections relate to one another.

3.   Review by partial rereading.   If you've underlined the chapter and made margin notes, you can review by rereading what you've marked and written. Since you've been concentrating on marking the main ideas, reading what you marked should be like reading a summary of the chapter. However, don't simply *read* what you've underlined. Stop after each section, close your eyes, and recite the ideas you underlined to yourself.

You might also reread selected parts of the chapter, particularly those you felt that you didn't understand fully the first time through. Now, information you've gotten from the instructor's lecture or from the rest of the chapter may help you understand those sections.

4.   Review by writing.   Perhaps the best way to review a reading assignment is with pen in hand. Try writing a one-page summary of the reading assignment—an integrated summary of the chapter or selection in paragraph form. The process of writing such a summary will be a learning experience in itself, as it will lead you to reflect on what you have read and its significance. You can keep these summaries together in a journal notebook or in the back of your class notebook. Later on, you can use the summaries to review for an exam.

An alternative is to do a more personal type of writing after each reading assignment by keeping a learning journal. A **learning journal** is a record of your responses and reactions to what you have read. Many instructors assign learning journals as part of the regular assignments for a course. When you make entries in a learning journal, think of yourself as answering the questions, "What did I learn from this reading assignment, and what do I think about it?" As the term progresses, a learning journal becomes a record of the development of your ideas. When you reread the pages you wrote, you will be able to see how your thinking has changed and matured through the term.

■ EXERCISE 5

Go back and review an earlier chapter in this textbook. Take the following steps:

1. Make up a series of questions based on the chapter subheadings and test yourself on them.
2. Reread the chapter objectives and the chapter summary to recall what you learned from reading that chapter.
3. Reread any margin notes or underlinings you made while reading.
4. Reread any sections of the chapter that you have forgotten, based on your self-testing or your review of the chapter summary and objectives.
5. Write a half-page summary of the chapter and a half-page response to the chapter.

SUMMARY

When you read actively, you use active ways of comprehending as you read. One technique for active reading is to use reading goals worded as questions to identify the main ideas in each section of a textbook. As you locate the information that answers each question, underline it. Other techniques are to be used when you have difficulty in understanding. Once you've reread the section rapidly to identify the problem, read it slowly and work at building up a picture of what's being said sentence by sentence. Often it's useful to verbalize what you don't understand as a question. Work with a glossary to check your understanding of key terms, and refer to any visual aid in the textbook as you read. If no visual aid was provided, try mapping the relation of ideas in the section yourself. You can also increase your participation during the reading process by writing margin notes as you read, as margin notes capture your reactions to the ideas you are encountering. Finally, part of your reading should be reinforcing your learning by reviewing. Review by testing yourself, by rereading chapter objectives and summaries, by reviewing what you underlined and wrote in the margin, by rereading sections of the text that you are still unsure of, and by writing summaries or entries in a learning journal.

■ JOURNAL WRITING

1. Have you ever marked your books while you were reading? Why or why not? If so, what did you do? If not, how do you react to the idea?

2. Compare the way you underlined one chapter in your text-book with the way one of your classmates marked his or her book. What differences did you observe? Did one person's markings seem more in accord with the principles outlined in this chapter? Whose book would be easier to review and why?

3. Keep a learning journal in one of your classes for a week. Include in it summaries of the readings that you do and your personal responses to them.

■
ACADEMIC WRITING

1. Read the chapter in the appendix, "Components of the Composite Arts," and, as you read, mark the chapter with under-linings and margin notes. Use any of the comprehension strategies suggested as needed when you reach a difficult passage.

2. Apply the skills of underlining, comprehension strategies, and responding to reading when you read a regularly assigned chapter in one of your textbooks. Report on what strategies you used and how effective they were.

PASSAGES TO PRACTICE READING STRATEGIES FOR EXERCISE 1 ON PAGE 113

REGULATION OF BREATHING

The amount of oxygen used by the body varies with different levels of activity. When you are engaged in a strenuous basketball game, for example, you require more oxygen than when reading quietly. Breathing is controlled by respiratory centers in the brain that are indirectly sensitive to increases in the amount of carbon dioxide in the blood (see Fig. 26–5). Nerves from the respiratory centers stimulate the contraction of chest muscles. During exercise greater amounts of carbon dioxide are produced. The carbon dioxide stimulates the respiratory centers to produce more rapid and more forceful breathing. In this way sufficient oxygen is provided to meet the body's increased need.

World of Biology, p. 552

Smell—an Ancient Sense

Smell is a unique sense in at least two important ways. First, it is perhaps the most ancient sense of all. Single-celled organisms could detect molecules in the water around them long before they became sensitive to sights or sounds. The fact that the olfactory nerve bypasses the thalamus and runs directly to the amygdala and other parts of the "old mammalian brain" (see Chapter 4) is good evidence of the ancientness of smell. All other sensory inputs pass through the thalamus before going on to the cortex.

Second, smell seems more directly related to emotion and motivation than are the other senses (see Fig. 6.7). In his 1982 book *The Perception of Odors*, Brown University psychologist Trygg Engen puts it this way: "Functionally, *smell may be to emotion* what sight or hearing is to cognition. . . . When odor is involved it may well cause a feeling before it elicits a concern with the meaning of odor." Engen notes, for instance, that many attacks of **mass hysteria** are set off by a new or unusual odor. And many epileptic patients report they experienced an "odd odor" (real or imagined) just prior to a grand mal seizure.

Understanding Human Behavior, p. 155

The Western

Usually set in the period following the Civil War and located in the West or Southwest of the United States, the Western tends to present characters who are clearly either good or evil and who are shown in situations that involve physical conflict and other forms of violence. Typically, the good characters—cowhands, farmers, sheriffs, and schoolteachers—represent the forces of order, law, and civilization. They oppose the representatives of disorder, lawlessness, and savagery such as train robbers, rustlers, and renegades. The confrontation between these two opposing factions leads to standard scenes including a chase and a final showdown [177]. Visually, these films—often shot in Monument Valley, Arizona—present immense open spaces which are contrasted with tiny outposts of civilization. The ability of film to capture motion by tracking and panning can make the chase and showdown scenes especially exciting.

The simple conflict between the forces of good and evil or civilization and lawlessness which is the theme of the ordinary Western has been treated with great subtlety in such outstanding examples of the genre as *My Darling Clementine* (1946), directed by John Ford (1895–1973), *High Noon* (1952), directed by Fred Zinnemann (b. 1907), and *The Wild Bunch* (1969), directed by Sam Peckinpah (1926–1984). In *High Noon,* members of the supposedly civilized community are shown to be weak and cowardly as they refuse to help the heroic sheriff in his struggle against a group of outlaws. Not only the community's but also the hero's behavior is atypical. At the end, although he has been successful, the disillusioned sheriff throws down his badge, leaving the town to its fate. In addition, this film is much more tightly constructed than the usual Western, for it strictly observes the unities of both action and time. Everything is directly related to the central conflict and takes place within a few hours. Its disillusionment with civilization and the concentrated action make *High Noon* far more thought provoking and powerful than most Westerns.

Explorations in the Arts, pp. 291–292

PASSAGES TO PRACTICE COMPREHENSION STRATEGIES FOR EXERCISE 3 ON PAGE 116

Harmony

The third important element of music after rhythm and melody is *harmony.* The term is used for the way in which different pitches sound together. When three or more different pitches are arranged to sound simultaneously, they form a **chord.** When they sound one after another in close succession, they form a **broken chord.** Harmony may, in fact, be defined as the structure and movement of chords.

Harmony may be the most complex element of music. When a composer writes a series of chords, a listener will normally hear only one note of each chord—the highest note—as the melody note. Since note succeeds note in performance, the listener is aware not simply of chords but also, over a period of time, of a melodic and rhythmic progression. In listening, we cannot isolate the harmony and deal with it as if it were independent of other musical elements.

Chords can be described by the *intervals,* the distance between pairs of pitches, that constitute each chord. This distance is expressed as an ordinal number (second, third, fourth, and so on), which can be quickly read on the musical staff by counting lines and spaces [see Example 4]. We must remember to count all the lines and spaces that are occupied by and are between each note of the interval.

Example 4   Some musical intervals.

Explorations in the Arts, p. 64

Muscle Tissue

In most animals muscle is the most abundant tissue. It accounts for nearly two-thirds of the body weight in a human being. **Muscle tissue** is specialized for contraction and is the basis for almost all movement in animals. Because they are long and narrow, muscle cells are referred to as fibers. Muscle fibers are usually arranged in layers or bundles surrounded by connective tissue.

There are three types of muscle tissue: skeletal, cardiac, and smooth (Fig. 20–9). **Skeletal muscle,** which is attached to the bones, can be contracted voluntarily. This muscle tissue permits us to walk, run, write, and move the body in other ways. Characterized by a pattern of light and dark stripes, or striations, it is also referred to as **striated muscle.** Each skeletal muscle fiber has several nuclei that lie just under the cell membrane.

Cardiac muscle, the main tissue of the heart, is a kind of striated muscle that is not under voluntary control. The fibers of cardiac muscle are joined end to end and branch and rejoin to form complex networks. One or two nuclei are found within each fiber. A characteristic feature of

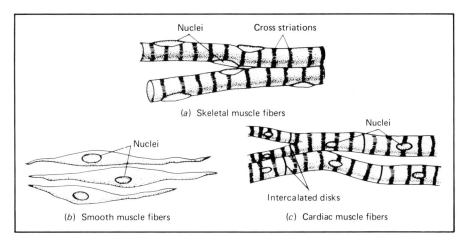

Nuclei Cross striations

(a) Skeletal muscle fibers

Nuclei

Nuclei

Intercalated disks

(b) Smooth muscle fibers (c) Cardiac muscle fibers

cardiac muscle tissue is the presence of **intercalated disks,** which mark the junctions between adjoining fibers.

The third type of muscle, **smooth muscle,** lacks striations and is involuntary. Its spindle-shaped cells contain only one nucleus. Found within the walls of many organs, smooth muscle is responsible for such internal movements as moving food through the digestive tract.

World of Biology, pp. 423–424

Eustress (YOU-stress). From the Greek word *eu,* meaning "good." Euphoria is "good feelings." Eulogy means "to speak good" of someone, eugenics means "good genes," and the eucalyptus tree gets its name from "good shade." Eustress is the amount of stress you need in order to operate at an optimum level of performance.

Eustress

In an interview published a few years before his death, Hans Selye talked at length about **eustress**, or "good" stress. According to Selye, we shouldn't try to avoid all stress. Rather, we should recognize what our typical response to stress is—and then try to adjust our lifestyles to take advantage of that response.

Selye believed that some of us are "turtles"— that is, we prefer peace, quiet, and a tranquil environment. Others of us are "racehorses," who thrive on a vigorous, fast-paced way of life. The optimum amount of stress we may require to function best is what Selye called *eustress.*

The problem with Selye's approach is this— he assumes you are born a "turtle" or a "race-horse." Thus, from Selye's point of view, there is little you can do about changing your response to stress other than trying to compensate for the genes that nature gave you. Few psychologists agree with Selye on this issue.

Society depends on eustress, for cultures are kept going by motivated people who are willing to learn how to cope with each other—and with their own individual needs and personalities. Thus, emotionality is necessary for life. The problem comes in discovering ways to make your emotions helpful to you rather than harmful. Needless to say, the more you know about your feelings, the better off you will be. And that means not only discovering what your emotions *are*, but learning effective ways of *handling them* as well.

Understanding Human Behavior, p. 333

PASSAGE TO PRACTICE MARGIN NOTES FOR EXERCISE 4 ON PAGE 117

"Sink or Swim" Learning

In 1980, Lt. Col. William Datel reported an interesting set of experiments performed during the 1970's on Army recruits at Fort Ord, near Monterey in California. Each year, thousands of recruits are given their basic training at Fort Ord. Most of the recruits find the situation fairly stressful. They have little privacy, they are punished (often severely) for any mistakes, they are not allowed to talk back or argue with orders, and they are restricted to camp for the first several weeks of their stay at the camp.

Many recruits survive this stressful ordeal rather well, but a large number fall by the wayside. Some try to escape the situation by "going AWOL"—that is, by being absent without leave. Others become ill or depressed. A few commit suicide.

When Colonel Datel was asked if he could find better methods of providing basic training, he first analyzed the situation psychologically. The philosophy in most army camps is that recruits must be "tempered in the fire of experience." Therefore, many trainers try to create the maximum amount of stress they can. One popular way of doing so is throwing recruits into dangerous situations to see who sinks and who swims.

Direct methods of coping—like all other habits—are usually learned best when you are rewarded for progress rather than being punished for failure. Knowing this, Colonel Datel set up an experimental unit at Fort Ord that trained a random selection of recruits using *positive reinforcement* rather than *punishment*. These men earned "points" for everything they did well, but were not severely penalized for their mistakes. The recruits in this experimental unit could trade in the points for various rewards—including the privilege of going into town the first night they were at the camp.

Colonel Datel followed his experimental recruits both while they were at Fort Ord and throughout their next several years in the Army. He compared their progress with that of a "control group"—namely, an equal number of recruits who went through the regular stress-oriented basic training at Fort Ord.

Datel's first discovery was that few of the men in the experimental program went "AWOL." This result alone saved the Army many thousands of dollars. Datel also found that his experimental subjects got better marks on such skills as rifle marksmanship and map reading than did recruits in the "control group." Furthermore, when the experimental subjects went into combat in Vietnam, they performed better under enemy fire than did the "control group" recruits. And more of the experimental group reenlisted at their end of their term of duty than did members of the "control group."

Despite Datel's data, the Army abandoned much of the experimental program a few years after Datel had set it up. Most military commanders apparently still believe that "sink or swim" techniques are the best way to help recruits learn to cope with stress.

FOUR

STUDYING

10

STUDYING TO LEARN

In this chapter you will learn techniques for studying effectively, including:

- ▲ reviewing a unit
- ▲ making study aids, including summary sheets, organizational charts, and flash cards
- ▲ specific suggestions for group study, studying for math tests, and cramming

What does it mean to study? Studying is more than spending time on school-related tasks. Knowledge is presented to you in your courses through the instructor's lectures, your readings, and your experiences. However, until you make the effort to internalize this knowledge, it remains "out there," and not in your possession. Studying is the process of making the material in your courses *yours;* in other words, studying is the process of learning.

Furthermore, studying is not a single activity, but a general name for a variety of activities you use to learn the material in your courses. As a college student, you need to have a range of study techniques under your command in order to meet the different study demands of different courses. This chapter presents a variety of study techniques that you can apply in your college courses.

REVIEWING A UNIT

You may not believe this until after you've faced your first exam period at the end of your first semester in college, but it's almost impossible to do all of your studying for all of your courses in the last week or two of the semester—there's simply too much material to master in that short period of time. The most effective way to study is at regular intervals during the semester. Specifically, each time you finish a unit in one of your courses, you should take time to study that unit. Since units represent subsections of a course, the end of a unit is an ideal time to study that material. At that point, the material is still fresh in your mind, and you can stand back and view it as a whole, perhaps using ideas from your text to help you interpret ideas from your lecture notes and vice versa. Furthermore, if you discover that there are some ideas you don't understand, you can easily ask your instructor to review the material.

What might a study session to review a unit look like? Here's an example. You have just finished a unit in your psychology course on language development. A study session for this unit might look like this:

1. Gather your materials.   Gather your notes for the unit, any handouts from class, and the book.

2. Make a study guide.   Use the chapter headings, chapter objectives, and titles from your notes to create a list of subtopics or study questions to guide your study. Note that these study questions are just like the reading goals used in directed reading of a textbook (see Chapter 9), except that now they are used to review instead of to guide your comprehension.

3. Review your notes.   Reread your notes, filling in any missing information and generally editing them.

4. Review the textbook.   Review the chapters in the unit by rereading your underlinings and margin notes or by reading the summaries of each chapter. Reread any sections you didn't understand the first time.

5. Review the material, topic by topic.   Now concentrate on one item from your study questions at a time. For each question, review all the material from the notes and from the textbook related to that topic and work to synthesize the ideas in your mind. For example, if one subtopic in the unit on language development is on how children acquire speech sounds, look over your notes and the material in the textbook on that topic and then try to answer in your own words the question "How do children acquire speech sounds?" When you trust your understanding of one subtopic, go on to the next.

6. Recite the material.   For maximum retention, use **reciting**—the use of speaking or writing to yourself to reinforce your learning. For example, after having reviewed and synthesized the material on how children produce speech sounds, you could produce a spoken or written summary of what you know. Or you might imagine that you were the instructor and give a lecture to your desk lamp on the topic. If you don't like talking to yourself, you could write a brief summary of the information. (Hint: if you tape your lecture or write your summary in a reserved place in your notebook, you'll be compiling a study guide that will be wonderfully useful the night before an exam.)

■
EXERCISE 1

At the end of the chapter beginning on page 145 are a page of notes from a psychology class on Maslow's theory of self-actualization and a selection from the psychology textbook *Understanding Human Behavior* on the same topic. Read the notes and the selection. Then use this material to practice an end-of-unit review.

Your study guide is five questions:

What are biological needs?
What are safety needs?
What are belongingness and love needs?
What are esteem needs?
What are self-actualization needs?

1. After reading the material, review the notes and the markings you made in the textbook excerpt to be sure you have a basic understanding.
2. Then review the material from the notes and from the textbook on the first topic—the sensory-motor period only. As you reread the notes on this topic and the material in the textbook, work to synthesize the information from the two sources. Drill yourself by answering the question, "What are biological needs?" When you are satisfied with your understanding of this topic, go on to the next topic, safety needs.
3. For each of the five topics, produce a summary. Either tape a lecture to yourself on the characteristics of the five types of needs or write a summary for each one.

Two days after you have completed this exercise, test yourself to see how much of the information you retained.

STUDY SHEETS

As was stated above, engaging in the language activities of writing and speaking while studying helps you to learn the material that you're studying. It also helps your concentration. In this section, you'll learn some more specific ways to use writing to study.

Remember "crib sheets" or "cheat sheets?" Half of the logic behind them was good. A student who composes a crib sheet is actually using a very effective study technique. The only problem is that trying to use them during an exam can have dire consequences, like causing you to fail the exam or get expelled from school. So make up crib sheets while you're studying but leave them in your bookbag during the exam. In fact, because you'll be using them honestly, call them study sheets instead of crib sheets. **Study sheets** are notes you write while studying that summarize the information you need to learn for an cxam.

Why are study sheets effective study tools? In the process of making up a study sheet, you're reviewing, synthesizing, and summarizing. As you write, you're also reciting. When you've finished, you have an effective visual aid to study from. In fact, the visual form of a well-laid out study sheet often helps you remember the material.

The most common type of study sheet is a summary sheet. Figure 10.1 is an example of a summary sheet of this type. It is a summary of the central ideas in one unit of a course, a unit on nutrition from a biology course. To construct a study sheet like this, after reviewing a unit, write a page that highlights the main ideas from the unit. Limit yourself to a single page so that you are forced to select the most important ideas. Write your summary in an informal outline format (like the format used for lecture notes), using indenting and graphics.

In studying for a test, you might make up a study sheet for each unit that the test would cover. Remember that the process of making up a summary like this is a useful form of studying in itself. Don't think that making up the study sheet is preparation for studying and memorizing it is studying.

Another type of study sheet is a vocabulary sheet, used for learning the meaning of technical terms in a course. (See Chapter 11, Figure 11.2, for an illustration.) A vocabulary sheet has four columns: the word itself, a sentence illustrating the word's context (a sentence taken from the textbook or your notes), a definition of the term, and an aid to remembering its meaning, such as an illustration, a synonym, or an example. If you've been kceping a vocabulary sheet all along for one of your courses, then you'll find it a great aid to studying for a test. If you've haven't, then part of your studying for the course might be to make up a vocabulary sheet.

■

E X E R C I S E   2

The appendix to this textbook contains a chapter from a humanities textbook entitled "Components of the Composite Arts," which you may have underlined as part of your work in Chapter 9. Review the chapter and make up a summary sheet for it, using the model in Figure 10.1. Limit your summary to a single page. In order to do so, you will have to concentrate on main ideas in the chapter.

Figure 10.1

STUDY SHEET FOR BIOLOGY CLASS

Study Sheet: Nutrition   Unit 6: Intro to Biology

Balanced diet proteins, carbohydrates, lipids, vitamins,
    minerals & water

Nutrients {

Vitamins: fat soluble (A, D, E, K)
          water soluble (B-complex & C)

Carbohydrates: used as fuel   Ex: rice, cereal, grains

Water: adult needs 2.5 quarts daily, gets most from food

Minerals: inorganic nutrients Ex: salt, potassium

Lipids: includes fats & dairy products. Used for fuel, as
components of cell membranes & to make complex lipid
compounds

Protein: most expensive & least available nutrient
essential to cell building

Metabolism
Nutrients transported to hepatic portal vein & then to liver.
Liver stores surplus nutrients, sends rest thru blood stream.
Carbs: liver stores excess glucose, releases it into the blood
        stream as needed (like between meals) so glucose
        level is kept steady.
Amino Acids: excess are "deanimated" by liver & excreted in
        urine. Remaining keto acids are converted to carbs
        or to lipids & stored.
Fatty Acids: converted to molecules of acetyl-coenzyme A &
        used as fuel. Excess stored as fat.

Basal Metabolic Rate basic rate of energy used when resting.
BMR + energy used in activity = Total Metabolic Rate
If calorie input = energy output, weight remains constant.

FLASH CARDS

Flash cards are a kind of study sheet that are handy because they can be carried with you and reviewed frequently in spare moments. Particularly good subjects for flash cards are math formulas, vocabulary terms, or short-answer questions, like, "What are the three main types of X?" Figure 10.3 on pages 136 and 137 illustrates different types of flash cards.

A new-age version of flash cards is a self-testing tape that you can play on a walkabout tape recorder. On a self-testing tape, you ask yourself a question, pause for an appropriate amount of time for the answer, and then feed back the answer. See Figure 10.2 below for an example of a script for this kind of tape.

Figure 10.2

SELF-TESTING TAPE SCRIPT FOR LEARNING POETIC METER

What is poetic meter?

(pause for 30 seconds to allow you to answer)

Poetic meter is a pattern of rhythm in a line of poetry established by the alternation of accented and unaccented syllables.

OK, next question.

What is a foot in poetry?

(pause for 30 seconds to allow you to answer)

That's right; a foot in poetry is a part of the line of a poem that includes a stressed or accented syllable.

Name the four most common feet.

(pause 15 seconds for answer)

They are iamb, trochee, anapest, and dactyl.

What is the pattern of iamb?

(pause 10 seconds for answer)

It's an unstressed syllable and a stressed syllable. Here's an example from the book: "Come LIVE with ME and BE my LOVE."

Figure 10.3

SAMPLE FLASH CARDS

What is poetic _meter_ & what are some common _feet_?

> Meter: pattern of rhythm established by pattern of accented & unaccented syllables.
> Foot/Feet: part of a line in poetry with one stressed syllable.
> Ex: Iamb (ˇ´) Come live/with me/and be/my love
> Trochee (´ˇ) Kiss me/dear u/pon my/dy ing
> Anapest (ˇˇ´) And the sheen/of their spears
> Dactyl (´ˇˇ) High on a/moun tain top

What is arithmetic mean?

> Mathematical average of all scores
> symbol - $\bar{X}$
> formula - $\bar{X} = \frac{\Sigma x}{N}$
>
> Mean = $\frac{\text{sum of all scores}}{\text{number of scores}}$
>
> example $\begin{cases} \bar{X} = \frac{4+3+6+8+2}{5} \\ \bar{X} = \frac{23}{5} = 4.6 \end{cases}$

Figure 10.3 cont.

SAMPLE FLASH CARDS

median

In a set, the median is a point on the score scale which divides the scale into two equal parts, with half the scores above and half below. It's the 50th percentile.

Ex: 2, 4, 8, 11, 12   median

5, 7, 9, 12, 14, 15   10.5 would be median

avoir faim

to be hungry

Ex: J'ai faim.

■ ——————————
E X E R C I S E   3
Select some material from one of your courses that lends itself to flash cards and make up a set of flash cards or a self-testing tape for that material.

ORGANIZATIONAL CHARTS

Another form of study sheet is an **organizational chart**. This kind of chart organizes information into columns and rows. Making up such a chart forces you to be systematic in ordering the material that you're studying.

Study the sample organizational charts (Figures 10.4 and 10.5), for example. In setting up the categories and filling in the chart, the student needed to think about what kinds of information were critical to his understanding of memory systems and then to search his notes and underlinings for appropriate information to fill in each box. Studying a chart like this is easier than studying a linear set of notes, because the chart is organized visually. Students who use organizational charts have reported that they could almost see the chart in their minds while taking a test.

The chart itself is useful for predicting a variety of questions, such as, "Compare and contrast the accuracy of long-term and short-term memory," or "Name two types of memory and their features."

■ ——————————
E X E R C I S E   4
Make up a chart that could be used to study the chapter on "Components of the Composite Arts." Use the following categories:

	Treatment of time	Treatment of space	Special techniques
Theater			
Film			

STUDYING FOR MATH COURSES

Studying for a math course sometimes throws students—it's difficult to figure out how to study or what to study. Some suggestions for study sheets for a typical math course follow on page 140.

Figure 10.4

EXAMPLE OF ORGANIZATIONAL CHART: MEMORY SYSTEMS

	Duration	Capacity	Storage	Accuracy
Short-term Memory	around 30 seconds (info can be re-inserted to lengthen time, like when you say a phone # over and over)	7±2 (from 5 to 9 items)	temporary storage. When item is gone it's not retrievable	more accurate for familiar items: overall petty accurate.
Long-term Memory	potentially permanent (but the older the memory, less accurate it will be). However, a lot gets forgotten, & once it's gone, it's not retrievable.	limitless (but not all events get stored in LTM)	seem to store items in categories along with info about how to retrieve it.	unreliable — memories get distorted or forgotten.

Figure 10.5

EXAMPLE OF ORGANIZATIONAL CHART: IMMUNITY

	Type of Immunity	When developed	Memory cells	Duration of Immunity
Active	Naturally Induced (developed from exposure to antigens: ex you get measles)	Through natural encounter — you may get sick but then develop antibodies	Yes	many years
	Artificially Induced (immunization shots)	After you're given an immunization shot — a vaccine	Yes	many years
Passive	Naturally Induced	After mother transfers her antibodies to fetus, or to infant (through breast feeding)	No	several months
	Artificially Induced	after given shot of gamma globulin (contains another person's antibodies)	No	several months

1. Make up a list of technical terms (terms like absolute value, integer, median, etc.) and make up a vocabulary sheet for them.
2. Make up a second vocabulary sheet for new symbols used in the course, like < for less than, > for greater than, Σ for sum, and so on.
3. For each type of problem or formula learned, make a two-

column study sheet. In the first column, work the problem step by step using simple numbers. In the second column, write an explanation of each step.

4. For each topic on the syllabus, make a summary of the major concepts (a summary sheet).

See Figure 10.6 for an example of study sheets for a math unit on measures of central tendency.

GROUP STUDY

Studying in a group can be very effective or a real waste of time. How effective a group study session is depends first of all on the *motivation* of the people in the group. If even one member of the group wants to turn the group study session into a social hour, he or she probably can. So it's important that everyone in the group (even if there are only two of you) agrees to abide by certain ground rules in a study session.

The other key to a successful study session is *organization.* All the people in the group need to agree on when and where to meet, how long to meet, what they will do to prepare for the session, and what they will do during the session.

Here's an illustration of how a study session might operate. Four of you in your Introductory Biology class decide to study together for your upcoming midterm. You agree to meet in the group study room (it has few distractions) in the library Thursday night at six, and one person takes responsibility for reserving the room. There are four chapters to be reviewed for the test, so each of you takes responsibility for reviewing the notes and readings for one unit and preparing four copies of a two- to four-page summary of that chapter. During the session, each of you in turn presents your summary and explains it. People ask questions as each summary is presented, including asking questions that they think might be on the exam, and you all try to determine the answers from your notes and the text, making notes on what you learn. After an hour or so, you take a fifteen-minute break for coffee, and then get back to work. As this example shows, group study can be a very effective way to study if (and only if) everyone does what he or she has agreed to do.

Another type of group study that is surprisingly effective is tutoring a weaker student. Teachers have always known that one of the best ways to master something is to teach it. If you're strong in a certain subject and offer to help someone else study, while you're explaining and demonstrating material, you're reviewing it yourself and reinforcing your knowledge of it.

CRAMMING

It's true that cramming—doing all the studying for a test in one marathon study session—isn't as effective as studying throughout

Figure 10.6

EXAMPLE OF STUDY SHEETS FOR A MATH COURSE
Topic: Measures of Central Tendency

I. Technical Terms
  <u>Mean</u> – arithmetic average of a set of scores
  <u>Median</u> – midpoint when scores are arranged in rank order
  <u>Mode</u> – most frequently occurring score

II. Symbols
   Σ – sum
   $\bar{x}$ – arithmetic mean
   Mdn – median
   Mo – mode
   x – a score
   N – number of scores

III. Formulae

Finding
the mean: $\bar{x} = \frac{\Sigma x}{N}$

Mean ($\bar{x}$) equals the sum of
all scores divided by the
number of scores

Ex: Scores: 7, 9, 8, 4, 7

$\bar{x} = \frac{\Sigma x}{N}$

$\bar{x} = \frac{7+9+8+4+7}{5}$

$\bar{x} = \frac{35}{5} = 7$

Top of fraction is five scores
added up. Bottom is the number
of scores. Add & do division.

IV. Important Ideas
  <u>Mean</u> is the only measure that is mathematical & takes
  all scores into account; that means it's also sensitive
  to very high or very low scores.
  <u>Median</u> is often used in reporting the typical something,
  such as the typical weight of a 10-year old.

the course or spacing your final study sessions over a week or two. It's also true that everyone crams sometimes for a test. Here are some suggestions to make your cramming more effective:

1. Be realistic about the minimum amount of sleep you need. Falling asleep during the exam is nature's way of telling you that you overdid it.
2. Coffee and caffeine tablets can make you jittery. A cool shower will wake you up just as effectively; it also has more beneficial side effects.
3. Walking through the student lounge or your kitchen forty-seven times to announce that you still have 480 pages to review is dramatic but less effective than actual studying.
4. Begin by reviewing the last unit covered instead of beginning at the beginning of the syllabus. In general, instructors ask more questions about the last topic covered than the first.
5. If there are vast quantities of reading assignments that you haven't read, at least try to read summaries of them or skim them.
6. Be very selective in what you study. Concentrate on the material that the instructor emphasized. If the instructor gave you a study guide for the test, use it.
7. Many textbook aids like chapter summaries, chapter objectives (for predicting questions), and glossaries organize information for learning, and so function as preconstructed study sheets. Use reciting to learn the material in them.
8. Make up your own study sheets also. Making up summary study sheets will help you concentrate under pressure and will keep you on track doing the tasks you need to do: summarizing, synthesizing, and reciting.

SUMMARY

Studying is actually a cluster of mental and linguistic activities you engage in to learn information. The most effective study pattern involves reviewing each unit in each course after it is completed. To review a unit, gather your materials and make up a study guide that lists the questions you should be able to answer. Go through the unit one subtopic at a time by reviewing the notes and the textbook section on that topic. To reinforce your learning, prepare either an oral or a written summary of the information. Closer to exam time, study sheets are an effective study tool, as the process of composing them is a valuable form of learning and the sheets themselves are useful for rapid reviewing. Vocabulary sheets, summary study sheets, organizational charts, flash cards, and self-testing tapes are different types of study sheets. A study sheet for a math course will combine technical vocabulary, math symbols, sample problems, and the major concepts of a unit. Finally, two special study situations are group study and cramming. An effective group study session depends on participation from everyone in the group. Students might agree to each prepare a study sheet on one topic and share it with the group. Effective cramming depends on being realistic and selecting carefully where to concentrate your time and effort.

■
JOURNAL WRITING

1. Think of some subject or skill that you learned on your own because you wanted to. An example might be finding out about different types of stereo systems or cars, learning how to refinish furniture or to lift weights, or becoming an amateur photographer or investor. In your journal, discuss how you went about learning this subject—what you read, who if anyone you went to for instruction, what you had to learn, what was hard to learn, and what was easy to learn.

2. Explain how you would organize a group study session for one of your courses in which you have an upcoming test. Include the ground rules, place and length of study session, whom you would ask to participate, and what each person's obligations would be.

3. What's effective about the way you usually study? What's not so effective that needs to be changed? How might you change it?

■
ACADEMIC WRITING

Prepare a set of study materials for one unit in one of your courses. Include in your materials at least two items from the following list:

A summary sheet
An organizational chart
A set of flash cards or a self-testing tape
A vocabulary sheet
A plan for a group study session

NOTES FOR EXERCISE 1 ON PAGE 132

<u>Maslow's Theory of self-actualization</u>   3/14

[Motivation] - Theory in psychology to explain what makes people
act the ways they do.

Theory of motivation needs to include ⎰biological⎱
⎰social⎱   needs.
⎰psychological⎱

Abraham Maslow - studied characteristics of individuals who had
achieved a high degree of self-fulfillment.
• emphasizes characteristics of healthy personality, not
unhealthy one
• believes people have an active roll in shaping their
personality, not a passive one

His theory: people have a hierarchy of human needs.
[[hierarchy] - a series of steps from lower to higher]
① Infants begin with the most basic need: need to get | Biological Needs |
what you need to live/survive.
② Need to feel secure. Get this from knowing what to | Safety Needs |
expect from your surroundings.
③ Sense of belonging to family, community, church, etc. | Belongingness and Love |
Need to belong & be loved.
④ Need to be loved back. Get validation from | Self-esteem |
being loved. Provides <u>self-esteem</u>
⑤ Need to be socially useful - to achieve your | Self-actualization |
potential. Can only focus on this when other
needs are met.

READINGS FOR EXERCISE 1 ON PAGE 132

> **Hierarchy** (HIGH-er-ark-key). To make a hierarchy is to list things (or people) in order of their importance.

Maslow's Theory of "Self-Actualization"

According to Abraham Maslow, human needs can be placed on a **hierarchy**, or ladder. This hierarchy runs from the simplest biological motives up to the most complex of intra-psychic and social desires. As you develop in life, you move up the ladder until you reach the top rung, which Maslow calls *self-actualization* (see Fig. 10.1).

Maslow assumes that you start life at the lowest level of the motivational hierarchy. He believes you are born with innate reflexes that help you satisfy your basic biological needs. Once you are blessed with biological life, however, you must secure some control over your physical environment. Thus, almost immediately after birth, you begin to move up to the second level of the motivational hierarchy, that of safety needs.

The next two rungs of the ladder involve the social environment. You need people to love, and you need people to love you. Part of these needs are satisfied by your family, but there are also work groups and various social organizations you can join. These groups not only offer you rewards for performing well, they can also help you learn what self-respect is all about.

If you are fortunate, you will finally reach the top rung of Maslow's hierarchy and achieve *self-actualization*. This term is difficult to define. Put simply, it means reaching your own greatest potential, doing the things you do best in your own unique way, and then helping those around you achieve these goals too. But you can get to this final stage of human development only by first solving the problems associated with the four lower levels.

Now that we have given Maslow's theory in broad outline, let's look at what he says in more detail.

Maslow's Hierarchy of Needs

Maslow says there are five primary levels on the ladder of human motivation:

1. *Biological needs.* Bodily needs come first. You must always satisfy your physical needs or you won't live long enough to take care of any psychological or social needs you may have. You cannot take the next step up the motivational ladder unless, and until, your primary biological needs are met. (As we will soon see, *drive theory* operates at this rung of the ladder.)

2. *Safety needs.* Neither man nor woman lives by bread alone. Once an infant's basic needs are satisfied, the child is ready to explore the physical environment. But as we will show in later chapters, young children typically don't explore unless they feel secure. A predictable world is, generally speaking, a much safer environment than one that is unpredictable. Thus, one reason you "move about" in your environment is to reduce your uncertainty about what the world has to offer. With this knowledge, you can choose sensibly among the various physical inputs you need to sustain life. And once you know what to expect from the world, you can move on to the next rung of the motivational ladder. (Arousal theory operates in part at this stage of development.)

3. *Belongingness* and *love needs.* Once you have gained control over your physical environment, you can then turn your attention to social inputs. As the poet John Donne once said, "No man is an island, entire of itself." Donne knew quite well that, to be a *human* being, you must have other people around you. Therefore, according to Maslow, you have an innate need for affection and love that can be satisfied only by other people. You must *affiliate* with others, and identify yourself with one or more like-minded individuals. When you identify with someone else, you learn to perceive part of the world as that person presumably does. (As we will learn in Chapters 11 and 12, perceptual and emotional theories of motivation apply primarily to the first three rungs of the ladder.)

4. *Esteem needs.* One reason you need other people is to help you set your life's goals. Under the right conditions, the groups you affiliate with can offer you *models* or *feed-forward* on what your future behavior might (or should) be. Groups also offer you external *feedback* on how close you are coming to achieving your targets in life. And the better you get at reaching your goals, the more esteem you will likely have for yourself (and the more esteem you will probably get from others). According to Maslow, "esteem needs" are just as important for *human* life as are food and water. (Social learning theory and the various theories of social motivation we will discuss later in this book operate at levels 2, 3, and 4 of the hierarchy.)

5. *Need for self-actualization.* Until you have achieved self-esteem, you probably will not feel secure enough to become a "fully-actualized person." Unless you have confidence in yourself, Maslow says, you will not dare to express yourself in your own unique way, make your own special contribution to society, and thus achieve your true inborn potential.

And once you have achieved self-actualization for yourself, Maslow says, you will find you have a strong urge to help others get where you have gotten. And to do *that*, you will need to teach others the lessons you learned as you worked your way up the four lower levels of the motivational hierarchy. (The many theories of personality and human development discussed later apply to all the rungs of Maslow's ladder, but primarily to the fifth rung.)

Question: How far up the ladder would a frequently abused child be likely to climb? Or a student whose teachers gave the student nothing but criticism?

11

LEARNING SPECIALIZED VOCABULARY

In this chapter, you will find out how to learn the meaning of specialized vocabulary words by:

▲ observing how they are used in textbooks and lectures
▲ using prefixes and suffixes
▲ making vocabulary study sheets

What do the following exam questions have in common?

(from a psychology exam)
Distinguish punishment, negative reinforcement, extinction, and modeling. Explain how each might be used by a parent attempting to eliminate an undesirable behavior in a child.

(from a humanities exam)
Describe the following film techniques: close-up, panning, angle shots, tracking, framing, cutting, cross-cutting, dissolves, fade-out, fade-in, freezing, accelerated motion, flashback, and flash-forward.

(from a biology exam)
Give the functions of: (a) myelin, (b) ganglia, (c) neuroglia, (d) dendrites, (e) an axon.

The answer is that all of these questions are testing not only your knowledge of the subject matter but also your understanding of vocabulary that is commonly used in that subject area. Every academic subject area or discipline has a specialized sct of terms used by people who have studied that subject. The terms used in an academic discipline are called **specialized vocabulary** or **technical vocabulary**. As a college student, you can expect both your general vocabulary and your specialized vocabulary to expand as a result of the large amount of reading you will be doing.

A **general vocabulary** term is one that is not specific to one academic discipline. For example, the word *drab,* which means "dull," may be a new word for you, but it is not a specialized vocabulary term because it is not associated with any one academic area. In other cases, a word will have a general meaning that is familiar to you but will have a specialized meaning when it is used in one of your courses. As an example, consider a term like *freeze.* As a general vocabulary word, *freeze* has the meaning "to form into ice." But if a humanities professor uses the term *freeze* when discussing film, she is using the term in a technical sense to mean "stopping the action in a motion picture."

Each of us has four vocabularies: a *listening vocabulary* consisting of words that we recognize when we hear them, a *reading vocabulary* consisting of words that we recognize when we see them, a *speaking vocabulary* consisting of words that we use in talking, and a *writing vocabulary* consisting of words that we use in writing. Generally, a person's listening vocabulary is the largest, followed in order by his or her reading vocabulary, speaking vocabulary, and writing vocabulary. In college, your four vocabularies will expand along two dimensions. First, since you will be exposed to a much wider range of language users and language situations, all of your vocabularies will increase. Also, since you will be hearing lectures and reading about new academic areas daily, your listening and reading vocabularies will expand in the direction of absorbing more specialized terms. In fact, when you take an introductory course in a subject, a large part of your learning consists of learning the specialized vocabulary in that subject. Students often find introductory courses surprisingly difficult because so much specialized vocabulary is introduced in them. Therefore, particularly when you are taking your first course in a new academic area, expect that a large part of your study time will be spent in mastering new terms and the concepts they encode. You can help yourself in college by learning how to study the specialized vocabulary in your college courses, using the techniques introduced in this chapter.

USING THE CONTEXT: TEXTBOOKS

You will encounter many specialized vocabulary terms for the first time when you are doing reading assignments in textbooks. In many textbooks, specialized vocabulary terms are highlighted by **boldface** or *italicized* type. Often, the passage in which a new vocabulary item appears will suggest the word's meaning. Some of the common ways in which the meanings of words are indicated in context are illustrated below. As you read the examples, mentally define the word that is underlined.

1. *A definition of the term in the same paragraph:*

> The brain signals the adrenal medulla rapidly via neural connections to release <u>epinephrine</u> and <u>norepinephrine</u>, hormones that prepare the body for fight or flight.

> Your body goes through rather regular biological cycles every day. Many of these cycles reach a peak at some regular point during the day or night. These cycles are often called <u>circadian rhythms</u>, a technical term that means "a repeating pattern of activity that runs about 24 hours in length."

2. *Use of a synonym (a word with the same meaning) along with the new term:*

> In this instance, a dominant front view is supplemented by side, or <u>lateral</u> views.

> So somehow your eyes must translate or <u>transduce</u> these light rays into a pattern of neural messages.

3. *Explanation of a term by contrasting it with another term:*

> Unlike real time, <u>stage time</u> can be either longer or shorter than the duration of the actual performance.

4. *Use of an example to explain a term:*

> There are a variety of <u>mnemonics</u>, or "memory tricks," that psychologists have developed to help people remember things better . . . For example, if Mr. Bird looks like an owl, you can make an easy connection between his face and his name.

5. *Use of a visual to illustrate a term:*

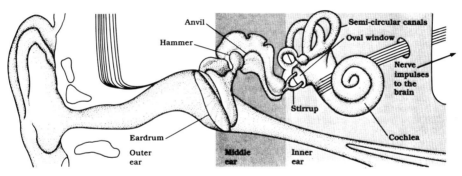

Structure of the human ear

As you do reading assignments, pay attention to these cues to meaning in the text surrounding a specialized term. As suggested in Chapter 9, if the key word is not in boldface or italics, box or highlight it. Then underline the information that explains or defines the term and draw a line connecting the definition with the term. Making these markings will force you to actively search for the meaning of a term as you read, and the markings themselves will be a study aid when you review.

■

EXERCISE 1

In each of the following passages, use the context to determine the meaning of the italicized terms. Mark each sentence to indicate the word's meaning and write a definition of the term in your own words.

Example: Still, the tragic hero is generally defined as someone who has not only great stature but also a *tragic flaw.* This flaw or weakness, first discussed by Aristotle (384–322 B.C.) in his *Poetics,* is usually pride.

tragic flaw *a weakness such as pride*

1. The general pattern of the tragic plot consists of the *reversal* of the hero's fortune from good to bad.

reversal _____

_____

2. In the opening two lines, Pope uses an especially clever device of satire, the *mock heroic.* This is an heroic or solemn treatment of an unworthy subject.

mock heroic _____

_____

3. However, according to Freud, the best way to discharge the pent-up tension is through *catharsis,* which involves the open expression of your feelings.

catharsis _____

_____

4.   At about a year of age, infants begin uttering *holophrastic* or one-word sentences.

holophrastic sentences _____

_____

5.   Each of us has about 30 trillion (3×10^{13}) red blood cells, more formally known as *erythrocytes,* suspended in our plasma.

erythrocytes _____

_____

6.   The normal heart rate is about 70 beats per minute and the *cardiac output,* the volume of blood pumped by a ventricle, is about 5 liters (5 quarts) per minute.

cardiac output _____

_____

SPECIALIZED VOCABULARY IN LECTURES

When introducing new terms, instructors will often include the same cues to meaning as those found in textbooks. In fact, instructors often will provide multiple context cues to a word's meaning, knowing that students can not go back and "reread" what they have said.

When you hear an instructor presenting a new term, skip a line or two, and write down the term. Guess at its spelling if necessary; you can check the spelling later. Then write down as much information as you can about the term's meaning: a direct definition, any synonyms or contrasting terms, and any diagrams or examples that illustrate the word's meaning. If the instructor provides multiple examples, aim to get at least one down. If you miss information, leave space for filling in later when you review your notes. After the class, check the spelling of the term and your definition of it. Also, box or highlight the word so that when you review your notes, it will stand out.

Instructors will not define every specialized term they use in their lectures, and students often have trouble comprehending lectures because they have difficulty with the specialized vocabulary used by the lecturer. If you have this problem in a course, prepare for each class by skimming the chapter to be covered and reading all new specialized terms and their definitions.

■
_____
E X E R C I S E   2

Here are three excerpts from lectures. Read each one, and after it, write down what you would write down in your notebook to define and illustrate the italicized term.

1. (from a psychology lecture on sexual motivation)
"Everyone knows what sex is, right? And you know what a role is—a part you play, like an actor's part. You also know what a stereotype is, a generalization about the behavior of members of a certain group, an idea like 'All older people are weak.' So then, *sex-role stereotypes* are generalizations about the way men act and the way women act. For example, if you've ever said to a child, 'Big boys don't cry,' or 'Girls shouldn't play with guns,' you were echoing sex-role stereotypes. In the twentieth century, psychologists have disagreed on the question of whether such stereotypes are genetically or culturally determined."

Notes:

_____

_____

_____

_____

2. (from a humanities lecture on internal motivation in film and novels)
"Another problem faced by both writers and directors is how to reveal the inner thoughts and feelings of characters. You can simply let people reveal themselves through their actions and let the audience infer what kind of person the character is, and often this is the way it's done. Sometimes, however, the writer lets the characters speak to themselves, as if they were thinking out loud. This type of character revelation is called an *interior monologue* and resembles the soliloquy of drama. In film, it often takes the form of a shot of the individual accompanied with a voice-over."

Notes:

_____

_____

_____

_____

3.   (from a biology lecture)
"Think of *blood pressure* as being like the water pressure in
your shower at home. It's the amount of force exerted by the
blood when it presses against the inner walls of your blood ves-
sels—your arteries and veins. For instance, if a person gets hurt
and loses a lot of blood, there would be less blood circulating in
his system and therefore less blood pushing against the walls of
his veins, so his blood pressure would drop."

Notes:

_____

_____

_____

_____

USING INFERENCE

In the examples above, there were definite clues to the meanings of specialized terms provided in the context in which the terms
appeared, whether written or spoken. However, even if there are no
direct aids to meaning, you can often **infer,** or make an educated
guess at, a word's meaning based on your comprehension of the context in which it appears. In order to see how this process works, do
the following exercise.

■ _____

E X E R C I S E   3

The following poem is a famous nonsense poem by Lewis Carroll, taken from the children's fantasy, *Through the Looking-Glass* (a
sequel to *Alice's Adventures in Wonderland*). Many of the words in
the poem are invented words, words that Carroll made up. Read the
poem and then offer a guess as to what some of these words might
mean.

Jabberwocky
Lewis Carroll

'Twas brillig, and the slithy toves   1
    Did gyre and gimble in the wabe:

All mimsey were the borogoves,
  And the mome raths outgrabe.

"Beware the Jabberwock, my son!   5
  The jaws that bite, the claws that catch!
Beware the Jubjub bird, and shun
  The frumious Bandersnatch!"

He took his vorpal sword in hand:
  Long time the manxome foe he sought—
So rested he by the Tumtum tree,
  And stood awhile in thought

And, as in uffish thought he stood,   13
  The Jabberwock, with eyes of flame,
Came whiffling through the tulgey wood,
  And burbled as it came!

One, two! one, two! and through and through   17
  The vorpal blade went snicker-snack!
He left it dead, and with its head
  He went galumphing back.

"And hast thou slain the Jabberwock?   21
  Come to my arms, my beamish boy!
O frabjous day! Callooh! Callay!"
  He chortled in his joy.

'Twas brillig, and the slithy toves   25
  Did gyre and gimble in the wabe:
All mimsey were the borogoves,
  And the mome raths outgrabe.

(from Carroll, Lewis. Through the Looking-Glass. New York: New American Library of World Literature, Inc., 1960, pp. 134–136.)

  1. Jabberwock (5) _____

  _____

  2. frumious (8) _____

  _____

  3. vorpal (9,18) _____

  _____

4. manxome (10) _____

_____

5. uffish (13) _____

_____

6. whiffling (15) _____

_____

7. burbled (16) _____

_____

8. galumphing (20) _____

_____

9. beamish (22) _____

_____

10. frabjous (23) _____

_____

11. chortled (24) _____

_____

12. brillig (1, 25) _____

_____

As you can see, you can often make a good guess as to a word's meaning by carefully reading the context in which it appears and using the clues that appear there to decide what kind of meaning would make sense. This process is called **inference**. For instance, even though we don't recognize the word "wabe" in line 2, the sentence makes it clear that it's where the toves (whatever they are) are, so it must be some kind of place. You can use this kind of inference to work at the meaning of an unfamiliar word you encounter as you read or take notes on lectures. Try it in the following exercise. This time, the words are actual words.

■
EXERCISE 4

1. *Farce* is an especially old type of film comedy, going back to the days before sound recording was invented. Pratfalls, horseplay, and other types of slapstick were emphasized by accelerating the speed of the film, as in the chases of Mack Sennett's Keystone Cops.

farce _____

_____

2. Many subjects reported disturbances in their *body images*. For instance, one student had the impression that his body had turned into twins. A second student stated that his mind seemed to leave his body and roam around the cubicle.

body images _____

_____

3. Normal blood pressure of a young adult would approximate 120/80. When the diastolic pressure consistently reads over 95 mm Hg, the patient may be suffering from *hypertension*. This disorder places a heavy burden upon the heart, which must pump against greater blood pressure.

hypertension _____

_____

USING STRUCTURAL CUES

Another aid to understanding vocabulary as you read is the structure of the word. Many specialized words contain word parts that are meaningful, and familiarizing yourself with these meaningful word parts will help you comprehend and remember a word's meaning. The meaningful parts of a word are called **morphemes**. Morphemes include **prefixes,** syllables attached to the beginning of a word; **suffixes,** syllables attached to the end of a word; and **roots,** core syllables of words.

When you use structural cues, you use your knowledge of the word's parts or morphemes to construct a meaning. For instance, let's say your roommate asked you to "un-park the car." Because you know what the word "park" means and you know that the prefix "un-" often means to reverse an action, you could figure out that you were being asked to take the car out of its parking space. With specialized vocabulary, you use the same process of analogy. Knowing the meaning of prefixes commonly used in specialized vocabulary terms is especially useful, as these prefixes are fairly common. Figure 11.1 lists prefixes that often appear in specialized or technical words.

Figure 11.1

PREFIXES COMMONLY USED IN SPECIALIZED VOCABULARY WORDS

Numerical Prefixes	Meaning
uni-, mono-	one
bi-, di-	two
ambi-	both
tri-	three
quadra-, tetra-	four
quint-, pent-	five
sex-, hex-	six
sept-, hept-	seven
oct-	eight
non-	nine
dec-	ten
semi-, hemi-	half
centi-	a hundred or one-hundredth

Some other common technical prefixes	
hetero-	different
homo-	same
omni-, pan-	all
poly-, multi-	many
oli-	few
hyper-	excessive, over
hypo-	less than or beneath
inter-	between elements
intra-	within an element
sub-	under, to a lesser degree
super-	above, to a greater degree
pseudo-	fake
endo-	inner
exo-	outer
matri-	mother
patri-	father
proto-	first, original
iso-	equal
para-	beyond or beside
retro-	backward
micro-	small
macro-	large
mal-	bad
neo-	new

While prefixes often alter a word's meaning, suffixes are more frequently used to allow a word to be used in another word class. For instance, the word *prohibit* means "to forbid." If we wish to talk about a rule that forbids a certain action, we can add a suffix to *prohibit* and call the rule a *prohibition*. From the same word we can also derive the words *prohibitive* and *prohibitively*. Words that are related in meaning like these four forms of prohibit are called **word families**. Often word families are formed around a common root. Knowing or learning the meaning of the root enables you to know something about the meaning of related words in the same family. For instance, the word root *arch,* from the Greek word *archien,* "to rule," appears in words describing different types of social organization. Use this information and the table of prefixes in Figure 11.1 to guess at the different types of social organization these words describe:

Monarchy _____

Oligarchy _____

Matriarchy _____

Patriarchy _____

As you encounter new words, pay attention to any explanation of the meaning of the word's parts. For instance, your instructor in your humanities class may mention that the word *chronological* is derived from the Greek word *chronos,* meaning "time." When you later come across the word *chronometer* in a science course, you will be able to guess that it is some kind of device used to measure time.

■
——————————
E X E R C I S E   5

Use the context and the meaning of the prefixes to complete the following sentences in a meaningful way.

1. *Intra-psychic* psychologists are primarily interested in the thoughts and processes _____ a person.

2. Hugo van der Goes's painting, *The Portinari Altarpiece,* is a *triptych* containing _____ separate but related panels.

3. Some materials such as lead and mercury exhibit a condition called *superconductivity* when they are cooled; that is, their ability to conduct an electrical current is greatly _____.

4. A *subcutaneous* injection is administered _____ the skin.

5. While vertebrates have an *endoskeleton,* a framework located _____ the organism, arthropods have *exoskeletons,* or _____ skeletons.

6. Whereas in *monophonic* music, all singers follow _____ melody line, in *polyphonic* music, there are _____ melody lines.

7. In *matrilineal* societies, property passes from a _____ to children; in a *patrilineal* society, property is inherited by offspring from the _____.

8. A *tetrahedron* has _____ triangular faces.

USING A GLOSSARY

As discussed in Chapter 7, many textbooks include a **glossary,** a dictionary of specialized terms and their definitions. Most frequently, the glossary is an appendix located in the back of the textbook with terms arranged in alphabetical order. In other textbooks, glossary definitions may be located directly on each page, at the end of each chapter, or as part of the index. You will find a glossary more useful than a desk dictionary for learning specialized vocabulary, as a desk dictionary primarily lists general vocabulary terms, while a glossary provides the specialized terms and definitions used in that academic area.

Use the glossary as a self-check of your own work to decide on a word's meaning. When you encounter a specialized term in a textbook, your first step should be to use the context to formulate a definition. Note any prefixes, suffixes, or roots which will help you decipher the word. Then use your comprehension of the passage as a whole to infer the meaning of the term.

When you have done these steps, check the text glossary to determine how accurate your understanding of the term was. Quite possibly the glossary definition will be more precisely worded than your own. Read the definition over a few times, and then reread the passage in which the term occurred to check your comprehension.

STUDYING SPECIALIZED VOCABULARY

Up to this point, you have been learning how to use various aids to determine a word's meaning. This is the first step in learning new vocabulary, as it lays the foundation. But there is also an important second step—studying the word in order to make it your own. You'll find that making lists or cards of specialized vocabulary terms in your courses is a most effective way of studying them. The act of writing the lists will force you to actively consider the word and its meaning, and then the completed list or cards will be a tool that you can use for review.

Students have found that the most effective format for a vocabulary entry contains four parts:

1. The word itself
2. The context in which the word appeared. The context should be an actual sentence either from your textbook or from your lecture notes, not an invented sentence.
3. A definition of the word
4. An aid that will help you remember the word's meaning. Possible aids to the word's meaning might be:
   a. A synonym for the word
   b. A contrasting term
   c. An explanation of any prefixes, suffixes, or roots used in the word.
   d. A nonsense association that will help you remember the word
   e. A drawing or diagram
   f. An example
   g. A cognate word in your first language, if you are bilingual

All of these aids are illustrated in the sample vocabulary list (Figure 11.2) and vocabulary cards (Figure 11.3).

Whether you decide to use a list or cards is an individual decision. If you use vocabulary lists, you can place them with your notes for each course, perhaps on the back pages of your notebook. You can refer to your lists during a lecture when your instructor uses a word you're unfamiliar with, and you can use the lists as study sheets to review for tests. If you use vocabulary cards, you can carry them with you for review in spare moments, and you can use them like flash-cards. When studying, you can read the word and the context from the front of the card, give the definition orally, and flip the card to see if you were correct. You can put cards with words you know in one pile and cards with words you didn't know in a second pile for further study.

Figure 11.2

EXAMPLE OF VOCABULARY SHEET

Word	Context	Definition	Aid
mock heroic	Pope uses an especially clever device of satire, the <u>mock heroic</u>.	heroic or solemn treatment of a trivial subject	<u>mock</u> as in <u>mocking</u> (teasing)
catharsis	The best way to dissolve pent-up tension is through <u>catharsis</u>.	open expression of feelings to relieve your emotions	opposite of <u>suppression</u>
holophrastic	At about a year of age, infants begin uttering <u>holophrastic</u> sentences.	the act of expressing a complex idea in a single word or phrase	
interior monologue	<u>Interior monologue</u> is especially useful as a means of expressing the character's inner-most thoughts.	In film, the expression of a character's inner thoughts, heard while the character is not speaking.	Ex: The Color Purple
sex-role stereotypes	Several studies suggest that <u>sex-role stereotyping</u> is controlled by the environment.	a cognitive prototype that describes expected dress & behavior of males & females in a certain culture.	boys = guns girls = dolls
erythrocytes	Each of us has about 30 trillion (3×10^{13}) <u>erythrocytes</u>.	red blood cells	cytes = cells
cardiac output	The <u>cardiac output</u> of the normal heart is about 5 liters.	volume of blood pumped by the ventricle	
blood pressure	When cardiac output decreases, blood flow decreases, causing a fall in <u>blood pressure</u>.	the force exerted by blood against the inner walls of the blood vessels	think of water pressure in plumbing systems

Figure 11.3

EXAMPLES OF VOCABULARY CARDS

Front   **Back**

FARCE

At the other extreme from high comedy is low comedy or farce.

<u>Definition</u>: a type of comedy in which laughter is aroused more by slapstick action than by character analysis or by witty language.

<u>Aid</u>: the Marx Brothers

BODY IMAGES

Many students reported disturbances in their <u>body images</u>.

<u>Definition</u>: Internal representation of how we look from another's point of view.

<u>Aid</u>: Ex: A person who is hallucinating and thinks he is flying or melting.

HYPERTENSION

When diastolic pressure consistently reads over 95 mmHg, the patient must be suffering from <u>hypertension</u>.

<u>Definition</u>: high blood pressure

<u>Aid</u>: <u>hyper</u> — over, excessive

IMPROVING YOUR GENERAL VOCABULARY

This chapter has concentrated on ways to learn and study specialized vocabulary terms. But you may also need to expand your general vocabulary to cope with the reading demands on you. The author of one of the textbooks used as an example in this text, James McConnell, once asked his students to circle words in his textbook that they didn't understand, so he could decide which terms to include in the glossary. To his surprise, many of the words they selected were not specialized terms, but general vocabulary words.

Many of the same techniques that you have learned for specialized vocabulary can also be used to increase your general vocabulary. You can look for explanations of a word's meaning from the surrounding context, make inferences based on context, and use structural cues to help you figure out a word's meaning. The only difference is that you will not use glossaries or specialized dictionaries to check the correctness of your definition; you can refer to a general dictionary instead. In fact, a good collegiate (college-level) desk dictionary should be one of your prized possessions—and it should look more and more dog-eared each year.

If you want to expand your store of general vocabulary words, you can use the same techniques you used for studying specialized vocabulary—vocabulary charts and lists. Additionally, the more you encounter a new word in reading and listening or use it in speaking or writing, the more it will become your own. Sometimes you may use a word incorrectly, but that's O.K.—making mistakes is part of the learning process.

SUMMARY

Learning the technical or specialized vocabulary terms used in an academic area is a critical task in introductory courses. When you encounter a specialized term, either while reading a textbook or listening to a lecture, your first step should be to use the context to formulate a definition in your mind. Read the paragraph in which the term appears, looking for any clues that shed light on the word's meaning: a definition, a synonym, a contrasting term, an example, or an illustration. Use your overall comprehension of the context to infer the word's meaning. Note any prefixes common to technical words or other structural cues that can help. When you have taken these steps, check the textbook's glossary to determine how accurate your working definition was. While these strategies lay the foundation for learning specialized vocabulary, studying is necessary to master new terms. Learn specialized vocabulary by using either vocabulary lists or flash cards. For either format, your entry will include the word, the context in which it appeared, a definition, and an aid to remembering. Review these sheets or cards frequently and give yourself self-tests to learn them.

JOURNAL WRITING

1. At the beginning of the chapter was the information that every person has four vocabularies: a reading vocabulary (words you recognize in reading), a listening vocabulary (words you recognize when listening), a speaking vocabulary (words you use in talking), and a writing vocabulary (words you use in writing). Discuss how each of your four vocabularies is different. Which are adequate and which ones need to be expanded? Explain.

2. Choose a selection from one book or textbook you are using this term and read it. As you read, place a checkmark next to every word you don't know or aren't sure you know. List these words and count how many are general vocabulary words and how many are specialized vocabulary words.

3. Find ten vocabulary terms from courses that you are currently taking that contain prefixes from Figure 11.1. Write their definitions as given in the glossary and the context. See if the prefix's meaning is incorporated into the meaning of the word.

ACADEMIC WRITING

1. Select one of your courses in which learning specialized vocabulary is a major part of your studying. Make out a vocabulary sheet or vocabulary cards for at least twelve specialized vocabulary words from one chapter, following the models in Figures 11.2 or 11.3.

12

MEMORIZING

In this chapter you will learn skills for memorizing material, including:

▲ how to select what to memorize
▲ the importance of understanding in memorizing
▲ aids to memory, including organization, rehearsal, memory-aiding devices, and visualization

One study technique you will need frequently is memorizing. Everything you study doesn't have to be memorized, but nearly every time you're studying for a test, some things will. Since memorizing is time-consuming, you want to be efficient in your memorizing: to select what you choose to commit to memory with care and to use effective techniques in memorizing.

CHOOSING WHAT TO MEMORIZE

Since memorizing takes a lot of effort, you want to be very selective about what you memorize. In order to decide what to memorize, think about the kinds of questions you may be asked on a test, and whether or not they will require you to recall information exactly. Often the instructor will simply tell you what you should memorize. For instance, in a humanities class, the instructor may announce that the exam will be a list of twenty technical terms for you to define. If the instructor doesn't provide information like this, you need to select what to memorize. Here are some things you might need to memorize when studying for a test in different courses (depending on the type of questions to be asked on the test):

Algebraic formulas in math, physics, and statistics classes

Vocabulary words in vocabulary and foreign language classes

Titles and authors in a literature class, or major theorists and the names of their theories in a social science class

Maps in a geography class, or diagrams with labels in a biology class

Terms and their definitions in almost any class

Lists of ideas or steps in almost any class

If you're faced with large chunks of information to learn for a test, work up outlines for each chunk and memorize the outline. As a general rule, it's more efficient to memorize outlines or lists and to use the memorized outline or list as a framework to help you recall the descriptions or details of each item. For instance, if you thought you might be asked to identify and discuss Maslow's theory of self-actualization (presented in Chapter 10), you would want to have the names of the five types of needs memorized, but could probably depend on a thorough knowledge of what each one entailed for your descriptions. The list of the five types of needs that you memorize is short and serves as a tag to ensure that you include all parts in your answer.

UNDERSTAND TO MEMORIZE

You can memorize something you don't understand—parrots do it all the time. But the more you understand some information, the easier it is to memorize. As an example, the easiest phone numbers to learn are those with a pattern—the added knowledge of the pattern makes them easier to recall than an arbitrary string of seven digits.

So the preliminary work to any memorizing is to work on understanding. If you try to memorize something you don't understand, you have to work ten times as hard to memorize it, and even then you're less likely to retain it. Understanding should include not only learning what things are, but also how they are related, as the more connections you can make between ideas, the better able you will be to fix them in your mind. It's like trying to learn who the people are that you are working with when you start a new job. If they were just a roster of faces and names, it would take you a very long time to sort them out. Learning what their jobs are, what their backgrounds are, and what their relationships to other employees are helps you to remember them more easily.

EXERCISE 1

Try it. Return to the textbook passage in Chapter 10 that explains Maslow's theory of self-actualization. Review it, making sure you understand each stage. Then memorize the names of the five types of needs. After a decent interval—from several hours to a day—write down the names of the five types. Then see if you can reconstruct explanations of each of the types around this framework.

ORGANIZE TO MEMORIZE

An ordered list of items is easier to recall than an unordered list. The simplest kind of organization is numbering—if you recall that there are eight items on a list you need to recall, that information will tell your brain to keep searching after you recall seven of them.

Another type of organizing is classifying information into groups. As an illustration of how classifying helps, study the following list of eleven arts for fifteen seconds to see how many you can recall:

Painting	Sculpture
Architecture	Photography
Fiction	Music
Theater	Film
Opera	Dance
Poetry	

Now, try it a second time, but this time put the arts in three groups. Make sure you understand the basis for separating the arts into these three groups before you begin to work at memorizing:

Arts of space (arts that exist in space)
   Painting
   Architecture
   Sculpture
   Photography

Arts of time (arts that unfold along a temporal dimension)
   Music
   Poetry
   Fiction

Composite arts (arts with both a visual and temporal dimension)
   Theater
   Opera
   Dance
   Film

You probably found that you were able to remember more of the eleven categories the second time. You will also find that you'll retain the second list longer, because the categories help you to establish relations among the eleven arts.

■
────────────────────────

E X E R C I S E   2

Work out a simple classification system for the following list of art forms, and memorize them for your next class.

Symphony: a large-scale composition for orchestra

Novel: a long work of fiction, usually involving several subplots and many characters.

Ballad: a type of short narrative poem, often set to music, that celebrates folk heroes or common people.

Short story: a brief, concentrated work of fiction

Sonata: a large-scale musical work for solo instrument or for two instruments, generally in three or four movements.

Sonnet: a type of lyric poem in fourteen lines following a definite rhyme scheme.

Novella: a work of fiction longer than a short story but shorter than a novel

Concerto: a musical composition in which a single instrument joins with or is accompanied by the orchestra

Epic: a long narrative poem or story, told in an elevated style, that usually presents national heroes and gods in a series of exploits.

Lyric poem: a short poem expressing emotion

───────────────────────────────────

───────────────────────────────────

───────────────────────────────────

───────────────────────────────────

───────────────────────────────────

MNEMONIC AIDS

Another way to organize items to make them easier to recall is to use a **mnemonic aid**. A mnemonic aid is a device to aid memory. You probably have used these devices in the past. For instance, you may have learned the names of the Great Lakes by using their initial letters to form the word *HOMES* for Huron, Ontario, Michigan, Erie, and Superior. Or you may have learned the sentence "Every good boy does fine" to remember the names of the notes in the treble clef

(E, G, B, D, F). Another well-known mnemonic device is the name
ROY G. BIV for the colors in the spectrum (red, orange, yellow,
green, blue, indigo, violet).

These devices use two principles to help you remember: econ-
omy and memorability. Studies by psychologists have shown that our
memory is most effective for between five to nine unrelated items.
That's why phone numbers are seven digits long (and why eleven-
number zip codes are only used by computers). Also, we're more
likely to remember something odd than something ordinary, which
is why a mnemonic like ROY G. BIV sticks in our mind.

One common way to make up mnemonic devices is to use the
first letters of the words to be remembered to form a word like ROY
G. BIV. Words like this are called **acronyms**. For instance, the word
scuba is an acronym for "self-contained underwater breathing appa-
ratus," and BASIC, a computer language, is an acronym for Beginner's
All-Purpose Symbolic Instructional Code.

A second way to create a mnemonic device is to invent a sentence composed of words that start with the first letters of the words
to be remembered (like "Every good boy does fine"). Sentence mnemonics are somewhat less efficient than word mnemonics because
they're less compact. If you make up a sentence mnemonic, try to
make the sentence a bit absurd so that you'll remember it.

■
E X E R C I S E   3

1. As a warm-up, make up a mnemonic device to enable you to
   remember Maslow's five stages of self-actualization.
2. Figure 12.1 lists the ten organ systems of a mammal. Read it
   to familiarize yourself with the terms. Then work with a
   partner to make up a mnemonic device to help you remember the ten organ systems. Since there are ten items on the
   list (more than the recommended five to nine), strive for
   two words using the letters (or two sentences). Then practice recalling the list using your mnemonic device.

Mnemonic Device:

_____

_____

_____

_____

Test yourself a day later to see how many of the ten systems
you were able to recall.

Figure 12.1　　　　　　　　**ORGAN SYSTEMS OF A MAMMAL**

System	Components	Functions	Homeostatic ability
Integumentary	Skin, hair, nails, sweat glands	Covers and protects body	Sweat glands help control body temperature; as barrier, the skin helps maintain steady state
Skeletal	Bones, cartilage, ligaments	Supports body, protects, provides for movement and locomotion, calcium depot	Helps maintain constant calcium level in blood
Muscular	Organs mainly of skeletal muscle; cardiac muscle; smooth muscle	Moves parts of skeleton, locomotion; movement of internal materials	Ensures such vital functions as nutrition through body movements; smooth muscle maintains blood pressure; cardiac muscle circulates the blood
Digestive	Mouth, esophagus, stomach, intestines, liver, pancreas	Ingests and digests foods, absorbs them into blood	Maintains adequate supplies of fuel molecules and building materials
Circulatory	Heart, blood vessels, blood; lymph and lymph structures	Transports materials from one part of body to another; defends body against disease	Transports oxygen, nutrients, hormones; removes wastes; maintains water and ionic balance of tissues
Respiratory	Lungs, trachea, and other air passageways	Exchange of gases between blood and external environment	Maintains adequate blood oxygen content and helps regulate blood pH; eliminates carbon dioxide
Urinary	Kidney, bladder, and associated ducts	Eliminates metabolic wastes; removes substances present in excess from blood	Regulates blood chemistry in conjunction with endocrine system
Nervous	Nerves and sense organs, brain and spinal cord	Receives stimuli from external and internal environment, conducts impulses, integrates activities of other systems	Principal regulatory system
Endocrine	Pituitary, adrenal, thyroid, and other ductless glands	Regulates body chemistry and many body functions	In conjunction with nervous system, regulates metabolic activities and blood levels of various substances
Reproductive	Testes, ovaries, and associated structures	Provides for continuation of species	Passes on genetic endowment of individual; maintains secondary sexual characteristics

USING REHEARSAL TO MEMORIZE

How do you commit information to memory? Organizing and mnemonic devices are aids to memorizing, but the actual work of memorizing is **rehearsal,** the repeated recitation of information until it is preserved in your brain. You've used rehearsal to memorize many times in your life, such as when you learned the lines for a school play by reciting them again and again, or when you kept repeating a phone number while you were looking for a pen that worked. You usually erase these bits of information from your mind when you no longer need them, but there may be poems that you memorized as a child that you still remember today. The fact that you still remember them shows how effective a strategy rehearsal can be.

One way to rehearse information you want to memorize is to make up a self-test sheet or a set of flash cards, and carry it around with you, referring to it in odd moments throughout the day. A self-test sheet records questions or prompts in one column and answers in a second column. To study from it, you cover up the second column. Flash cards have questions or prompts on the front and answers on the back. (See illustrations of flash cards in Chapter 10.) As an example of how you would study with these aids, you might have written your mnemonic device for the ten organ systems of a mammal on one side of an index card and have written the organ systems on the reverse side. Then you might have tested yourself while waiting for the bus, during a pause in your work, or while drinking a cup of coffee, until you had memorized the list.

Another way to rehearse information you want to memorize is to make use of a tape recorder. It's fairly easy to make a self-testing tape: Ask yourself the question, leave a pause on the tape for the response, and then after the pause, supply the answer. (See Figure 10.3, Chapter 10 for a sample script of a self-testing tape.) Here's an example of how effective a study device these can be. One student had failed a critical test in French on the definitions of 100 idiomatic expressions. She had a chance to take a retest, and, to prepare herself for it, she made a study tape. On the tape she would hear herself saying "avoir faim." There was a short pause to give her time to say the answer, and then she would hear the answer: "to be hungry." She played the tape while she was getting dressed, while she was jogging, and while she was getting ready for bed. She passed the second test with an A.

Of course the time-honored way to rehearse is to ask a parent, sibling, or roommate to quiz you, but they tend to wear out more quickly than your tape recorder's batteries.

E X E R C I S E   4

Make a list of ten vocabulary terms that you need to know for one of your other classes. Either make a set of flash cards for the terms or make a self-testing tape for the terms. Study them five times a day for two days; then give yourself a test on the terms (no cheating!). Record your results and your reactions.

USING VISUALIZATION TO MEMORIZE

In many courses designed to help you improve your memory, participants are taught the techniques of visualization. **Visualization** is the use of visual imagery to record information in your brain—for instance, remembering that a professor is named Dr. Lamb by imagining him grazing in a field by the side of a mother sheep.

As you may know, the brain is asymmetrical—that is, the functions of the left side of the brain and the right side of the brain are different. For most people, the left side of the brain is specialized for analytical and language-based thinking, while the right side of the brain is specialized for holistic thinking (getting a sense of something as a whole as opposed to breaking it down into its parts), emotions, and visual knowledge.

In some learning, we use one side of the brain predominantly—cognitive psychologists theorize that mathematical reasoning is a left-brain activity, while sketching a painting is primarily a right-brain activity. However, much learning is interactive. Musicians, for example, appear to process music on both sides of their brain. The right side of their brain responds to the overall (holistic) impression of a piece of music and provides an emotional response, while the left side of their brain uses their knowledge of music theory to analyze the components of the music.

When you use visualization to help you remember language, you're involving both sides of your brain in learning—the left side for language-based thinking, and the right side for visualizing. Try it: as an aid to remembering Maslow's hierarchy of human needs, visualize five scenes: a person eating in a hut (biological needs), standing behind a crossing guard (safety needs), getting married (love needs), receiving an award (esteem needs), and recycling glass bottles (self-actualization needs).

The fact that visualization enables you to use both sides of the brain in learning also explains why tables, charts, maps, and graphs are useful learning aids, since they arrange information visually. For example, the organizational charts that you learned to create in Chapter 10 are effective study aids in part because they organize information visually.

E X E R C I S E   5

Figure 12.2 presents an outline of six types of play engaged in by children. Create a visual image to help you recall each of these six types of play. Rehearse recalling these several times during the next two days, and then test yourself. Report on how effective this form of remembering was for you.

Figure 12.2

SIX TYPES OF PLAY

Exploration Play	Roaming around and exploring objects in the physical environment by inspecting, touching, and moving them
Parallel Play	Playing alongside other children but without interacting with them
Instigative Play	Playing by mimicking someone or by responding to cues, as in peek-a-boo
Free Play	Unstructured play, like rough-housing
Formal Play	Play with rules to be followed, like sports and board games
Creative Play	Play involving imagining and making believe

SUMMARY

Memorizing is a time-consuming study technique, so you need to select what to commit to memory with care. Once you have selected what information to memorize, make sure you have a thorough understanding of it. Since organized information is easier to learn, any grouping of the information into meaningful categories will help. Students also use mnemonic, or memory-aiding devices, including acronyms and sentence mnemonics to make memorizing more efficient. The work of committing information to memory occurs with rehearsal—the repeated recitation of the information to be learned. Study aids such as flash cards, self-test sheets, and self-test tapes put information in convenient form for frequent rehearsals. Visualization also is an effective aid to memorizing, as it involves both the left and right sides of the brain in learning.

■
JOURNAL WRITING

1. How good would you say your memory is? Are you good at remembering faces? people's names? Do you remember trivial facts easily? What about phone numbers? Do you retain information that you've memorized for a long time or forget it quickly? Would you say your memory for visual information is better or your memory for words? What else have you noticed about your memory abilities?

2. What information—poems, lists of information, facts—that

you had to memorize for school can you still recall? What do you remember about how you memorized them?

ACADEMIC WRITING

Select the class in which you will have your next test. Review your notes, handouts, and textbook from that class, as well as any information you have about the upcoming test or typical test questions the instructor asks. Make a list of information you should memorize for that test.

Choose three sets of material that you named and write down the information you need to memorize. Make sure that you understand the material and have organized it in a meaningful way before you begin to memorize it.

Then use any of the techniques suggested in this chapter, including the use of flash cards, rehearsal, visualization, self-testing sheets and tapes, and mnemonic devices to memorize the information you selected. Finally report on what techniques you used and on how effective your memorization was.

PART
FIVE

TAKING COLLEGE EXAMS

13

TEST-TAKING STRATEGIES

In this chapter, you will learn how to:

▲ prepare for a major exam
▲ adapt your studying for different types of exams
▲ handle test anxiety
▲ follow exam directions
▲ decide on a time and order strategy for an exam

Clearly, knowing the material is an important factor in how well you do on a test. Another important factor, however, is how good a test-taker you are. Knowing how to take a test is an important academic skill—in fact, there is nothing more frustrating than the feeling that you knew the material for an exam but didn't do as well as you might have because you used a poor strategy when taking the exam. This chapter presents some overall strategies for preparing for and taking exams. Chapters that follow give specific advice on handling essay and objective questions.

PREPARING FOR TESTS

Studying for a test can sometimes seem to be an overwhelming task, especially when the test is a midterm or final that covers a lot of material. Here are some techniques that will allow you to organize your studying efficiently.

1. Organize your materials. Begin to prepare for a major test in one of your courses a week or two before the exam date by taking some time to get all materials together. Gather together your notes, handouts, and reading materials for the class. If some notes are sketchy or missing, make plans to get them from another student. At the same time, check to be sure that you've done all the reading assignments; read and underline any material that you overlooked.

2. Make up a study guide—an outline of the material that will be covered on the test. Some instructors routinely distribute a study guide before each exam. If your instructor does, this step is done for you. If not, make up your own. Start out with the course syllabus, if you have one, and use it as a guide. Compare the topics on the printed syllabus with the topics covered in your course notes. The instructor may have altered the order of topics, omitted or added topics, or omitted or added reading assignments. Write all changes directly on the syllabus. If there was no syllabus to begin with, then use the topic headings from your notes to outline the topics covered.

Figure 13.1 is an example of a student's outline for a unit test in his psychology course. Notice that in addition to topics, his study guide lists the readings and the pages and dates of the notes for each topic. This additional information is a guide to what material to review on each topic.

3. Find out about the test.   In order to study efficiently, you need to know as much about the test as you possibly can. Your best source of information is the instructor. A few weeks before the exam, ask the instructor to tell you about the test. Here's the information you want to know.

1. What material will the exam cover?
2. What material should be considered most important (later units as opposed to earlier units, notes and handouts as opposed to readings)?
3. What type of test will it be? (See Figure 13.2 for the different types of tests.)
4. What types of questions will be on the test: true–false, multiple-choice, fill-in-the-blank, matching, identification, short-answer, essay, problem-solving, other?
5. How long will the test be, and where will it be given?
6. How would the instructor recommend that you study for the test?
7. Could the instructor provide a study guide of what to study?
8. Will the test follow the format of earlier tests, and are any old tests available for examination?

4. Make a study plan.   After you've learned all you can about a test, make a list of what you need to do to prepare for it. This activity allows you to break down the large task of studying for a major test into a series of smaller tasks. A **study plan** is simply a TTD list for a

Figure 13.1

UPDATED SYLLABUS: INTRODUCTORY PSYCHOLOGY

Unit I: Biological Bases of Behavior

Date	Topic	Readings	Notes
8/25	What is Psychology? Three views of human behavior - biological - intra-psychic - social/behavioral	Ch. 1 Article: "What Does a Psychologist Do?"	pages 1 to 3
8/27	The Brain's Role - organization - hemispheric specialization	Ch. 2	4-6
9/1 & 9/3	Altered States Sleeping Dreaming Drugs	Ch. 3 "A Primer of Mind-altering Substances"	7-11
9/8	The mind-body problem Maclean's "Three Brains"	} Ch. 4	12-13
9/10	Aggression Three Views of Violence		14-17

Figure 13.2

TYPES OF TESTS

Objective test	A test consisting of multiple choice, true–false, fill in the blank, and/or matching questions.
Essay test	A test consisting of questions that you answer by planning, organizing, and writing an essay.
Problem-solving test	A test on which you're given problems to solve, like a math test.
Open-book test	A test during which you're allowed to consult materials from the class, such as your textbook or your notes.
Take-home exam	A test that's completed at home and turned in at a designated time.
Performance test	A test on which you're asked to perform some skill, like a swimming test.

specific exam. For example, a study plan for the introductory psychology exam used as an example earlier might look like the illustration in Figure 13.3.

Note that part of the study plan is an estimate of how long it will take to study. Most students underestimate how long it will take them to study for an exam. As a general guideline, figure on at least an hour of study time for each week of instruction. That means that if you were taking a test covering four weeks of classes, you'd need to study four hours to prepare for the exam. If the exam covers an entire sixteen-week semester course, you should plan on studying sixteen hours for the final. That probably seems like a huge amount of study time, especially if you were used to studying an hour or two for a final exam in high school, but college courses require more independent work on your part than high school courses did.

■
EXERCISE 1

Construct a study guide and a study plan for an upcoming exam in one of your courses. Use the samples in Figure 13.1 and Figure 13.3 as guides.

PREPARING FOR MIDTERM OR FINALS WEEK

If you're facing a series of exams, like a set of midterms or finals, you should allot time for all the courses you are studying for and plan your study time for each day the week before the exams. Figure 13.4 is an example of a calendar for studying for a set of final exams. As you can see, the student has provided time for studying for each sub-

Figure 13.3

SAMPLE STUDY PLAN

STUDY PLAN: 9/15 Psychology Test

1. Review notes & underlinings — pages 1 to 3 notes & Chapter 1, & Article. (What does a psychologist do?)
2. Make up study sheets on "What Is Psychology" & "Three Views of Human Behavior".
3. Review notes (p4-6) & underlinings in Ch 2 "The Brain's Role".
4. Study sheets on "Organization of the Brain" "Hemisphere Specialization"
5. Review notes & underlinings in "Altered States" (notes pp 7-11, Ch 3).
6. Study sheet: sleeping, dreaming, drugs.
7. <u>Memorize</u> primer of mind altering substances. (Instructor says <u>impt</u>)
8. Make up organizational chart — 3 views of violence & <u>learn</u> it. (Note: skip "mind — body problem" & "Maclean's Three brains" — won't be on test.)
9. Review study sheets & memorize <u>Primer</u> chart.

1½ to 2 hours Sunday am

1 hour Sunday evening

1 hour Sunday evening

1 hour Monday afternoon

ject proportional to the amount of material to be reviewed, has planned for breaks, and has tried to vary the activities in accord with her own study preferences.

If the schedule looks like a lot of hours and a lot of work, it is. Finals week is the time to make every other demand on your time a secondary priority—the laundry, your social life, your hobbies— and to make studying your top priority. If you work, see if you can get time off during exam week.

At some colleges, there's a study week before exams—a week before finals week with no classes scheduled to allow students time to prepare for exams. Often it's difficult for students to use a study week effectively, because it's totally unstructured time. A calendar like the one shown in Figure 13.4 is essential for you if you're facing a study week. It provides some structure, and enables you to budget your time for each course so that you don't neglect any subject.

Figure 13.4

STUDY WEEK SCHEDULE

	Thurs 12/10	Fri 12/11	Sat 12/12	Sun 12/13	Mon 12/14	Tues 12/15	Wed 12/16
9-12:00	Humanities	10-12 Humanities Exam	Biology	Biology	9-10 Math Test	10-12 Intro Psych Exam #5	
12-3:00	Biology	Break!	Break	Math	Last minute review - Biology	off until dinner	
3-6:00	} Break	} Study Math &	Intro Psych	Work-out	3-5 Biology Exam	↓	3-5 English Final
6-9:00	Study Humanities	Biology	↓ Break	} Biology	} Psych	Review notes do practice essay for English final	out to dinner - Exams over!
9-12:00	↓	Early to bed	Biology	}		↓ Get some sleep	

STUDYING FOR DIFFERENT TYPES OF EXAMS

As you learned in Chapter 10, studying includes a cluster of activities: reviewing, making study aids like study sheets and organizational charts, and memorizing. What study techniques you choose and how you adapt them will depend on the type of exam you're studying for. Here are some specific suggestions.

Studying for Essay Exams.   In studying for essay tests, stress predicting questions, making study sheets, and memorizing outlines. It's particularly useful to have a study guide when you're preparing for an essay exam, as you can study by predicting what essay questions might be asked about each topic listed on the study guide and then making up study sheets directed to the questions you predict. Even though the exact question you predict will usually not appear on the exam, your rehearsal will prepare you for many related questions.

You will also want to commit outlines of important chunks of information to memory as suggested in Chapter 12—such as a list of four parts of an important theory or the steps in a process. When answering an essay question, these outlines will provide the framework for your answer.

Studying for Objective Exams. Students often assume that, while essay questions focus on concepts and theories, objective questions concentrate on facts and details. Here are some examples of objective questions on the psychology of aggression that refute that idea:

1. Aggression
   a. is entirely a learned behavior
   b. is not related to frustration
   c. is related to cultural values
   d. is not related to watching TV

(The correct answer is c.)

2. Violence is caused by many factors, including social, psychological, and _____ factors.

(The correct answer is *biological.*)

3. True or False: People who view films that show violence against women are more likely to develop the attitude that violence against women is acceptable.

(The correct answer is *true.*)

As you can see, these questions require as thorough an understanding of the psychological theories about aggression as an essay question might. When you study for an objective test, concentrate on learning the important concepts in each unit, using the study techniques suggested in Chapter 10. The only exception would be when the instructor has specifically said that the test will concentrate only on memorized facts—a history test on dates or an art test on famous artists and the names of their paintings, for example.

Studying for Problem-Solving Exams. You might encounter problem-solving exams in math, computer, or business courses. To study for an exam of this type, make a list of the different types of problems that might appear on the test. Work each type of problem using simple data and outline the steps in solving the problem and the principles involved.

Studying for Open-Book Exams. Open-book exams require a special type of preparation. Students underestimate how difficult this type of exam is, and often don't study or prepare well for it, thinking that they can rely on their books. In preparing for an open-book exam, you need to study the material just as you would for any exam. Furthermore, you need to organize your materials well so that you can look up information during the exam.

For example, an instructor might declare a math exam an open-book exam so that you can use the book to look up math formulas and won't have to memorize them. In studying for an exam like this, you would want to review the formulas that you had been taught, know their names and what type of problems they were used to solve, and practice working sample problems of each type. You also need to prepare to be able to locate the right formula during the exam quickly and accurately. You might highlight the formulas in your textbook's index or table of contents, or list formulas and page references on the inside cover of the book, or put tabs on the pages you think you'll need to find. Without this kind of preparation, you'll waste a lot of time during the exam turning pages trying to find information.

Studying for Take-Home Exams. A take-home exam is like an essay exam in the type of questions it contains, but is unlike an essay exam in that in most cases you can use the materials of the course to plan your answer and you usually have a longer time to write your answer. Since there is no set time limit on a take-home exam, you need to set your own time limits. Work out a realistic schedule for planning your answer, writing it, and revising it. Pay attention to any restrictions on the length of your answer, the materials you should use, the use of outside help, and the form of your answer. Make sure that you will be finished well before the deadline for handing the exam in; most instructors will penalize students severely if a take-home exam is handed in late.

When planning your answer, consult the course materials. Look through your notes and readings on the topic. Write down ideas that relate to your answer, but be sure to paraphrase them. Your answer should be in your own words, not in the textbook's words.

If possible, write a first draft, edit it, and then write a second draft. While drafting is not suitable for in-class essay exams, it is suitable for take-home exams. Try to write a rough draft two days before the exam is due, and then review and revise it the day before the exam is due. Since you have more time, your take-home exam should be carefully proofread. Take-home exams are often typed.

Studying for Performance Exams. Not all courses require you to learn a body of knowledge; some courses, or parts of some courses, instead challenge you to acquire or learn skills. Examples would be a physical education course like beginning tennis or swimming, a course in beginning drafting, a writing course, or a class in computer programming. For skills-oriented courses like these, a large part of your study time will be practicing the skill. For example, in a group piano class that one student was taking to fulfill the humanities requirement at his college, the final was a performance final—to play one of four music pieces for the instructor. Studying for this class consisted of practicing the piece he had selected each day for two weeks, until he could play it flawlessly. In fact, because he knew that he would be nervous when he played it for the instructor, he overlearned the piece to compensate for his nervousness.

As this example suggests, short, frequent practices are better than one long practice session right before a performance test, and practicing for a performance that will be evaluated usually means overlearning a skill to compensate for the nervousness that performing for a critical audience involves.

PHYSICAL AND MENTAL PREPARATION

Studying for midterms and finals is a real endurance test. Yet, when it's time to take an exam, you need to be in decent shape physically and mentally in order to perform well. Therefore, you have to remember to be good to yourself while you're working hard. Being physically prepared means having had enough sleep so that you're alert—and only you know how much sleep you need to function reasonably well. You should also have had something to eat beforehand, preferably something with a reasonable amount of nutritious value. Don't experiment with drugs, thinking they'll help you through the test—you're inviting disaster. One story that makes this point dramatically is about a student who tried a mind-altering substance before a heavy test in his major, and wrote a brilliant essay. Unfortunately, he wrote it all on the same line of the test booklet.

Be sure you know when and where the exam will be given and allow yourself enough time to get there, and, if necessary, to find the room. You certainly don't need the added tension of running around campus looking for your exam. This kind of situation is so anxiety-producing that many people report that years after they have finished college they still have dreams about getting lost when they're supposed to be taking a final exam.

Another common-sense kind of preparation is to have all your equipment with you and in good working order—paper, pencils, pens, erasers, and any special equipment that's allowed, like a dictionary or a calculator (make sure batteries are fresh). You might also want to bring some gum or hard candy if it helps you concentrate.

Being mentally prepared means knowing the material, but it also means putting yourself in a positive state of mind for the exam. You can expect to be anxious, but you want that anxiety to be under control—to work for you by pushing you to work at your best, instead of disrupting your concentration.

HANDLING TEST ANXIETY

Don't be surprised if your level of anxiety increases as a test approaches. It's very common for students to feel nervous before a test of any kind. If you think about it, you probably feel nervous almost any time when you know your performance is being observed and evaluated—when trying out for a school squad, when performing in a recital, or when a supervisor observes you doing your job. Realizing that anxiety is a natural feeling when you're being evaluated should help to put test anxiety into perspective for you—it's really a normal reaction to the situation.

In fact, test anxiety can work to your advantage. Any coach will tell you that such nervousness often helps players to push themselves to higher levels of performance during a game. You may be able to harness your anxiety and use it to push yourself to work at top level during an exam.

Sometimes, however, anxiety gets out of hand, and you might find yourself so nervous about an exam that you can't even study, or so panicky during an exam that you're unable to recall a single thing you studied. What do you do then? There's no single answer to this question. Different people have different ways of reducing their anxiety. Here are some suggestions you can try.

1. Make a phone call.   Talk over your anxieties with someone else, instead of keeping them to yourself. Think of your most supportive friend or family member, call him or her up, and explain what's on your mind. You're not necessarily looking for advice; just the activity of sharing your concerns often makes them more manageable.

2. Take an exercise break.   Studying is not a very physical activity. Running around a track, swimming a few vigorous lengths in the pool, biking around the campus, or even running up and down

Reprinted by permission of UFS, Inc.

the stairs often discharges a lot of the anxiety you have collected around exam time.

3. *Take a meditation break.* One student said that when she is studying hard for an exam, her stress level keeps rising until she's doing more worrying than studying. At that point, she goes and sits in her most comfortable chair, closes her eyes, and lets her mind escape to a tranquil moment from her last vacation. Relaxation exercises and deep breathing exercises can be used for the same effect.

4. *Learn one thing well.* Decide what item on your study plan is most likely to appear on the test and learn it. If your anxiety comes from knowing that you're not prepared to take an exam, then studying is a remedy. Learn one thing, and tell yourself, "Well, at least I can handle a question about that."

It's very common to have an attack of panic when you're in the exam room and are given the exam. ("I don't know any of this stuff. I'm going to flunk. I don't belong here. Help!") If that happens, close your eyes for a few minutes and meditate or do relaxation exercises until you calm down a bit. Then say to yourself, "I'll do the best I can—that's all I can do," and get to work.

If your level of anxiety is really interfering with your studying, talk to a school counselor. He or she has seen many students with the same problem over the years and will offer a sympathetic ear and some good advice.

Finally, sometimes circumstances beyond your control leave you in no physical or mental shape to take an exam—you catch the flu, or there's a major crisis in your life. It you decide that it's absolutely impossible for you to take the exam, you must contact the professor before the exam, explain the circumstances, and ask permission to take a make-up exam at a later date. If you don't contact the instructor *before* the exam, you will most likely be given a failing grade, even if you were in the hospital.

FOLLOWING EXAM DIRECTIONS

Fellow professors tell me that every time they give an exam, at least one student does poorly because he or she ignored the directions on the exam—answering all the questions instead of selecting a certain number, or failing to answer the questions the right way, or omitting a section. It's understandable why mistakes of this type occur. When you finally have in your hands a copy of that exam you've been worrying about, what you're interested in is what the questions are, not in that little paragraph at the top that provides the directions. So look over the questions first to satisfy your curiosity, but then go back and read the directions carefully. Then read them a second time.

Remember that some exam directions may be given orally. Again, you have to put aside your nervousness and listen carefully to the directions the instructor is giving.

It's a real help if you're allowed to make notes on the exam. Ask the instructor. If you can write on the exam, underline all the key instructions, and even make notes on each section to remind you of the instructions. Figure 13.5 shows an example of exam instructions that a student has marked.

Be especially on the alert for directions like these:

1. Answer two questions from section 1, two from section 2, and all questions in section 3.
2. Answer all questions.
3. Answer Question 1 and any two other questions. Question 1 is worth 50 points. Your other two answers are worth 25 points each.
4. Mark each question true or false. If you decide the statement is false, cross out the incorrect part of the statement and correct it so that the statement will be true.
5. Circle the correct answer for each question. Some of the questions have more than one correct answer.
6. Do not write on this exam. Record all answers in your answer booklet.
7. Write all answers on this exam.
8. Do not write your name on this exam. Instead, write the exam number that has been assigned to you in the space provided.
9. Write your name on each page of your answer booklet.
10. You may use your notes in preparing your answer.
11. Do not consult any materials during the exam.
12. (for a math test) Solve the following problems. Show all your work on your answer sheet.
13. (for a math test) Solve the following problems. Do not show your work; record the answers only on your answer sheet.
14. Label each section of your answer clearly.
15. Start each answer on a separate page in your blue book.

If you're unclear about any directions, ask the instructor. Most instructors will answer any reasonable question during a test. ("What's the answer to question #5?" is not considered a reasonable question.)

■
─────────────────
EXERCISE 2   Here are some directions from a biology exam. Read them and underline the key information.

Figure 13.5

SAMPLE TEST

Introductory Psychology — Test #1

General Directions: Write your name on this test, and record your answers for Part 1 (multiple choice) on these pages. Write your answers for Part 2 (identification) and Part 3 (essay answers) on the paper that is provided. Put your name on each page, and record the number of the question you are answering. Do not consult any outside material while you work. You have 2 hours.

Part 1 Multiple Choice Questions (30 points)   *end by 2:30*
Directions: Answer all questions. Each question has only one correct answer. Write the correct answer in the blank space provided. Do not write on the test copy.

Part 2 Identification (20 points)   *end by 2:50*
Directions: Identify 10 out of 13 of the following by writing a short phrase or sentence indicating what each term refers to. Write your answers on the paper that has been provided. Underline the term you are identifying.

biological view of human behavior
intra-psychic view of human behavior
social/behavioral view of human behavior
the cerebrum
neurotransmitters
hemispheric specialization
REM sleep
stimulants
hallucinogens
endorphins
Broca's area
psychosurgery
frustration-aggression hypothesis

Part 3 Essay Questions (50 points)
Select two of the following essay questions to answer (25 points each). Write the number of the question you are answering on your answer page, and clearly label all parts of your answer. Write in complete sentences and paragraphs.

1. Discuss violence and aggression:
    a. from an intra-psychic viewpoint
    b. from a social-behavioral viewpoint, and
    c. from a psychobiological viewpoint

✓2. Select five drugs studied in class and discuss, for each one, its effect on the nervous system and its effect on behavior.   *end by 3:20*

✓3. Explain the four stages of sleep and the typical behaviors observed in each stage.   *end by 3:50*

4. Explain the different functions generally associated with the two hemispheres of the brain.

Directions: Answer all questions in Part 1. In Part 2, answer question #1 and two other questions of your choice. Write all answers in your exam booklet and number each question clearly. Question 6 is a bonus question—you may answer it if you wish. If you do, label the diagram directly on the page.

PLAN YOUR TIME

A common problem, particularly on any exam that involves essay questions, is not planning your time well. If you're taking a two-hour exam, and you wait until the last fifteen minutes to start the fifty-point essay question, you're inviting disaster. The basic principle of planning your time for an exam is to allot the time in proportion to the amount of credit given for each section.

Here's an example: a biology test has three sections:

Twenty-five multiple-choice questions (25 points)
Ten definitions (25 points)
Two essay questions (50 points)

Students taking this exam should allow a maximum of thirty minutes for the multiple-choice questions, thirty minutes for the definitions, and a half hour for each essay question. To plan a time strategy for an exam, look at the point value for each section or question on the exam and the total time allowed, and divide the time proportionally. If point values for different questions or sections aren't given, ask. Otherwise, as a general guideline, estimate that objective questions (true–false, multiple-choice, matching, and sentence completion questions) will take you from a half minute to a minute each. An essay answer can take as much time as you can spend on it. The longer the exam and the more points assigned to the essay question, the longer the time you should allow for each essay question.

To apply your time strategy when you are taking the exam, write down your deadline for each section, as in the example in Figure 13.5. When you see your deadline for that section approaching, wrap up your work on that section and go on to the next part. If you finish work on one part before your deadline, you've saved valuable time for the next section, or for proofreading and reviewing.

■
EXERCISE 3

Here are some sample exam formats. Work out a time strategy for each one.

Time strategy

1. *(a humanities exam: one hour)*
Part 1:   Ten short answer questions (25 points)   _____

Part 2:   Three essay questions (25 points each)   _____

2. *(a biology exam: two hours)*
Part 1:   A matching column (10 points)

Part 2:   Ten multiple choice questions (20 points)

Part 3:   Four essay questions (10 points each)

Part 4:   Two diagrams to label (15 points each)

3. *(a sociology exam: two hours)*
Four essay questions, one worth 40 points, and the others
worth 20 points each

4. *(a math exam: one hour)*
Part 1:   Ten problems (30 points)

Part 2:   Ten identifications (20 points)

Part 3:   Two essay questions (25 points each)

PLANNING AN ORDER STRATEGY

Many times you don't have to answer the questions on a test in the order in which they were written. Instead, you may work in an order that is best for you. Here, for example, are some different order strategies that students used on the psychology exam in Figure 13.5.

First, I'll answer all the multiple-choice questions I know. Next, I'll write the essay answers. Then I'll do the identifications. Then I'll go back and work on the multiple-choice questions I wasn't sure of. Finally, I'll reread the essay answers I wrote.

I would start by outlining all the essay answers. (This calms me down by showing me that I have something to say.) Then I would work on the first two sections. As I'm working on those sections, if more ideas occur to me about the essay answers, I write little notes to myself. Then I'd spend the last hour on the essay answers.

I always do the essay answers first to get them out of the way and to make sure I spend enough time on them. It's easier to speed through the multiple-choice and identification sections if I run short of time.

As these examples show, there's no one correct strategy for test-taking. The only thing you have to be sure of is that when you finish the exam, your answers are arranged in the same order as the questions, so that the instructor doesn't have to hunt around to find them.

■ EXERCISE 4

Describe the time and order strategy you would use on the psychology exam in Figure 13.5 and explain why you chose that strategy.

SUMMARY

Begin your preparation for a test by organizing your materials, including getting any missed notes and handouts. Next, construct a study guide (a list of topics to be studied) and find out about the test from the instructor. Your study plan for an exam should include a list of what you will do and a realistic time estimate for each activity. If you are facing a series of exams or a study week, use a calendar to make a master plan for studying for all your exams in that time period.

Adapt your studying to the type of exam you're facing. To study for an essay test, emphasize predicting questions, making study sheets, and memorizing outlines. Study the same way for an objective test: don't assume that an objective test calls only for the memorization of facts. If you're facing an open-book exam, emphasize understanding concepts in your study, and organize your materials with care so you can find critical information quickly. A take-home exam requires little recall of information, but wise time planning and an application of writing skills. To study for a performance exam, try short, frequent practices and overlearning to compensate for nervousness.

Physical preparation for a test includes taking care of yourself by getting enough sleep, eating well, and staying away from body-abusing substances. Mental preparation includes coping with test anxiety. Some ways to reduce test anxiety are by verbalizing it, using exercise to discharge tension, trying relaxation or meditation techniques—and studying.

Strategies during the exam are equally important. Exam directions are easily overlooked, so take time to read them carefully and, if possible, to mark them. Once you have an overview of the exam, work out a time and order strategy. Allot your time in proportion to the credit value of each section, and plan to answer questions in an order that is comfortable for you.

■ JOURNAL WRITING

1. What strategies have you learned that are effective for dealing with stress and anxiety in your life? Describe what the strategies are and the situations in which you have employed them.

2. Figure 13.2 lists different types of exams. Which types do you prefer and why? In stating your preferences, draw on yourown experiences as a student.

3. Write a letter to yourself telling yourself what you should and should not do to be physically and mentally prepared for an exam. In deciding what advice to include in your letter, draw on your own experiences of strategies that worked and mistakes you made in the past.

4. In what order do you prefer to work on a multi-part exam that includes both essay questions and objective questions? Explain.

■
ACADEMIC WRITING

A. Prepare for an open-book test in this course based on Chapters 10, 11, 12, and 13. Take the following steps:
   1. Make up a study outline by using the headings and dates in your notes. Include any additional readings and hand-outs in your study outline.
   2. Question your instructor about the test, using the questions on page 179.
   3. Based on the information from 1 and 2, make up a study plan that lists what to study and estimates how long to study each item on your list.

B. The following is a one-hour, open-book exam based on information in Chapters 10 to 12 in this textbook. Work out a time and order strategy for the exam. Then take the exam, applying your time and order strategies.

Review Test: Chapters 10 through 13

Directions: You are limited to an hour's time. Answer all questions in Part 1, and 3 out of 4 questions in Part 2. You may consult your book and your notes.

Part 1 (40 points) Identify each of the following terms briefly.

Rehearsal
Organizational charts
Study sheets
Mnemonic devices
Self-testing tapes
Study outline
Open-book exam
Study plan
Visualization
Order strategy for an exam

Part 2 (60 points)

1. Explain why study sheets are useful study tools and give some examples of different types of study sheets.
2. What are the advantages of a study plan? What information should be included in it?
3. Why is understanding an important step in memorizing?
4. What are the advantages and disadvantages of test anxiety?

14

Answering Essay Questions

In this chapter, you will learn:

▲ how to read essay questions to understand what is being asked of you
▲ how to plan essay answers
▲ how to write an essay answer that clearly conveys what you know
▲ how to learn from reviewing your tests

Essay exams have always been a popular type of exam with instuctors, and they are becoming ever more common because of the increasing emphasis on writing abilities and cognitive skills in college. They are generally less popular with students, because they demand more of students than objective questions do, and also because they really test students on their writing abilities as well as on their knowledge of the material in the course. This may seem unfair, but part of a college education involves learning how to express ideas in writing. If you can project ahead to the kind of career you'd like to have, you almost certainly will have to write frequently, but you won't need to demonstrate your knowledge of your field on an objective test after college.

   This chapter will help you apply your writing skills to answering essay questions on tests, but it is not aimed at improving your general writing abilities. If doing any college writing assignment is a hurdle for you, you need to get advice on what writing courses you should be taking, and you need to take those courses as early in your college career as possible. Taking courses is the easiest way to improve your writing skills, and there will be immediate transfer to the writing assignments in all your classes.

READING ESSAY QUESTIONS

An essay test is also a test of reading ability. An overwhelming number of the students who do poorly on an essay question either fail to answer the question or fail to answer all parts of the question.

The first step in answering an essay question is understanding what the question is asking. Essay questions can be divided into five types, based on the kind of answer you are being asked to write. Studying these five types will help you to comprehend essay questions on tests. Directive words commonly used in each type of question are pointed out. However, as you will see, it's the whole sense of the question that determines its type, not the use of any one word.

I   FEEDBACK QUESTIONS

Feedback questions ask you to feed back or summarize information from the course. Here are some examples.

1.   Explain the principle of the "tragic flaw," using one example of a drama read in the course to support your analysis.

2.   Describe the structure and function of a leaf.

3.   Summarize the physical reactions of the body to stress.

II   PROCESS ANALYSIS QUESTIONS

Process analysis questions ask you to present the steps in a process, such as a procedure that takes place as a sequence of events or steps or stages.

4.   Outline the stages of moral development.

5.   Briefly trace the evolution of drama in the sixteenth century.

6.   Explain the process by which blood is pumped through the human body.

III   RELATIONAL QUESTIONS

Relational questions ask you to examine the relationship between two ideas. Some questions of this type will ask you to discuss the similarities and differences of two topics. The directive *compare* almost always means to discuss similarities and differences. Other relational questions will direct you to concentrate on differences. Questions of this type often contain the directive *contrast*. Less frequently you will be asked to explore only the similarities shared by two ideas.

7.   How were theaters designed differently in ancient Greece, in Renaissance England, and in eighteenth-century Europe? What changes in society might account for these changes?

8.   Compare and contrast photosynthesis in desert and non-desert plants.

9.   Contrast the sympathetic nervous system and the parasympathetic nervous system.

IV   ARGUMENT QUESTIONS

Argument questions ask you to write an essay defending a position by using information you've learned in the course. One type of argument question calls on you to *evaluate* something. When you evaluate something, you discuss its benefits and disadvantages and reach a conclusion, deciding that your topic is good on the whole or bad on the whole. Here are some examples of argument questions.

10.   Agree or disagree with the following: "A work of art should be judged as if it were timeless, with no regard for its relation to the political or historical climate in which it was produced."

11.   Do you believe that control of population is necessary to improve the quality of life in the world? Explain, citing real examples to support your position.

12.   Evaluate whether IQ tests measure intelligence accurately or not.

V   APPLICATION QUESTIONS

Application questions ask you to explore how principles you learned in the course might be applied in a specific situation, as in these examples.

13.   Imagine that you were to direct a filming of one of the short stories read in class this term. Tell what short story you selected, and explain what settings you would use, what characters and scenes you would select, and which ones you would leave out. Give the artistic reasons for your decisions.

14.   You've read several articles about water pollution in this area. Based on what you've learned, outline a plan of action for combating water pollution to be presented to the city council. Present the steps you think should be taken in priority order, from most to least important, and explain why each step you select is necessary.

15.   Black and white workers at your office don't seem to get along well. You've been asked to design a program to improve the situation. How would you assess the causes of the problem? What options would you consider to improve the situation?

Figure 14.1   **COMMON DIRECTIVES IN ESSAY QUESTIONS**

I   Feedback questions
describe, discuss, explain, summarize, outline, identify, review.

II   Process analysis questions
trace, give the steps, present the stages, describe the process.

III   Relational questions
compare, compare and contrast, contrast, discuss the differences, show the relationship, differentiate, distinguish between, relate.

IV   Argumentative questions
agree or disagree, argue, justify, criticize, evaluate, prove, support.

V   Application questions
what would you do, how would you, what steps would you take?

As a general strategy, read an essay question several times to identify what type it is. One suggestion is to read it as if you were reading it out loud. This practice forces you to slow down and pay attention to each word.

A second useful strategy is to work at **paraphrasing** the question—putting it into your own words—until you're sure that you understand what is being asked of you. As you read, pay attention to the direction words, as they often signal the type of question being asked. (See Figure 14.1 for a list of common directive words classified according to type.) Paraphrasing is another way to focus your attention on the question. For example, for the question, "Describe the structure and function of a leaf," you could paraphrase it by saying, "What are the parts of a leaf? What does each part do?"

■
EXERCISE 1

Identify the type of each of the following questions.

1. If you were a therapist, how would you treat a person with an irrational fear of dogs? Discuss the overall approach you would take and the specific steps in your treatment plan. _____

2. Agree or disagree: all women over the age of 35 who become pregnant should be tested for genetic disorders. _____

3. List and describe the seven classes of vertebrates. Give an example for each class. _____

4. Discuss the physical, emotional, and interpersonal effects of anger. _____

5. Describe the stages in the life cycle of a butter-fly. _____

■
─────────────────
E X E R C I S E   2

Read sample essay questions 3, 5, 8, 10, and 14 to yourself as if you were reading them out loud. Then write a paraphrase of them. Compare your paraphrases with those of two other students to see if you interpreted the questions accurately.

3. _____

_____

5. _____

_____

8. _____

_____

10. _____

_____

14. _____

_____

PREDICTING PARTS

A real aid in answering essay questions is to use the question as a guide to planning the parts your answer will have. Many essay questions imply the parts your answer should have. Let's look at each type of question in turn.

For *feedback* questions, pay attention to key words that indicate how the question asks you to break down information. For example, for the question, "Describe the structure and function of a leaf," you should plan your answer to include two sections, one on leaf structure, and one on leaf function. However, for a question like, "Summarize the physical reactions to stress," you're given no guidelines on how to break down your answer, and must rely on your own knowledge—that's when you use the outlines that you memorized in studying.

For *process analysis* questions, you know that you'll be presenting a series of steps or stages. Again, a memorized outline of the names of the steps or stages is a real help in constructing your answer. Even without this information, you should try to plan your answer as a numbered series of steps.

For *relational* questions, you might have two topics and be asked to discuss their similarities and differences. Here is how you might organize an answer to the question, "Compare and contrast photosynthesis in desert and non-desert plants":

1. Photosynthesis in non-desert plants
2. Photosynthesis in desert plants
   a. Similarities to non-desert plants
   b. Ways in which the process is different

Or else you might break down the question like this

1. Similarities in photosynthesis in desert and non-desert plants
2. Differences in their photosynthesis

Either way, you want to be sure to discuss both desert and non-desert plants and both similarities and differences.

For *argument* questions, your response should include your **thesis** (the position you are taking), several reasons that support your thesis, and explanations of each reason. For instance, a plan for an answer to sample question 10 might look like this:

Thesis: Works of art cannot be judged as if they were timeless.

Reason 1
Reason 2
Reason 3
Reason 4

If the argument question calls on you to *evaluate* something, you will typically discuss its pros and cons, and come to a conclusion about its worth. Your conclusion in this case is your thesis. An answer to question 12, for instance, would include: a discussion of the extent to which IQ tests do measure intelligence, a discussion of the extent to which they do not measure intelligence accurately, and the student's conclusion, which might be something like, "Although IQ tests do measure some types of intelligence, they do not measure many other types of intelligence, so I conclude that they do not measure intelligence accurately."

For *application* questions, your plan for a response should include a statement or restatement of the problem you are solving, and a breakdown of the solution you posed, following the guidelines in the question. For example, for question 13, your response should include the title of the short story you selected, a section on the type of stage you would choose, a section on settings, a section on characters, and a section on scenes. Each section, according to the directions, should include both what you would choose and the artistic reasons why you would make that choice.

As these examples show, specifically worded essay questions suggest outlines of the answers you should write for them. Instructors will read your answers looking for each part of the answer specified in the question and will only give full credit if all the parts are there. So it's important that you teach yourself to predict the parts of an answer from the question when possible.

■
—————————————
E X E R C I S E   3

For each of the following essay questions, identify the type of question and make up a short outline that specifies the parts of the answer based on the cues in the question. You don't have to be specific as to what the parts will contain—you can say "reason 1, reason 2, reason 3," or "example 1, example 2, example 3."

Model:
How were theaters designed differently in ancient Greece, in Renaissance England, and in eighteenth-century Europe? What changes in society might account for these changes?
Type of question: <u>relational question</u>
Outline:
1. Theater design in ancient Greece
2. Theater design in Renaissance England
   Differences from ancient Greece
3. Theater design in eighteenth-century Europe
   Differences from Renaissance England
4. Social reasons for differences

1. Explain what is meant by sex-linked genes and give three examples.

Type of question: _____

Outline: _____

_____

_____

_____

_____

2.   Compare and contrast insects and spiders.

Type of question: _____

Outline: _____

_____

_____

_____

_____

3.   Trace the life cycle of a leaf through four seasons.

Type of question: _____

Outline: _____

_____

_____

_____

_____

4.   How does punishment differ from negative reinforcement?

Type of question: _____

Outline: _____

_____

_____

_____

_____

5.   What are the effects according to Adler of being the first-born, an only child, the "baby," or a middle child?

Type of question: _____

Outline: _____

_____

_____

_____

_____

6.   Explain three ways this society encourages people to smoke and three way in which it discourages people from smoking. What type of pressure do you think is most effective? Explain.

Type of question: _____

Outline: _____

_____

_____

_____

_____

PLANNING YOUR ANSWER

The first steps in answering an essay question, then, are to read the question carefully, decide what type of question it is, and paraphrase it until you are sure you understand what is being asked. Then study the question to see what parts your answer should have. Your next step should be to write a scratch outline of your answer.

A scratch outline is an informal outline that plans the content of your answer. It is written for your eyes only. Figure 14.2 shows three samples of scratch outlines for essay answers. As you can see, these planning notes are lists of the ideas students will include in their answer.

Students often don't plan essay answers before they begin to write them, because the pressure of time on an exam makes them feel that they don't have time to waste on planning. Think about the

Figure 14.2

SAMPLE SCRATCH OUTLINES

<u>Question</u>: Agree or disagree with the following: "A work of art should be judged as if it were timeless with no regard for the relation to the political or historical climate in which it was produced."

Thesis: Disagree: can't judge works as if timeless

why {

1 — artist is a product of his time, molded by society's economic & political structure →Rivera (Mexican muralist)

2 — many works of art are political, or at least a comment on the times - Warhol - religious art

3 — if we don't look at political/historical climate, we limit ourselves (like blinders on)

<u>Question</u>: Describe the structure and function of a leaf.

Answer   <u>Structure</u>:   petiole
midribs
vein
blade

blade
midribs
petiole
veins

<u>Function</u>: limit water loss
perform photosynthesis
carry material to & from tissues

<u>Question</u>: Outline the stages of moral development

Moral Development Stages [Laurence Kohlberg]

1. pre-moral level - base moral decisions on considerations of reward/punishment

2. conventional level - conform to other people's rules & expectations

3. principled level - apply abstract moral principles

logic of planning—you have to plan your answer at some point, either before you write or while you write. It's actually more efficient to plan before you write, as you can see what ideas you have and organize them before you start writing. Students tell me that when they have planned their answers first, the actual writing goes much more quickly, so there's actually no loss of overall time.

Writers use many different techniques to plan, but some are not suited to an exam situation. For example, in writing a paper for class, you might write several rough drafts. An essay exam is not suited for draft writing. Your valuable time on an exam should not be spent drafting or copying an answer. Scratch outlines are a more suitable writing technique for an essay exam. They're quick and they can be revised quickly. They enable you to preview your answer and correct any problems quickly before you begin to write.

Begin your scratch outline with a breakdown of the parts of your answer. Next to each part, write down any ideas related to that part that occur to you. As you work, cross out ideas that don't seem relevant, add ideas that you think of, and number ideas in the order in which you'll present them. Spend up to one-quarter of the total time you've allotted for answering the question on planning. So if you have twenty minutes to answer an essay question, take up to five minutes for planning.

One strategy many students use is to begin planning their essay answers as soon as they get the exam in front of them. As they're working on other parts of the exam and other ideas occur to them, they jot them down on their outlines. By the time they're ready to write the answer, they have a good collection of ideas. After a few minutes of editing and rearranging those ideas, they're ready to begin to write.

EXERCISE 4

Each of the following essay questions is based on material in this textbook. After reading the question and identifying the type of question and the parts your answer should have, work up a scratch outline for an answer.

1. What are some causes of test anxiety? Identify some strategies that you can use to handle test anxiety. (Chapter 13)

_____

_____

_____

_____

2. Evalute the extent to which grades help learning. (Chapter 2 plus your own experiences)

3. Explain the strategy you should use to learn specialized vocabulary terms. (Chapter 11)

Feel free to review the chapter on which the question is based as you plan your answer.

WRITING YOUR ANSWER

An aid to writing a good essay answer is knowing what instructors look for when they grade essay answers. A good essay answer:

   Answers the question as stated
   Answers all parts of the question, with the parts clearly labeled
   Reflects knowledge of the course material
   Reflects understanding of course material and ability to reason independently (particularly on argument and application questions)
   Is clearly stated and well-organized
   Is easy to read

Figure 14.3 gives two examples of essay answers that meet these criteria. Let's look at each point in turn:

1. A good essay answer answers the question as stated. First, be sure that you have used slow, careful reading and paraphras-

Figure 14.3

TWO ESSAY ANSWERS

Question: Outline the stages of moral development

Psychologist Lawrence Kohlberg outlined three stages of moral development.

In the <u>first</u> stage, which he calls the <u>pre-moral</u> level, a person bases decisions on considerations of reward or punishment. So moral values are imposed by whoever is handing out the rewards & punishments.

In the <u>second</u> stage, which he calls <u>conventional</u> level, moral decisions conform to the peer group's or society's views of right & wrong. So a teenager whose friends shoplift & who believe shoplifting is ok because "everyone does it" would be at this stage.

In the <u>third</u> stage, which he calls the <u>principled</u> level, a person is guided by internalized abstract principles such as, "It's wrong to steal" (no matter what society thinks or what my friends do.)

These are stages in that you have to pass through one to get to the next, but ~~there are no age categories~~ they don't necessarily correspond to any stage in maturation. An adult could still function at Stage 1.

Question: Agree or disagree with the following: "A work of art should be judged as if it were timeless with no regard for the relation to the political or historical climate in which it was produced."

I <u>do not agree</u> that a work of art should be judged as if it were timeless.

<u>First</u>, an artist is a product of his or her time and has been molded by the social, economic, & political structure in which the artist lives. So the artist as an individual is responding to & reacting to

Figure 14.3 cont.

the context in which the artist was raised. In order to understand
what an artist is saying, it helps to understand who the artist is.
For example, many movements in art such as impressionism in art &
modernism in architecture are responses to earlier movements.
It helps us to understand them if we understand what the artist
was reacting to.

Second, many works of art are comments by the artist on his/her
times, and so could not be understood at all if we ignored their
historical context. At one extreme, we have the religious art of the
middle ages. At the other extreme, there is revolutionary art of a
modern artist like Rivera, the Mexican muralist. The subjects
chosen by these artists were not chosen in a vacuum. When we look
at the values of the society in which the artists lived, we understand
their meaning more fully.

Third, if we ignore the historical climate - the time dimension - in which
works of art were produced, we limit ourselves meaninglessly
unnecessarily. Why try to limit ourselves to what's inside the frame
when the other information is available to us? Any information that
is useful to help us appreciate & understand a work of art should
be used.

ing to understand the question. Then, to convey the topic of your answer, begin your answer with a one- to three-sentence introduction that paraphrases your answer and possibly presents the parts of your answer. This brief introduction clearly communicates to the instructor that you understand the question; it also helps you stay on track. Examples:

> A leaf has X main parts, each with a distinct function.

> If I were to direct a film production of "Gift of the Magi," here is how I would handle decisions about staging, setting, character, and scene selection.

More elaborate introductions are not needed in essay answers.

2. A good essay answer answers all parts of the question.   When you analyze a question to predict the parts of the answer, you're planning your answer so that it will fulfill this criterion. When you write your answer, be sure to place each part of your answer in a separate section. Label each section clearly by using numbers, by skipping a line between each section, by using subheadings, or by underlining key words to clearly identify each section. The instructor should be able to look at your essay answer and tell in a glance where each part of your answer is. Study the examples for model answers with the parts clearly labeled.

3. A good essay answer reflects knowledge of course material.   One problem students often have with writing essay answers is the paradox of writing information to someone who already knows the answer. When you're answering an essay question, the goal of your writing isn't to inform your reader, but to demonstrate your knowledge. Instead of thinking of the instructor as your audience, it's useful to compose your answer as if you were addressing it to another college student who hasn't taken the course yet.

Another related problem occurs on argument questions, when you're asked to present arguments for a position. Students often ask, "How can I be graded on my opinion?" What the instructor will be evaluating in your answer won't be the opinion you chose, but will be how well the arguments you use to support your opinion reflect your learning in the course. Don't use arguments that are outside the scope of the course. For example, if you are arguing the position that IQ tests do not measure intelligence accurately, a story about your cousin whose IQ was measured to be below average but who went on to become a neurosurgeon isn't appropriate, because it doesn't reflect your knowledge of the material in the course. Instead, select arguments from your readings and lecture notes on this topic.

4. A good essay answer reflects your understanding of the course material and your ability to reason independently.   In part, how well you meet these criteria will depend on how well you have understood the central ideas in the course. But you can strive to make your answer reflect your understanding by explaining clearly the thinking behind your answer, especially on argument and application questions. Each time you make an assertion, explain your thinking behind your position, using examples and explanations that reflect your thinking. Don't assume the instructor will know why you think the way you do. Look at the model essay answers to see how these students explained the thinking behind their answers.

5. A good essay answer is clearly stated and well-organized.   In writing your essay answer, try to be crystal clear. An essay answer should be written in a clear, simple, direct style. It is not the place for hints, or for elaborate similes or metaphors that leave the reader puzzled as to your meaning. For example, if you say, "A work of art is deeply rooted in the historical period in which it is produced just as a tree is deeply rooted in the ground," be sure that you then explain clearly what you mean by this simile.

Part of clear writing is organization. Your answer to one part of a question shouldn't be scattered over four paragraphs of your answer. Estimate how many essay answers to the same question your instructor will be reading—the instructor's patience in searching through an essay answer to find the parts of the answer is going to become limited very quickly. That's why it's essential that you organize your answer before you begin writing, so you're not simply writing ideas down as they occur to you.

6. A good essay answer is easy to read.   You want your instructor to be able to read your answer without struggling. But you do not want to take time out on your exam to copy your answer over to make it perfectly neat. Instead, write with wide margins so you have room for adding words or sentences in the margins. Also, skip lines between parts of your answer.

When you have finished writing, read over your answer once to see if you've left out anything important. If you have, add a sentence or two in the margins, and draw an arrow from the place where it should be inserted to the insert. If you decide to delete a sentence or a paragraph, cross it out neatly.

If you have time, proofread your answer. **Proofreading** means looking your writing over for errors in grammar and spelling and making corrections. Make all corrections neatly, right on the page. Do not copy your answer over.

■

E X E R C I S E   5

Select one of the questions you worked on in Exercise 4. Write an essay answer to the question, following your outline. Begin your answer with a short summary sentence. Write each part of your answer with a short summary sentence. Write each part of your answer as a separate section. Skip lines between each section, and label each section clearly. Write your answer as if you were writing to a student who hadn't taken this course. Give supporting arguments for any broad statements or generalizations you make. Write clearly. When you have finished, reread your answer twice, once to make sure it's clear, and once to proofread it. Make any changes you want to make legibly.

REVIEWING YOUR TESTS

You can expect to continue to improve your ability to answer essay questions throughout your college career if you work at it. Working at improving your essay writing skills implies that you will profit from your mistakes. Always try to get back any exams you have taken as soon as possible. Look at the questions you did well on and at the ones you didn't do well on, and analyze the problems.

> Was it a study problem? Perhaps you didn't leave enough time for studying or emphasized studying the wrong things.
> Was it a problem in understanding the question or in identifying the type of question? You may need to spend more time reading the question.
> Did you understand the question, but miss out on predicting the parts of the question so your response was judged incomplete? If so, you may need to spend more time planning your answer.
> What about the way you wrote your answer? Did the instructor have difficulty locating the parts of your answer? Did your answer not reflect the course content? Did you fail to explain your reasoning? Or was your answer marked down because it was poorly organized, unclearly written, or just plain hard to read?

As these questions suggest, a weakness on an essay question can be traced back to how you studied, how you understood the question, or how you planned or wrote the answer. Analyzing what part of the process was the weak link for you will help you to improve your performance on future tests.

SUMMARY

Essay questions include feedback questions, process analysis questions, relational questions, argument questions, and application questions. Knowing the type of question helps you understand the type of answer you're being called upon to write, and also to predict the parts of your answer. If comprehending an essay question is difficult, try reading it slowly and work at paraphrasing it. The first step in writing an essay answer is to plan your answer. The most efficient way to plan your answer is with a brief scratch outline. In writing your answer, aim for a brief introduction that summarizes your answer. Then, answer all parts of the question, and use graphics like underlining or numbering to clearly indicate where each part is. Base your answer on the material in the course and explain clearly the reasoning behind assertions you state. Since your purpose is to demonstrate your knowledge, write your answer as if your audience were another student who hasn't taken the course, not the instructor. Finally, make your answer legible. When essay exams are returned, study the comments and the grades to determine your strengths and weaknesses and diagnose what areas need improvement.

■
JOURNAL WRITING

Evaluate your reactions to essay questions versus objective questions. Which type of question do you think is easier? Which type do you think allows you to demonstrate your knowledge more? Which type do you learn more from? Give reasons for your opinions.

■
ACADEMIC WRITING

Select a unit from one of your courses and make up a feedback question, a process analysis question, a relational question, an argument question, and an application question based on it. Now write essay answers for two of your questions, applying the principles suggested in this chapter.

CHAPTER

15

ANSWERING OBJECTIVE QUESTIONS

In this chapter, you will learn:

▲ how to evaluate true–false questions
▲ how to evaluate multiple-choice questions
▲ strategies for answering sentence completion and matching column questions

Objective questions are questions which are designed to have only one correct answer. Types of objective questions include true–false questions, multiple-choice questions, sentence completion questions, and matching columns. They're called objective questions because no one has to subjectively evaluate whether an answer is correct or not.

ANSWERING TRUE–FALSE QUESTIONS

True–false questions are deceptively simple. After all, without studying, you have a 50/50 chance of getting the right answer. That's true, but a grade of 50 percent on most scales is an F.

In order to evaluate whether a statement is true or false, you need to read it carefully and determine exactly what it states. In order to be true, all parts of a statement must be true. However, a statement is false if even part of it is false. Here are some examples.

_____ Narcolepsy is a very common disorder related to muscle paralysis.
(The correct answer is *false,* because part of the statement is false.

Reprinted by permission of UFS, Inc.

Narcolepsy is related to muscle paralysis, but it is not a very common disorder.)

_____ Comedies always have non-serious themes.
(The correct answer is *false*, because the word "always" makes it false. Many comedies have serious themes, while others do not.)

_____ Blood pressure is highest in arteries and lowest in veins.
(The correct answer is *true*, both parts of the statement are true.)

_____ In both a play and a movie, an actor's performance can vary from performance to performance.
(The correct answer is *false*, since part of the statement is false. The statement is true about plays, but not about movies.)

One factor that you need to evaluate in deciding whether a statement is true or false is whether it is an absolute statement or not. An **absolute statement** says that something is always true, or, if it's a negative absolute statement, that something is never true. A **qualified statement** says that something is true most of the time or some of the time. For instance, look at these statements:

> All dogs bite.
>   (absolute statement)
> Dogs bite.
>   (absolute statement)
> Most dogs bite.
>   (qualified statement: high degree)
> Some dogs bite.
>   (qualified statement: low degree)
> Dogs usually don't bite.
>   (negative qualified statement: low degree)
> Dogs never bite.
>   (negative absolute statement)

If we were to translate these statements into rough percentages, they would look like this:

All dogs bite. (100% of dogs bite)
Dogs bite. (100% of dogs bite)
Most dogs bite. (around 80% of dogs bite)
Some dogs bite. (around 25% of dogs bite)
Dogs usually don't bite. (only around 5% of dogs bite)
Dogs never bite. (0% of dogs bite)

As the above examples show, an absolute statement can either state a fact without using an absolute term (like, "Dogs bite.") or can specifically include an absolute term like *all* or *always*. Qualified statements will include qualifying terms or phrases, some of which are high degree (indicating they apply to a high percentage of a group) and some of which are low degree (indicating they apply to a low percentage of a group). Negative absolute statements will include negative terms but no qualifying terms.

To assess what a true–false statement on a test is stating, you need to be sensitive to whether the statement is absolute, qualified, or negative.

■
EXERCISE 1

Rank order the five statements in each group from 1 for absolute to 5 for absolute negative, as in this model:

____2____ Winters are usually delightful.

____3____ Sometimes winters are delightful.

____1____ Winter is a delightful season.

____5____ Winters are never delightful.

____4____ Winter is not usually a delightful season.

_____ Some college libraries are good places to study.

_____ College libraries are often good places to study.

_____ College libraries aren't good places to study.

_____ College libraries are good places to study.

_____ College libraries are generally not good places to study.

_____ All students take naps in the library lounge.

_____ Students never take naps in the library lounge.

Figure 15.1

WORDS AND PHRASES WHICH AFFECT
A STATEMENT'S TRUTH VALUE

Absolute	Qualified (high degree)	Qualified (low degree)	Negative
always	in most cases	sometimes	no
in all cases	usually	occasionally	not
all	frequently	seldom	never
every	often	rarely	don't
	typically	some	
	most	few	
	many		
	almost always		
	generally		

_____ Students usually don't take naps in the library lounge.

_____ Students occasionally take naps in the library lounge.

_____ Students frequently take naps in the library lounge.

_____ The library is typically crowded on Friday night.

_____ The library is sometimes crowded on Friday night.

_____ The library is never crowded on Friday night.

_____ The library is crowded every Friday night.

_____ The library is usually not very crowded on Friday night.

EXERCISE 2

Directions:

A.   Read through the following statements and underline any words which affect the statement's truth value, using Figure 15.1 as a guide.

B.   Label each statement

      AP   (absolute positive),

      AN   (absolute negative),

      QH   (qualified high),

      QL   (qualified low), or

      QN   (qualified negative).

C.   Then evaluate each statement as to whether it is a true or false statement about you.

Examples:

Label	T/F	
QH	false	Hats <u>usually</u> make me look ugly.
AP	true	Blue is my favorite color.
AN	false	I <u>never</u> drink tea.
QL	false	I <u>sometimes</u> eat fresh fruit.
		(false because I often eat fresh fruit.)
AP	false	<u>All</u> of my friends are women.
QN	true	I <u>don't usually</u> like cartoons.
————	————	1. I always remember my dreams.
————	————	2. I usually don't eat a big breakfast.
————	————	3. I almost always remember to brush my teeth in the evening.
————	————	4. I rarely get colds.
————	————	5. I never exercise.
————	————	6. I always watch TV in the evenings.
————	————	7. I usually don't play the radio when I'm studying.
————	————	8. I'm always late for dates.
————	————	9. I usually forget people's birthdays.
————	————	10. I go to the movies frequently.
————	————	11. I occasionally go shopping for clothes.
————	————	12. I usually don't drink coffee in the morning.
————	————	13. I don't like chocolate.
————	————	14. I am overworked and underpaid.
————	————	15. I seldom ask questions during class.

Some students believe that absolute statements are generally false, but if you examine your own answers in Exercise 2, you'll probably find that you marked several statements that you labeled AP or AN as true. The same will be true of test items: when you encounter an absolute statement, you need to evaluate whether it corresponds with what you learned. If you assume that it's false just because it's absolute, you're merely guessing.

■
EXERCISE 3

Read the following passage. Then read the true–false statements based on it, underline any absolute or qualifying phrases in them, and decide if each statement is true or false.

Amount of Sleep

Generally speaking, the younger you are, the more you sleep and the deeper your sleep is likely to be. Newborn infants sleep about 16 hours out of 24. This sleep is scattered in six or more short bursts of a few hours each. Newborns sleep as much during the day as at night. During the first year of life, the amount of sleep decreases by two hours or more. By six months of age, 80 percent of the infants in one recent study were "sleeping through the night" and taking short naps during the day. By age two, the child sleeps about 12 hours a day, including about 90 minutes of daytime naps. According to Wilse Webb, the major change during the infant's first two years is a decrease in the *amount of daytime sleep*. This change occurs in almost all infants. Therefore, this developmental sequence probably is controlled primarily by genetic factors.

By adolescence and early adulthood, the amount of daily sleep has dropped to about 8 hours. Wilse Webb found that University of Florida students averaged about 7 hours and 40 minutes of sleep at *night*. In addition, they napped about 25 minutes per day. During the two-week period the students were studied, 84 percent of them took at least one nap and about 42 percent napped daily or almost every day. There was considerable variation, however. Some students averaged but 6 hours per day; others got as much as 10 hours of sleep per 24-hour period. And almost all the students slept more on weekends than during the week.

Older people tend to sleep less deeply than do infants or young adults. By 40 or 50 years of age, people wake up more frequently during the night. And by age 60, almost everyone naps on a regular basis. A recent study of 77-year-old men and women suggests these older individuals nap (on the average) twice a day and get about 10 percent of the daily sleep during the day.

These data, however, are for people in the US living in more-or-less normal circumstances. In other countries, a nap or "siesta" is part of the daily routine for people of all ages. And in the US, people in institutions, individuals who work at night, and persons who are sick or experiencing other unusual situations will often show quite different sleep patterns, no matter what their age.

_____ 1.   In adults, sleep patterns are in part cultural.

_____ 2.   In young children, sleep patterns are genetic.

_____ 3.   Illness usually doesn't disrupt normal sleep patterns.

_____ 4.   All students nap during the day.

_____ 5.   Older people sleep more deeply than younger people.

_____ 6.   Newborns sleep more during the day than at night.

_____ 7.   There's very little variation in how many hours different people sleep.

_____ 8.   Most infants are sleeping through the night by the time they're six months old.

Discuss your answers and the reasons for them with your classmates.

As these examples show, true–false questions are not always easy to answer. Sometimes you worry if you're interpreting the questions correctly. For example, suppose one question had been, "People sleep less as they grow older." You know that children gradually reduce the number of hours they sleep, but the article also suggests that people over sixty sleep more, so you're not sure. If "people" in the question means children and adults, the answer is true, but if "people" refers to adults and older adults, then the answer is false. In cases like this, if you can write on the exam, write down the answer that you prefer and add a note to explain:

People sleep less as they grow older. T(F)   *older people sleep more*

In fact, some tests direct you to edit any statement you labeled false to make it true. If you were given these directions, your answers to the sample statements on pages 214–215 might look like this:

F _____ Narcolepsy is a very ~~common~~ *rare* disorder related to paralysis.

F _____ Comedies ~~always~~ have *both serious and* non-serious themes.

F _____ In ~~both~~ a play ~~and a movie~~, an actor's performance can vary from performance to performance, *but not in a movie.*

■

E X E R C I S E   4

Edit any statements in Exercise 3 that you labeled false to make them true.

A note: If you're not sure whether an answer is true or false, guess. What you shouldn't do is try to write a letter like this 𝓕 that looks like it could either be a T or a F. Teachers have seen this ploy before. In fact, it's best to write out the whole word "true" or "false" so there's no mistake as to which answer you wanted.

MULTIPLE-CHOICE QUESTIONS

Multiple-choice questions are perhaps the most common type of objective exam question. A multiple-choice question consists of a **stem** (the first line of the question, often a partial statement or a question) and four or five **options** (the choices) for you to pick, as in these examples:

1. The most important factor in endangering a species is
    a. pollution
    b. introduction of a hostile species into the environment
    c. reduction of a food source
    d. destruction of a habitat

(The correct answer is d.)

2. Which of the following does not directly affect population growth?
    a. control of infectious diseases
    b. widespread use of birth control
    c. an increase in technology
    d. an increase in longevity

(The correct answer is c.)

3. Which of the following countries has achieved zero population growth?
    a. Sweden

b. the United States
c. Mexico
d. India

(The correct answer is a.)

4.   A source of water pollution is
a. water filtration plants
b. industrial waste
c. deforestation
d. automobiles
e. all of the above

(The correct answer is b.)

READ THE STEM CAREFULLY

The same principles that apply to a true–false statement should be applied to the stem of a multiple-choice question: specifically, that you should be on the alert for absolute, qualifying, and negative terms. As with true–false questions, it's helpful to underline any terms of this type in the stem. For instance, in the first example above, you should underline the word *most*, and in the second example, you should underline the word *not*.

CONSIDER ALL ALTERNATIVES

To answer a multiple-choice question well, you must consider all the options, even if one immediately strikes you as good. As you read the other choices and evaluate them, another one might strike you as better, or you may find that all the options are possible and consider "all of the above" as an answer.

A useful strategy is to consider each question as a set of true–false statements and to evaluate each option separately. For instance, consider the last example as a series of five separate statements:

Water filtration plants are a source of water pollution.
(False: water filtration plants clean water.)

Industrial waste is a source of water pollution.
(Possibly true: Factories dump chemicals into water systems.)

Deforestation is a source of water pollution.
(False: Deforestation means loss of trees in a forest—doesn't seem related to water pollution.)

Automobiles are a source of water pollution.
(False: Air pollution, yes, but not water pollution.)

All of the above are sources of water pollution.
   (False: I've already ruled out three of the answers.)

So the correct answer must be b.

■
E X E R C I S E   5

Apply the strategies outlined above to answering these questions. First, read each stem and mark any absolute, qualifying, or negative terms in it that affect its truth value. Then read all four options. Mentally convert each option into a statement and evaluate each statement as to whether it is true or false before choosing your answer.

1. The strongest influence on my decision to go to college came from
   a. my parents
   b. my friends
   c. school counselors
   d. teachers

2. Which of the following statements is most true about yourself?
   a. I went to college because I wasn't ready for a full-time job.
   b. I went to college because I wanted to change careers.
   c. I went to college because I couldn't find a full-time job.
   d. My decision to go to college was not related to a job decision.

3. Which type of reasons was least important in your decision to go to college?
   a. financial reasons
   b. social reasons
   c. educational reasons
   d. emotional reasons

4. Which type of reasons for going to college would you say was most important to other students at your college?
   a. financial reasons
   b. social reasons
   c. educational reasons
   d. emotional reasons

5. Which of the following is not particularly important as an educational goal for you?
   a. learning about many subjects
   b. learning about a specific subject
   c. learning many skills
   d. learning a specific skill

6.   What was the primary reason why you selected the college you are attending?
   a. its overall academic reputation
   b. its location
   c. its academic reputation in a specific field
   d. financial reasons
   e. social reasons

STRATEGIES FOR MULTIPLE-CHOICE QUESTIONS

Most experienced test-takers agree that an effective strategy for working through a multiple-choice section or test is to go through the questions twice. The first time, answer any questions that you're sure of. For the others, cross out any options you can eliminate, but if you get stuck deciding between the remaining choices, go on to the next question. After you've answered all the questions you know, go back and struggle with the ones you didn't answer. Sometimes, something you read in one question helps you recall the answer in another; sometimes the delay between your first pass and your second pass gives your mind a chance to work. If you run out of time, then you'll be guessing on the ones you left for the second pass—in other words, the ones you weren't sure of anyway. A word of caution: if you're marking questions on an answer sheet, make sure that the right answer goes next to the right number. It's easy to get crossed up when you're skipping questions.

PLAYING THE ODDS

A real advantage with multiple-choice questions is that all the choices are presented to you, so you don't have to construct an answer, you just have to choose one. Any option you can eliminate increases your chances of choosing the correct option. If there are four options, your chances of guessing the correct one blindly are 1 out of 4 or 25 percent. If you can eliminate 1 option, your chances of choosing the correct answer rise to 1 out of 3 or 33.3 percent, and if you can eliminate 2 options, your odds are now 1 out of 2 or 50 percent.

The fact that most multiple-choice questions have only one option that is the correct answer is a help in selecting the correct answer. For example, consider the following question:

Many people experience a hypnotic-like state when they are
a. sleeping
b. staring
c. listening
d. napping

Options a and d are almost synonyms. Since there will be only one correct answer to this question, and since these two choices mean almost the same thing, it's likely that neither of them is correct. That helps us eliminate two choices and leaves us with two to consider. (The correct answer is b, although c might be an appealing answer if you've ever sat through a long, droning lecture.)

If two of the options are absolute opposites, then both of them cannot be the answer. Either one of them could be correct, or both of them could be wrong and a third option could be correct. That's useful information when one of the choices is "all of the above," as in this example:

Objectivity means
a. evaluating something in light of personal feelings
b. evaluating something in light of societal standards
c. evaluating something unemotionally
d. all of the above

Because options a and c are opposites, both of them can't be true, so "d—all of the above"—is eliminated as an option and you only need to decide among the other three choices.

MYTHS ABOUT MULTIPLE-CHOICE QUESTIONS

More myths exist among students about multiple-choice questions than about any other kind of test item. Most of them are not true, except on the most poorly constructed test. If you believe the myths, you'll be hurting yourself more than helping yourself. To be specific:

1. Don't look for a pattern to answers. If the answers to the first three questions were a, b, and c, don't expect that the next answer will be d. Assume that on each question, each option has an equal chance of being correct.

Reprinted by permission of UFS, Inc.

2. *C is* not *the most common correct option.* And neither is
a, b, d, or e. Teachers usually edit tests before they print them to
make sure that answers are distributed randomly.

**3. *The longest answer is not usually the correct an-
swer.*** Correct answers come in all lengths.

**4. *Middle values aren't more likely to be correct than low
or high values.*** If the options involve numbers, the lowest and
highest numbers are as likely to be correct as the two middle
numbers.

**5. *If "all of the above" or "none of the above" are given as
options, they are not necessarily the right answer.*** In other
words, on each multiple-choice question, all of the options need to
be evaluated on their merit alone, not on the basis of anything else.
Always begin to examine the options with the assumption that any
one of them could be the right answer, and eliminate options for real
reasons, not by applying any of these student myths.

■
──────────────
E X E R C I S E   6

Read the following passage. Then answer the multiple-choice
questions based on it.

Proteins

Protein consumption is an index of a country's (or an individual's) economic status, because high-quality protein is the most expensive and
least available of all the nutrients. Protein poverty is one of the world's
most pressing health problems; millions of human beings suffer from
poor health, disease, and even death as a consequence of protein malnu-
trition.

Proteins are critical as nutrients because they are essential building
blocks of cells. Indeed, 75% of body solids consists of protein. These
nutrients also serve as enzymes and are used to make many needed substances in the body.

Ingested proteins are degraded in the digestive tract to their molec-
ular subunits—amino acids. These are absorbed and used by the cells to
make the types of proteins needed. Of the 20 or so amino acids important
in nutrition, the body is able to make several by rearranging the atoms of
certain organic acids. About eight of the amino acids (nine in children)
cannot be synthesized by the body cells at all, or at least not in sufficient
quantity to meet the body's needs. These, which must be provided in the
diet, are called the **essential amino acids.**

Not all proteins contain the same kinds or quantities of amino
acids, and many proteins lack some of the essential amino acids. High-
est-quality proteins, those that contain the most appropriate distribution

of amino acids for human nutrition, are found in eggs, milk, meat, and fish. Some foods, such as gelatin or soybeans, contain a high proportion of protein but do not contain all the essential amino acids, or they do not contain them in nutritional proportions. Most plant proteins are deficient in one or more essential amino acids, usually lysine, tryptophan, or threonine.

The recommended daily amount of protein is about 56 grams—only about an eighth of a pound (half a quarter-pound burger). In the United States and other developed countries most people eat far more protein than required. It has been estimated that the average American eats about 300 pounds of meat and dairy products per year. In some underdeveloped countries an average of only 2 pounds per person per year is consumed.

Most human beings depend upon cereal grains as their staple food— usually rice, wheat, or corn. None of these foods provide an adequate proportion of total amino acids or distribution of essential amino acids, especially not for growing children. In some underdeveloped countries starchy crops, such as sweet potatoes or cassava, are the principal food. Total protein content of these foods is less than 2%, far below minimum needs.

1. Protein is essential to the human body for
   a. calcium absorption
   b. waste elimination
   c. fuel
   d. cell building
2. High quality protein is
   a. the most expensive and most available of all nutrients
   b. the most expensive and least available of all nutrients
   c. the least expensive and most available of all nutrients
   d. the least expensive and least available of all nutrients
3. Essential amino acids are
   a. amino acids that cannot be manufactured by the body's cells
   b. contained in plant protein
   c. amino acids manufactured by the body's cells
   d. inorganic nutrients
4. In most countries of the world, the primary food is
   a. meat
   b. fish
   c. cereal grains
   d. vegetables
5. People in developed countries generally
   a. consume more protein than their bodies can use
   b. consume about 56 grams of protein daily
   c. get most of their protein from cereal grains
   d. suffer from protein poverty

SENTENCE COMPLETION QUESTIONS

Sentence completion, or fill-in-the-blank, questions are difficult for an instructor to write and difficult for a student to answer. Perhaps that's why they are less common than true–false and multiple-choice questions. A well-written sentence completion question will have only one correct answer that can go in the blank, which means that to answer the question, you have to produce the correct word. Here are some examples:

The hormones that create the physical changes associated with strong emotional feelings like fear and anger are _____ and _____. (adrenalin and nor-adrenalin or epinephrin and nor-epinephrin)

In literature, a narrator who speaks from that character's limited point of view is called a(n) _____ narrator. (first-person)

A non-prescription drug that has been implicated in causing ulcers is _____. (aspirin)

As these examples suggest, the best types of information to turn into sentence completion questions are identifications and definitions, so if you know you're facing a section of sentence completion questions, you might concentrate part of your studying on learning technical terms and items you could be asked to identify.

One good strategy for answering sentence completion questions is to turn the statement into a question, asking, for example, "What is a drug that seems to cause ulcers?" This often helps you see the implied question you're being asked. It also helps you to see the class of word that you're looking for, whether a noun, adjective, or verb. Sometimes the sentence pattern will provide grammatical clues. For instance, in the first statement, the *and* between the two blanks tells you that you're looking for a pair of terms. But that's not much help if you have no idea what the terms are. Note also that in the second question, the blank is preceded by the word *a(n)*, so you have no clue as to whether the word will begin with a consonant or a vowel. Be alert for instances when the word before the blank is either *a,* indicating that the target word starts with a consonant, or *an,* indicating that the target word begins with a vowel.

■
EXERCISE 7

Review this chapter, and then answer the following sentence completion questions.

1. The choices on a multiple-choice question are called

_____.

2. An example of a qualifying term is the word _____.

3. The most common type of objective question is the

_____ question.

4. If you see the option "all of the above" in a multiple-choice ques-

tion, you _____ assume that it is the right answer.

5. In true–false questions, underline absolute, qualifying, and

_____ terms.

MATCHING COLUMNS

Like sentence completion questions, matching columns are best suited for identification and definition questions, as in the exercise that follows. Before you begin to answer a matching column, read both columns to get an idea of the scope of the responses. Count the number of options in each column so you know if there is an even set. Often instructors will provide more choices in the first set, so that answering the last question isn't just a matter of elimination.

To work a matching column, begin with the answers you are sure of. As you work, mark off the items you have chosen in the left column. This way you are limiting your options for the choices you are less sure of. Keep working in this way until you've matched as many items as you can: if you're left with only two or three unmatched pairs at the end, you can guess on them.

■
EXERCISE 8

See if you can do this exercise independently; then refer back to page 215 to check your answers.

a. absolute positive
b. qualified (high degree)
c. qualified (low degree)
d. absolute negative
e. negative qualified (high degree)
f. negative qualified (low degree)

_____ Many cats are fussy.

_____ Cats aren't fussy.

_____ Some cats are fussy.

_____ Cats usually aren't fussy.

_____ A few cats aren't fussy.

_____ Cats are fussy.

REVIEWING TESTS

As with essay tests, you should review any objective tests you have taken as soon as you possibly can. Look over the questions you got right and the ones you missed. See if there is a pattern to your wrong answers. If most of the questions you missed were on one topic, then that's a topic you need to review. If many of the questions you missed were of the same type, or were questions about a topic that you knew, then you need to work on your skills for answering that type of question.

When you review your exam, if you think one of your answers that was marked wrong was actually correct, ask the instructor, either when he or she goes over the exam in class or during the instructor's office hours. Have your evidence with you. If you can convince an instructor that your answer was correct, you can raise your grade, and perhaps raise the grade of some of the other students in the class as well.

SUMMARY

Objective questions include true–false questions, multiple-choice questions, sentence completion questions, and matching column questions. In order for a true–false statement to be true, all parts of it must be true. In evaluating the truth of a statement, consider whether it is an absolute statement or a qualified statement, and whether the statement is positive or negative. In answering multiple-choice questions, read the stem carefully and note any absolute, qualifying, or negative terms, underlining them if possible. Then consider each option separately. When you're not sure of the answer, try to eliminate some of the options before guessing. Don't be guided by the myths concerning multiple-choice questions: there need not be a pattern to the answers, c is not a better guess than other letters, and neither is the longest answer, a middle value, or the option "all of the above." Sentence completion questions are often identifications or definitions; in answering them, try turning the statement into a question, and note any clues in the sentence structure. When doing a matching column, begin with the answers you're surest of and work back and forth, checking off answers as you choose them.

■
JOURNAL WRITING

1. Explain three of the statements that you marked *true* or *false* in Exercise 2.
2. Comment on what motivated you to go to college, based on your answers to Exercise 5.

■
ACADEMIC WRITING

One of the best ways to learn how to answer objective questions is to gain some insight into how they are written. Select one chapter from this textbook and write a set of objective questions for it, including two true–false statements, two multiple-choice questions, two sentence completion statements, and a short five-item matching column. Try to construct your questions so that there are no unnecessary clues to the correct answer, but so that all questions have only one correct answer. Then give the test to another student in the class.

P A R T

SIX

DOING ACADEMIC ASSIGNMENTS

USING A COLLEGE LIBRARY

In this chapter you will learn

▲ how to orient yourself to your college library
▲ how to locate books in your library
▲ how to locate periodicals in your library
▲ how to find information on a specific subject in your library

There are two main educational resources on a college campus: the faculty and the college library. During your college career, the college library will be a place that you use frequently. This chapter will guide you as you orient yourself to using this valuable resource.

Here are some typical assignments from college instructors that will send you to the campus library:

Read the two articles on reserve on schizophrenia for the next class.

For your next assignment, find an article about acid rain written in the last two years. Read it and summarize it.

Were the original reviews of the play *Death of a Salesman* favorable or unfavorable? Write a report based on your reading of three or four reviews.

Write a report on how the Food and Drug Administration tests a chemical for toxicity.

Listen to a recording of Handel's *Messiah* and write a one-page report on its use of counterpoint.

LIBRARY RESOURCES

You couldn't do most of the assignments listed above in your neighborhood or public library, but a college library will have the resources for you to do all of them, and, in fact, to do nearly all of the assignments you will be given in college. Of course, no two college libraries are the same, but you can expect your college library to have many of the following resources.

Study areas.   College libraries are usually designed with large tables, study carrels or booths, and reserved rooms for study. These are a real service when you need to work without the distractions of your home or college dorm room.

Circulation desk.   This is the desk, usually located right by the entrance of the library, at which you check out and return books.

Card catalog and/or an on-line catalog.   These catalogs serve as the index to the library, showing you what books and other materials the library has and where they are located.

The stacks.   The stacks are the shelves that contain the library's book collection. Books will be arranged by a classification system, either the Library of Congress classification system or the Dewey Decimal System. If a library has open stacks, as most libraries do, you can retrieve your own books once you know their call numbers. If a library has closed stacks, you give the call number of the book you want to a staff member, and the book is brought to you.

Periodical section.   Periodicals are any materials that are published at regular intervals, including newspapers, popular magazines, and scholarly journals. In the periodical section, you'll find current issues of a wide range of newspapers and magazines on open shelves for browsing, indexes which can be used to find articles on specific topics in back issues of periodicals, bound volumes and microfilms of back issues of periodicals, and microfilm readers and photocopy machines. In some libraries, there is a separate reference desk in the periodical section where you can get help locating periodicals.

Reserve section.   The reserve section contains any material that instructors have asked the library to place on reserve for students in their classes during the current term. Usually these materials circulate on a much more limited basis than regular library materials, so that all students in the class will have access to them. Materials on reserve change from term to term.

Reference section.   The reference section contains noncirculating books that are used for reference, including encyclopedias, dictionaries, yearbooks, handbooks, and bibliographies (lists of books and articles on a certain topic).

Reference desk.   The reference desk is where you'll find the most useful guide to the library, a staff librarian trained to help college students locate materials. It will also house some of the more commonly used reference materials.

Pamphlet file or vertical file.   These are files of booklets and pamphlets, arranged by subject matter and located in file cabinets.

Audio-visual materials.   Audio-visual materials include videotapes, filmstrips, records, and possibly computer software, along with equipment for viewing and listening to these materials.

Special collections.   College libraries may have books of certain types shelved separately. For example, there may be a *curriculum materials section,* containing elementary and high school textbooks and audio-visual materials, children's books, and local curriculum guides. *Government documents*—books and periodicals published by various agencies of state and federal governments—are sometimes kept in a separate section. Law books and medical books may also be kept in special collections, especially at colleges with professional schools in these fields. A library might also have unusual or unique materials kept in a separate area, such as a collection of rare books or materials on the history of the region.

Additional services.   Many libraries provide *interlibrary loan* services, enabling you to search the holdings of other libraries and borrow materials from them. Usually you'll find this service at the reference desk. College libraries may also provide *instructional services,* such as instruction in how to use the library, computerized instruction as academic support for some campus courses, or tutorial centers. Many libraries now have computers and software for *computerized searches,* so you can find books and articles on a topic by using a computer instead of by using indexes.

As the above list of resources suggests, a college library is more than a collection of books and study tables. To become an informed consumer of your library's resources, you need to find out what materials and resources your library has and where they're located. Most college libraries offer informational tours of the library for students and publish guides to the library for its users. You should make a point of orienting yourself to your campus library early in your first term at college.

■

E X E R C I S E   1

Research and answer the following questions about your campus library, either by giving yourself a tour of it and reading the printed guides to the library or by taking a guided tour of the library.

1. What are the library hours?
2. What are good places in the library to study?
3. What identification do you need to check out a book? How long does a book circulate for? What fines are charged for overdue books? Can you renew books over the phone?
4. Does the library have a card catalog? Does it have a computer catalog? Where are the catalogs located?
5. What classification system does the library use—Library of Congress system or Dewey Decimal System?
6. Does the library have open or closed stacks?
7. Where is the library's periodical section? How many periodicals does the library subscribe to? Where is there a list of the periodicals the library has? Does the library have some magazines and newspapers on microfilm? Where are the microfilm readers located? Where are the photocopiers?
8. Where is the library's reserve section? What are the regulations for using reserve materials?
9. Where is the reference section?
10. Where is the reference desk? When is a reference librarian on duty? What services does the reference desk provide?
11. Does the library have a curriculum materials section? Where is it located, and what does it include? Where is the catalog of curriculum materials located?
12. Does the library have a government documents section? Where are the government documents cataloged?
13. Where is the library's pamphlet file or vertical file? How are materials arranged in it?
14. What kinds of materials are in the library's audio-visual materials collection? Do they circulate?
15. With what libraries does your library have interlibrary loan arrangements? How long does it usually take to get something through interlibrary loan? Is there any charge?
16. Can you do computer searches of topics through your library? How do you arrange to do so, and is there any charge?
17. What special collections does your library have and where are they located and cataloged?
18. What other facilities or services does your library offer?

FINDING A BOOK

How do you go about locating a specific book in the library? Let's say that your instructor has assigned you to read two chapters of a book by Robert D. Nye entitled *Three Psychologies: Perspectives from Freud, Skinner, and Rogers*. Here is the process you would follow to locate it.

You'd begin by using the library's card catalog. A book like this has at least three cards in the catalog that refer to it: an author card, a title card, and one or more subject cards. Figure 16.1 shows the set of cards a catalog would have for *Three Psychologies*. On the *author card,* the first line is Nye, Robert D. This card will be alphabetized in

Figure 16.1

SET OF CATALOG CARDS FOR A BOOK

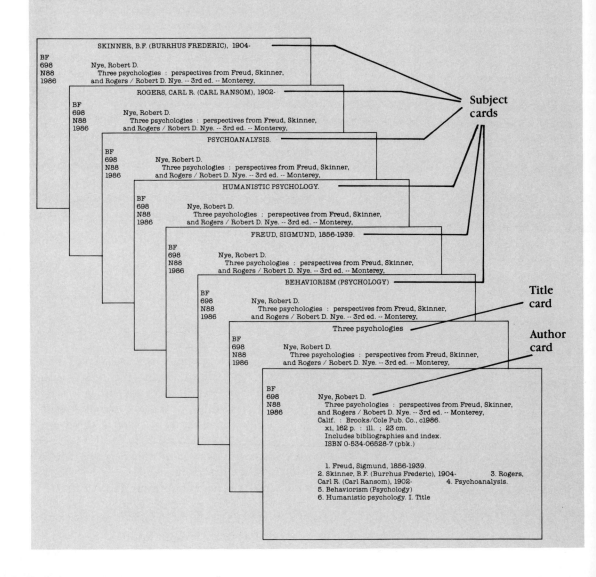

the card catalog under NY. The *title card* has the book's title on its first line, and will be alphabetized under TH. Under the subject heading "BEHAVIORISM (PSYCHOLOGY)" a *subject card* referring to Nye's book is placed under BE along with other books about behaviorist psychology. There are also subject headings for each of the three psychologists that Nye's book focuses on. For example, one card has "FREUD, SIGMUND, 1856–1939" on the top line. That card would be alphabetized along with all the other books the library had about Freud under FR.

Students often have difficulty distinguishing a subject card from a title card and an author card, a problem which can leave you looking for a book entitled *Sigmund Freud,* 1856–1939 that doesn't exist, or for a book by Sigmund Freud called *Three Psychologies* that Freud never wrote. If you study the sample cards in Figure 16.1, you can see the differences in the cards. On the author card, there is no heading at the top of the card. The first line, next to the call number, is the author's name, written in capital and small letters. On the title card, the title is at the very top of the card, also in capital and small letters. Now, notice that on the subject cards the subject heading is entirely in capital letters. In most libraries, the use of all capital letters indicates that you're looking at a subject heading, not at a book title or an author's name.

The rest of the information on a book's catalog card is the same whether it's an author card, a title card, or a subject card (see Figure 16.2). The numbered list at the bottom of the card is a list of all the subject headings under which the book is cataloged. The number in the upper left corner is the book's call number, which indicates its location in the library stacks.

If you were looking for Nye's book, since you know the author and title, you'd look under NY or TH in the card catalog. When you found the card for the book, you'd write down the book's call number. Library of Congress books are arranged by letter and then by number, so this book would be located among other BF books right before BF 700. Consult a map of the library, and go to the area where BF books are shelved to locate the book.

If the book isn't on the shelf where you expect it to be, it could be on reserve, in the reference section, checked out to another patron, or missing. In order to find out, ask at the reference desk or circulation desk. If the book has been checked out, you can usually have it recalled. The library will send you a notice when it's returned and hold it for you.

In many libraries, the catalog is also on computer, and you can type in the name of the author and/or title of a book you're looking for, following the directions on the screen or next to the terminal, to find its call number. The first time you use a terminal in a new library, it's a good idea to ask someone to show you how.

Figure 16.2

PARTS OF CATALOG CARD

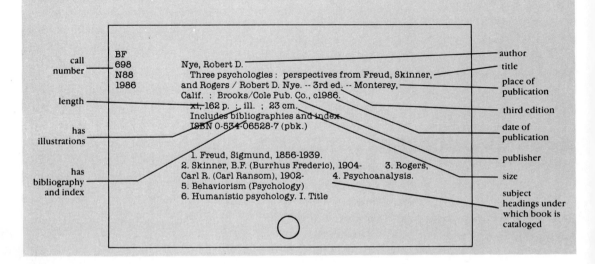

call
number

BF
698
N88
1986

length

has
illustrations

has
bibliography
and index

Nye, Robert D.
    Three psychologies : perspectives from Freud, Skinner,
and Rogers / Robert D. Nye. -- 3rd ed. -- Monterey,
Calif. : Brooks/Cole Pub. Co., c1986.
    xi, 162 p. : ill. ; 23 cm.
    Includes bibliographies and index.
    ISBN 0-534-06528-7 (pbk.)

1. Freud, Sigmund, 1856-1939.
2. Skinner, B.F. (Burrhus Frederic), 1904-   3. Rogers,
Carl R. (Carl Ransom), 1902-   4. Psychoanalysis.
5. Behaviorism (Psychology)
6. Humanistic psychology. I. Title

author
title
place of
publication
third edition
date of
publication
publisher
size
subject
headings under
which book is
cataloged

EXERCISE 2

Locate the call number for five of the following books in your college library by using the card catalog or on-line catalog and looking up the book by title or author.

> *The Forbidden Experiment* by Roger Shattuck
> *Mythology* by Edith Hamilton
> *What Color Is Your Parachute?* by Richard Nelson Bolles
> *Broca's Brain* by Carl Sagan
> *The Language and Thought of the Child* by Jean Piaget
> *The Civilization of the Renaissance in Italy* by J.C. Burkhardt
> *Silent Spring, Secret Spring* by Rachel Carson
> *A Death in the Family* by James Agee

Then look for two of the books in the stacks. Report if the books were on the shelf or not, and if not, where they currently arc. Be sure to ask a librarian for help if you have trouble locating any of these books.

Book No. 1 _____

_____

_____

_____

ASKING FOR HELP

Colleges hire librarians who are trained to help college students find the materials they need for their classes, but many students are reluctant to ask for help in using the library. Don't be—college libraries are complex, and everyone needs trained help sometimes. As a general rule, first try locating something on your own, but as soon as you start to feel frustrated, ask. Many students hesitate to ask for help because they're influenced by the stereotype of a librarian as someone whose job is to make sure that you keep quiet and don't write in library books. Like all stereotypes, this one is harmful. In fact, since you can expect to be using the college library frequently in your college career, it's a good idea to get to know some of your college librarians by name.

Book No. 2 _____

_____

_____

_____

FINDING PERIODICAL ARTICLES

The procedure for finding a magazine or journal article is somewhat different from that for locating a book in a library. As an example, suppose your psychology instructor had assigned an article for you to read and summarize. The listing he gave you read:

J.D. Blum On Changes in Psychiatric Diagnosis over Time *American Psychologist* 33 (11) 1017–1031

What you need to locate in the library is an article by J.D. Blum entitled "On Changes in Psychiatric Diagnosis over Time," which appeared in a journal called *American Psychologist,* volume 33, issue number 11, on pages 1017 to 1031.

In most libraries, back issues of magazines are either bound into books and shelved or on microfilm. To locate them, you need to find out whether your library has that particular magazine from that date and, if so, in what form. In most libraries, you'll find this information by consulting the library's **periodical holdings list,** which lists the journals the library has, the volumes of each journal and their location: whether they're in bound volumes or on microfilm. Figure 16.3 is an example of part of a periodicals holdings list. Note that in most cases, you do not look for periodicals in the card catalog. Most libraries do *not* have their periodical holdings in their card catalog, and no library has references to individual periodical articles in its catalog.

Once you've gotten the information from the periodicals holding list, you can locate the periodical you need. If journals aren't shelved by call number, they're usually in alphabetical order by title. Microfilmed volumes are kept in cabinets, also in alphabetical order. A librarian at the periodical desk can help you find the specific volume you need and show you how to use a microfilm reader. According to the information in Figure 16.3, volume 33 of *American Psychologist* should be in the stacks. Once you've found where the bound volumes of *American Psychologist* are shelved, look for volume 33. In volume 33, locate issue number 11, page 1017. Ask the librarian if you have any difficulty.

FINDING MATERIALS ON A SPECIFIC SUBJECT

Often, when you enter the library, you're not looking for a specific book or article, but for information on a certain subject. As an example, let's say that you've been asked to write a short report on osteoporosis (a condition in which the mass of bone in a person's skeleton becomes reduced and the bones become brittle). Where do you start?

Actually, the time to start is before you get to the library. As your first step, define what you're looking for. How many sources do you need? Do you need very recent sources (within the last five years) or sources from a specific time period? Are there certain kinds of sources you need, as specified by the instructor? Are books or periodicals preferable or doesn't it matter? What kind of information are you looking for about your topic? Usually the answer to these questions is in the specifics of the assignment the instructor has given. If you're not sure, ask the instructor before you begin. If there's no reason for using sources from a particular time period, use the most recent sources you can locate, preferably sources from the past five or ten years.

See if you can find the titles of some books or articles on your topic before you go to the library. Look through your textbook to see if there are any articles listed in a bibliography at the end of the chapter or in the appendix. Look through your notes also, if the instructor has lectured on the topic, to see if any books or articles on the topic were mentioned. You might even ask the instructor to recommend some materials. If you have specific titles to search for in

Figure 16.3

PERIODICAL HOLDINGS LIST

AMERICAN MUSIC TEACHER
18 (1968/69) — CURRENT
FILM I (1951) — 16 (1967)

AMERICAN NATURALIST
V.98 (1964) — CURRENT
FILM V.82 (1949) — V.101 (1967)

AMERICAN NOTES AND QUERIES
1 (1962) — CURRENT

AMERICAN OPINION
SUPERSEDED BY NEW AMERICAN IN SEPT. 1985
CURRENT TWO YEARS ONLY
FILM V.1 (1958) — V.28 NO.7 (1985)

AMERICAN PHILOSOPHICAL QUARTERLY
5 (1968) — CURRENT

AMERICAN PHYSICAL SOCIETY BULLETIN
SEE BULLETIN OF THE AMERICAN PHYSICAL
SOCIETY

AMERICAN POLITICAL SCIENCE REVIEW
V.42 (1948) — V.43 (1949), V.45 (1951) — CURRENT
FILM V.1 (1906/07) — V.61 (1967)
CUM IND V.1 (1906/07) — V.62 (1968)

AMERICAN POLITICS QUARTERLY
V.1 (1973) — CURRENT

AMERICAN PREFACES
CEASED PUBLICATION WITH V.8 (1943)
V.1 (1935) — V.8 (1943)

AMERICAN PRESERVATION
CEASED PUBLICATION WITH V.4 NO.2 (1981)
V.1 (1977/78) — V.4 NO.2 (1981)

Name of
journal

AMERICAN PSYCHOLOGIST
V.1 (1946) — V.17 (1962), V.19 (1964) — CURRENT
FILM V.16 (1961) — V.20 (1965)

Volumes 1 to 17 (1946-1962)
and volumes 19 to present
(1964 to this year) are on the
shelves in bound volumes

Volumes 16 to 20 (1961 to 1965)
are on microfilm

the library, your task will be much easier, because you'll have a place to begin.

IDENTIFYING SUBJECT HEADINGS

Once you've outlined what kinds of information you're looking for, the next step is to identify and list the subject headings under which materials on your topic are cataloged. It's important to know which terms the library uses to catalog information about your topic. For example, if you were writing a paper about "high blood pressure" and looked in the card catalog, you might be distressed to find no books on your topic. That's because the library catalogs books on high blood pressure under the heading "hypertension."

A useful tool for finding subject headings is a reference book entitled *Library of Congress Subject Headings,* a two-volume reference work which lists the subject headings the Library of Congress uses in cataloging books. Figure 16.4 is an example of an entry from the *Library of Congress Subject Headings*.

The Library of Congress Subject Headings will also direct you to other possible subject headings for your topic. If you looked up "osteoporosis," for example, you would find the following listing:

Osteoporosis
BT—Bones—Diseases
       Vitamin D deficiency
NT   Sudeck's atrophy

This tells you that, in addition to looking under "osteoporosis," you could also look under the broader headings "Bones—diseases," or under the related heading, "Vitamin D Deficiency." You could also check the narrower term "Sudeck's atrophy."

FINDING REFERENCE BOOKS

Once you've made a list of useful subject headings, your next step might be to find a reference book with information on your topic. Books in the reference section will include general encyclopedias like the *Encyclopaedia Britannica,* specialized encyclopedias that survey current knowledge in a field (such as the *McGraw-Hill Encyclopedia of Science and Technology*), handbooks, yearbooks, general and specialized dictionaries, and books which are important resources in their field. The reference librarian can usually assist you by suggesting some sources of information. You can also use a guide to reference books such as the *Guide to the Use of Libraries and Information Sources* by Jean Key Gates (McGraw-Hill, 1983) to identify the main reference books for the academic area in which you're doing research.

Figure 16.4

LIBRARY OF CONGRESS SUBJECT HEADINGS

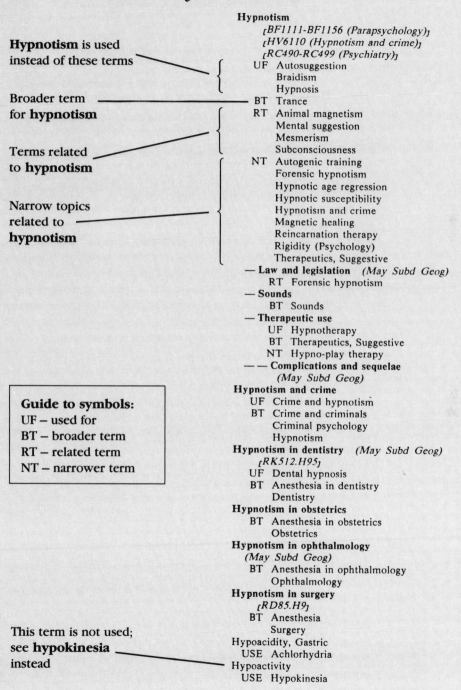

Hypnotism
  ₍BF1111-BF1156 (Parapsychology)₎
  ₍HV6110 (Hypnotism and crime)₎
  ₍RC490-RC499 (Psychiatry)₎
  UF Autosuggestion
      Braidism
      Hypnosis
  BT Trance
  RT Animal magnetism
      Mental suggestion
      Mesmerism
      Subconsciousness
  NT Autogenic training
      Forensic hypnotism
      Hypnotic age regression
      Hypnotic susceptibility
      Hypnotism and crime
      Magnetic healing
      Reincarnation therapy
      Rigidity (Psychology)
      Therapeutics, Suggestive
  — Law and legislation   *(May Subd Geog)*
      RT Forensic hypnotism
  — Sounds
      BT Sounds
  — Therapeutic use
      UF Hypnotherapy
      BT Therapeutics, Suggestive
      NT Hypno-play therapy
  — — Complications and sequelae
          (May Subd Geog)
Hypnotism and crime
  UF Crime and hypnotism
  BT Crime and criminals
      Criminal psychology
      Hypnotism
Hypnotism in dentistry   *(May Subd Geog)*
  ₍RK512.H95₎
  UF Dental hypnosis
  BT Anesthesia in dentistry
      Dentistry
Hypnotism in obstetrics
  BT Anesthesia in obstetrics
      Obstetrics
Hypnotism in ophthalmology
  (May Subd Geog)
  BT Anesthesia in ophthalmology
      Ophthalmology
Hypnotism in surgery
  ₍RD85.H9₎
  BT Anesthesia
      Surgery
Hypoacidity, Gastric
  USE Achlorhydria
Hypoactivity
  USE Hypokinesis

Hypnotism is used
instead of these terms

Broader term
for **hypnotism**

Terms related
to **hypnotism**

Narrow topics
related to
hypnotism

Guide to symbols:
UF – used for
BT – broader term
RT – related term
NT – narrower term

This term is not used;
see **hypokinesia**
instead

Note that rarely will the information you find in general reference sources be your main sources for an academic paper at the college level. However, information in general reference sources like encyclopedias is useful in giving you a rapid overview of information on your topic. In other words, general reference sources are good places to start your research, but bad places to end it.

FINDING BOOKS

After the reference section, your next step would be to compile a list of books on your topic from the card catalog. Using the subject headings you've identified, look for books listed under those subject headings. Select the books that are suited to your purpose and list them in a **working bibliography,** a list of books you will try to locate, along with enough information so that you can find them. For books, the essential information would be their title, author, and call number. See Figure 16.5 for a sample of a working bibliography on osteoporosis. As a general rule, list twice as many books as you need on your working bibliography, assuming that you won't be able to locate all of them.

FINDING PERIODICAL ARTICLES

Many times articles in periodicals will be more suitable for your purpose than material in books, as the information in them tends to be more current and each article concentrates on a narrower aspect of a topic than an entire book does.

In order to understand the process by which you would locate articles on a topic for a college assignment, let's use the same example, that of writing a short report on osteoporosis. You could, of course, select a journal that you know prints articles on topics like this and then look through each issue for the last five years or so, hoping to spot some article on your topic, but there are more efficient ways to proceed. Every academic field has indexes that group articles in journals in the field by subject heading. One that you may be familiar with is the *Reader's Guide to Periodical Literature,* an index of articles in popular magazines, like *Time, Newsweek,* and *Consumer Reports.* Since the *Reader's Guide* also indexes popular magazines in certain subject fields such as *Art News, Natural History, Scientific American,* and *Psychology Today,* it's a useful starting place.

As when finding books on a topic, you need to begin with a list of useful subject headings on your topic. Once you have a list of subject headings, go to the periodical section and find the *Reader's Guide.* The most recent issues are paperbound and index either one month's or three month's articles. Instead of starting with these smaller issues, begin with the most recent hardbound volume, which is an index of articles for an entire year. That way, you'll find the fullest current listing of articles on your topic.

Figure 16.5

EXAMPLE OF WORKING BIBLIOGRAPHY

BOOKS

	Subject headings	{ osteoporosis Bones - diseases Vitamin D deficiency Sudeck's atrophy	
Call #	**Author**	**Title**	**Notes**
WE 250 N911s	Notelouitz, Morris	Stand Tall: the informed women's guide to preventing osteoporosis	popular book, but has 10-page. bibliography
HE 20. (gut doc) 364/2 84-3	Kenton, Charlotte	Osteoporosis: Jan 1980 thru March 1984	bibliography with 355 citations put out by US Dept Health / Hum Sr.
microfiche gut. doc. 1043 A & B	US Congress, Senate Committee on Aging	Osteoporosis	hearings + bibliographies
RC 931 073079 1987	Avioli, Louis	The Osteoporotic Syndrome	1987 book w/ biblio & index
WE 255 c976 1985	ed Hans K. Uhthoff	Current Concepts of Bone Fragility	collection of articles from a conference

PERIODICAL ARTICLES

Author	Title	(In) Journal	Vol. / Date & pages	Notes
G. Kolata	How impt is dietary calcium in preventing osteoporosis?	Science	V. 233, Aug. 1, 1986 pp 519-520	
LH Allen	Calcium & Osteoporosis	Nutrition Today	V. 21 May-June 1986	has biblio
	Extra calcium may not ease bone disease	New Scientist	V. 113 Feb 12, 1987	p. 24
CW Callaway	Dietary Effects on Osteoporosis	Journal of the American Medical Assn.	V. 257 Mar. 27, 1987 p. 1652	
B. Riis and others	Does calcium supplementation prevent post-menopausal bone loss?	New England Journal of Medicine	V. 316 Jan 22, 1987 p 173-177	report on a study - has bibliography

Look under the different subject headings on your list and read the titles of the articles under that subject heading to see which heading or headings seems the most useful for your purposes. Figure 16.6 is an example of a page from the 1986 *Reader's Guide,* and Figure 16.7 is from a more specialized index, *General Science Index,* including listings on osteoporosis. As when browsing through the card catalog, you want to note on your working bibliography list articles that you might want to find. For periodicals, include the article's author and title, the name of the journal, the volume and/or date of the issue in which the article appeared, and the page numbers. This is the information you'll need to locate the article in the library.

To get the information for your worksheet, you must be able to decipher the information in the *Reader's Guide*. Figure 16.8 shows a sample entry and an explanation of it.

On your working bibliography, list twice as many periodical articles as you will eventually need, anticipating that you won't be able to find every article that you list. But be selective in what you choose for your worksheet. For example, some of the articles listed in Figure 16.6 from the *Reader's Guide* are probably too general, while some of the articles listed in the *General Science Index* (Figure 16.7) are probably too technical. Which articles you choose would depend on what aspect of osteoporosis you were interested in: you would select different articles if your topic was "Detection of Osteopososis" than if your topic was "Calcium and Osteoporosis."

Usually, the *Reader's Guide* is a starting point for college research. In addition, you'll be expected to have consulted an index of scholarly journals in whatever academic field you're doing research in, such as the *General Science Index* for a paper in the natural sciences. Several other indexes follow the same format as the *Reader's Guide,* so if you know how to use the *Reader's Guide,* you'll quickly be able to figure out how to use other indexes that follow its format. If the index you consult has a different format, a librarian can show you how to use it.

ON-LINE SEARCHES

It's now possible to do the same kind of search of indexes on a computer. To search for articles on osteoporosis, for instance, you could select a data base such as InfoTrac, type in your subject headings, and get a printout of all the articles published in a given period on that topic. Your success in doing a literature search this way depends on your identification of the right subject headings for your topic and your selection of the right data base. Reference librarians are trained to help students do computer searches. There is often a fee for a computer search. You'd elect to do a computer search when you needed a comprehensive listing of all articles on a topic and when the cost was low enough to fit your budget.

Figure 16.6

SAMPLE PAGE: READER'S GUIDE TO PERIODICAL LITERATURE

Osborne (New York, N.Y.: Apartment house) *See* New York (N.Y.)—Housing

Osbourne, Ozzy
about
Father's way. il pors *People Wkly* 25:111-13+ Je 16 '86

Osburn, Margaret
Cast iron artisan. il pors *Americana* 14:34+ S/O '86

Oscar Farris Agricultural Museum
On the farm in Nashville. il *South Living* 21:40+ D '86

Oscars (Prizes) *See* Academy Awards

Osceola (Iowa)
Industries
Small towns scramble for new jobs. C. Tevis. il *Success Farm* 84 no6:14-15 Mr '86

Oscillations
Conversion in matter may account for missing solar neutrinos. B. M. Schwarzschild. bibl f il *Phys Today* 39:17-20 Je '86
The Devil's staircase. P. Bak. bibl il *Phys Today* 39:38-45 D '86
Giant resonances in hot nuclei. G. F. Bertsch and R. A. Broglia. bibl f il *Phys Today* 39:44-52 Ag '86
Going back and forth on neutrino oscillations. D. E. Thomsen. *Sci News* 130:88 Ag 9 '86

Oscillators
See also
Multivibrators
555 design program. J. Holtzman. il *Radio-Electron* 57 ComputerDigest:8-9 Ja '86
An audio oscillator. R. Grossblatt. il *Radio-Electron* 57:83 Ag '86
How to design oscillator circuits (I). J. J. Carr. il *Radio-Electron* 57:65-6+ Jl '86
How to design oscillator circuits (II). J. J. Carr. il *Radio-Electron* 57:54-6 Ag '86
How to design oscillator circuits (III). J. J. Carr. il *Radio-Electron* 57:58-60 S '86
How to design oscillator circuits (IV). J. J. Carr. il *Radio-Electron* 57:72-4+ O '86
How to design oscillator circuits (V). J. J. Carr. il *Radio-Electron* 57:63-4+ N '86
How to design oscillator circuits (VI). J. J. Carr. il *Radio-Electron* 57:71-2 D '86

Oscillatory chemical reactions *See* Chemical reactions

OSHA *See* United States. Occupational Safety and Health Administration

O'Shea, James
The real nuts and bolts of Pentagon contracts. *Bull At Sci* 42:19-20 O '86

Osherson, Samuel, 1945-
about
'Each father shapes the life of a son in a different way' [interview] A. P. Sanoff. il por *U S News World Rep* 100:60-1 Je 16 '86

Oshima, Nagisa
about
Japan's 'world citizen'. H. Vinke. *World Press Rev* 33:55 Ap '86

Oshinsky, David M., 1944-
Teddy White's successors. il *New Leader* 68:21-5 D 16-30 '85

Oshkosh (Wis.)
Airports
Beehive air-do: controlling the swarm into Oshkosh. E. Weiner. il *Flying* 113:54-8 D '86

Oshkosh Fly-In *See* Aviation—Exhibitions

Osiek, Carolyn A.
about
How to prevent Bible baffle [interview] il *U S Cathol* 51:33-8 Je '86

Osing, Gordon, 1937-
Upon a news item [poem] *New Yorker* 62:38 S 1 '86

Osmond Boys (Musical group)
Oh, brother! Here comes another generation of Osmond Boys making beautiful music together. D. Clayton. il *People Wkly* 25:70-2 My 5 '86

Osmoregulation

OSS *See* United States. Office of Strategic Services

Ossman, Vess, 1868-1923
about
Vess L. Ossman and his ensembles. B. Ault. il *Hobbies* 91:50-2 My '86

Ossoli, Margaret Fuller, 1810-1850
Bibliography
The genius of Margaret Fuller. E. Hardwick. il *N Y Rev Books* 33:14-22 Ap 10 '86

Ossoli, Sarah Margaret Fuller, marchesa d' *See* Ossoli, Margaret Fuller, 1810-1850

Osteoarthritis *See* Arthritis

Osteoporosis
Bone up! M. Larkin. il *Health* 18:33-4+ O '86
Boning up. K. Freifeld. il *Health* 18:6 My '86
Boning up on calcium. C. SerVaas. il *Saturday Evening Post* 258:58-61+ Ap '86
The calcium connection: reducing the risk of osteoporosis now. H. Twidale. il *Work Woman* 11:186+ O '86
Calcium versus osteoporosis [study by Paul D. Miller] L. Vaughn. *Prevention* 38:44 O '86
Early milk drinking: will it prevent bone loss? *Prevention* 38:95 My '86
Estrogen effective against osteoporosis. il *FDA Consum* 20:2-3 Jl/Ag '86
A fishy cure [salmon calcitonin used to treat osteoporosis; research by G. F. Mazzuoli and Charles Chesnut] P. McCarthy. *Health* 18:23 S '86
How America's weakening bones could have been strengthened. R. Rodale. il *Prevention* 38:22-4+ Jl '86
How important is dietary calcium in preventing osteoporosis? G. Kolata. *Science* 233:519-20 Ag 1 '86
Let them eat calcium [food additives] D. Ceruti. il *Health* 18:9 O '86
New aid for bone victims. A. Finlayson. il *Macleans* 99:42-3 Ap 7 '86
New bones to pick about osteoporosis and calcium supplements. il *Discover* 7:8-9 O '86
Osteoporosis: a second look. C. A. McNurlen. *Better Homes Gard* 64:64+ Ap '86
Reasons for boning up on manganese. J. Raloff. *Sci News* 130:199 S 27 '86
The truth about osteoporosis. J. Schein. il *Consum Res Mag* 69:11-17 Ag '86
Who gets osteoporosis? M. Mihalik. il *Prevention* 38:40+ Ag '86
Women don't outgrow their need for milk. *Prevention* 38:9 Ja '86
Diagnosis
Disease of the week [osteoporosis screening and the media] M. Napoli. *New Repub* 195:17-18 D 1 '86
Osteoporosis testing. D. Farley. il *FDA Consum* 20:32-6 O '86

Osteosarcoma *See* Bone—Cancer

Ostergard, Don
Have a good trip. il *Flying* 113:94 Mr '86

Osterlund, Peter
(jt. auth) See Brooks, David, and Osterlund, Peter

Osthaus, Karl Ernst, 1874-1921
about
Historic architecture: Henry van de Velde. J. Rykwert. il *Archit Dig* 43:140-5+ S '86

Ostia (Ancient city)
A Roman apartment complex [Garden Houses of Ostia] D. J. Watts and C. M. Watts. il *Sci Am* 255:132-9 D '86

Oston, Ann
The gift of love. il pors *Harpers Bazaar* 120:176-9+ D '86

OSTP *See* United States. Office of Science and Technology Policy

Ostriches
Our gang, ostrich style [Nairobi National Park, Kenya] L. M. Hurxthal. il *Nat Hist* 95:34-41 D '86

Ostriker, Alicia
American poetry, now shaped by women. il *N Y Times Book Rev* 91:1+ Mr 9 '86

Figure 16.7

SAMPLE PAGE: GENERAL SCIENCE INDEX

Osmosis—*cont.*
The roles of osmotic stress and water activity in the inhibition of the growth, glycolysis and glucose phosphotransferase system of Clostridium pasteurianum. R. P. Walter and others. bibl il *J Gen Microbiol* 133:259-66 F '87

Ultrafiltration and reverse osmosis of the waste water from sweet potato starch process. B. H. Chiang and W. D. Pan. bibl il *J Food Sci* 51:971-4 Jl/Ag '86

Osmotic pressure *See* Osmosis

Ossification
Suspensory tuberosities for aging and sexing squirrels. M. L. Colburn. bibl il *J Wildl Manage* 50:456-9 Jl '86

Osteitis deformans
Case records of the Massachusetts General Hospital: case 44-1986 [An 80-year-old woman with Paget's disease and severe hypercalcemia after a recent fracture] S. R. Goldring and A. L. Schiller. bibl il *N Engl J Med* 315:1209-19 N 6 '86

Paget's disease: radiographic highlights. S. V. Kattapuram and S. A. DeLuca. bibl il *Am Fam Phys* 34:121-6 N '86

Osteitis fibrosa disseminata
McCune-Albright syndrome: long-term follow-up. P. A. Lee and others. bibl il *J Am Med Assoc* 256:2980-4 D 5 '86

Treatment of precocious puberty in the McCune-Albright syndrome with the aromatase inhibitor testolactone. P. P. Feuillan and others. bibl il *N Engl J Med* 315:1115-19 O 30 '86

Osteoarthritis *See* Arthritis

Osteoarthropathy
See also
Arthritis

Osteochondritis
Legg-Calvé-Perthes disease. il *Am Fam Phys* 34:218+ O '86

Osteogenesis
Cells of bone: proliferation, differentiation, and hormonal regulation. P. J. Nijweide and others. bibl il *Physiol Rev* 66:855-86 O '86

Do bones stop growing at zero gravity? il *New Sci* 108:30 Mr 20 '86

Osteogenic sarcoma *See* Tumors—Sarcoma

Osteolysis *See* Bones—Resorption

Osteomyelitis
Case records of the Massachusetts General Hospital: case 12-1987 [a 28-year-old woman with pain in the buttocks and leg and lesions of the sacrum and ilium] G. S. Lodwick and A. E. Rosenberg. bibl il *N Engl J Med* 316:736-42 Mr 19 '87

Case records of the Massachusetts General Hospital: case 28-1986 [An eight-year-old girl with multiple osteolytic lesions during the preceding six months] J. R. Kasser and A. E. Rosenberg. bibl il *N Engl J Med* 315:178-85 Jl 17 '86

Case records of the Massachusetts General Hospital: case 37-1986 [A 50-year-old woman with back pain, extensive travel, and exposure to farm animals] J. H. Maguire and A. E. Rosenberg. bibl il *N Engl J Med* 315:748-54 S 18 '86

Cephalhematoma complicated by osteomyelitis presumed due to Gardnerella vaginalis. L. M. Nightingale and others. bibl *J Am Med Assoc* 256:1936-7 O 10 '86

Pseudomonas osteomyelitis. *Am Fam Phys* 33:281 Ap '86

Therapy
Savings from outpatient antibiotic therapy for osteomyelitis: economic analysis of a therapeutic strategy. J. M. Eisenberg and D. S. Kitz. bibl il *J Am Med Assoc* 255:1584-8 Mr 28 '86

Osteopathy
Sectarian medicine. N. Gevitz. bibl *J Am Med Assoc* 257:1636-40 Mr 27 '87

Osteoporosis
Back pain in the elderly: updated diagnosis and management. S. Gandy and R. Payne. bibl il *Geriatrics* 41:57-2+ D '86

It came from outer space [osteoanalyzer] G. Ertel. *Health* 19:23 F '87

Mild postmenopausal serum calcium elevation. B. L. Riggs. *J Am Med Assoc* 256:3156-7 D 12 '86

Nurses detect osteoporosis. *Nurs 86* 16:17 Mr '86

Osteoporosis and pregnancy. R. Smith. *J Am Med Assoc* 255:2495 My 9 '86

Osteoporosis: bone loss is associated with back strength. *Geriatrics* 41:87 Ag '86

Osteoporosis: how to avoid its crippling effects. A. V. Beil. bibl il *RN* 49:14-17 Ag '86

Osteoporosis: most answers yet to come. J. Silberner. *Sci News* 131:116 F 21 '87

An "osteoporosis nurse" clinic. il *Am J Nurs* 86:890 Ag '86

Osteoporosis reexamined: complexity of bone biology is a challenge. B. J. Culliton. il *Science* 235:833-4 F 20 '87

Predicting osteoporosis. *Am J Nurs* 86:1095-6 O '86

Predicting the predisposition to osteoporosis. Gonadotropin-releasing hormone antagonist for acute estrogen deficiency test. R. Abbasi and G. D. Hodgen. bibl il *J Am Med Assoc* 255:1600-4 Mr 28 '86

Preventing osteoporosis: the new significance of hyperparathyroidism. L. V. Avioli. bibl il *Geriatrics* 41:30-2+ O '86

Reasons for boning up on manganese. J. Raloff. *Sci News* 130:199 S 27 '86

Transient osteoporosis puzzles researchers. H. L. Nash. *Physician Sportsmedicine* 14:27 N '86

Animal models
Effects of NaCl on calcium balance, parathyroid function and hydroxyproline excretion in prednisolone-treated rats consuming low calcium diet. A. Goulding and J. McIntosh. bibl il *J Nutr* 116:1037-44 Je '86

Nutritional aspects
Boning up. K. Freifeld. il *Health* 18:6 My '86

Calcium and osteoporosis. D. M. Hegsted. bibl il *J Nutr* 116:2316-19 N '86

Calcium supplements can help prevent steroid-induced osteoporosis. *Am J Nurs* 86:1389 D '86

Calcium, vitamin D may help reduce bone loss with hypothyroid therapy. *Geriatrics* 41:22 Ap '86

Dietary effects on osteoporosis. C. W. Callaway. bibl *J Am Med Assoc* 257:1652 Mr 27 '87

Does calcium supplementation prevent postmenopausal bone loss? A double-blind, controlled clinical study. B. Riis and others. bibl il *N Engl J Med* 316:173-7 Ja 22 '87

Extra calcium may not ease bone disease. il *New Sci* 113:24 F 12 '87

How important is dietary calcium in preventing osteoporosis? G. Kolata. *Science* 233:519-20 Ag 1 '86

Meat and manganese build stronger bones. D. Franklin. *New Sci* 111:31 S 18 '86

New bones to pick about osteoporosis and calcium supplements. S. Boxer. il *Discover* 7:8 O '86

No calcium fix. *Sci Am* 256:72 Ap '87

Osteoporosis: 'first step' diet treatment. L. Hengstler. *Geriatrics* 41:77-8+ Jl '86

Preventing osteoporosis: evidence for diet and exercise. B. Dawson-Hughes and X. F. Li. bibl *Geriatrics* 42:76-7+ Ja '87

When your patient needs extra calcium. P. L. Cerrato. il *RN* 49:51+ Ag '86

Therapy
Bone up! Make these 10 exercises your secret weapon against osteoporosis. M. Larkin. il *Health* 18:33-4+ O '86

Broken bones among elderly could be prevented. S. Kingman. *New Sci* 111:20 Jl 3 '86

Calcium: chief menopausal value as estrogen supplement? *Geriatrics* 41:27 N '86

FDA approves oral estrogen for osteoporosis therapy. *Geriatrics* 41:12 Jl '86

A fishy cure. P. McCarthy. *Health* 18:23 S '86

Good for the old bones. K. S. Zimmeth. il *Health* 19:16 F '87

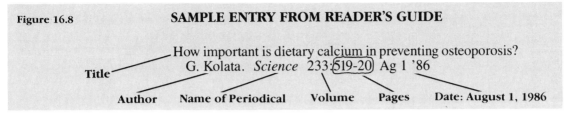

Figure 16.8

SAMPLE ENTRY FROM READER'S GUIDE

How important is dietary calcium in preventing osteoporosis?
G. Kolata. *Science* 233:519-20 Ag 1 '86

Title   Author   Name of Periodical   Volume   Pages   Date: August 1, 1986

OTHER SOURCES

In addition to books and periodicals, don't ignore other excellent sources of information in the library.

One is *newspapers*. Certainly, it would be impossible to find a newspaper article on a topic you're interested in without an index, but fortunately, several major newspapers have indexes, in particular, *The New York Times*. *The New York Times Index* dates back to 1851, so it's an excellent source for original material—like the newspaper articles that appeared in 1919 about the race riots in Chicago, or the coverage of Herbert Hoover's campaign for president, for instance. Additionally, since its coverage is so broad, you can often find a very up-to-date article reporting the latest findings on any topic you're researching. *The New York Times Index* is set up somewhat differently from indexes to magazines, so you would need directions for how to use it. Many libraries have *The New York Times* on microfilm so that you can easily locate an article that you find of interest.

Another excellent source of information is *government documents*. Students often don't think of government documents when they are researching a topic unless it's a topic in political science, but the government publishes literature on a wide range of topics. For example, a recent flyer put out by the Superintendent of Documents listed a book on protecting computer data from electronic theft published by the Office of Technology, a pamphlet on fetal alcohol syndrome published by the Department of Health and Human Services, a book on dropouts in education from the Department of Education, and a book on fusion energy published by the National Aeronautics and Space Administration.

A useful source of information about education and about the psychology of learning is ERIC (Educational Resource Information Center). ERIC indexes materials on microfilm, including many unpublished articles. Since the material is on microfilm, it's very easy to obtain. The ERIC index contains **abstracts** (brief summaries) of the articles, so you can judge whether the article is useful before you select it.

SUMMARY

Since many college assignments involve library work, it is essential that you familiarize yourself with the resources in your college library as soon as possible. Specifically, you want to be able to locate books in the library by using the card catalog or on-line catalog, and to use the periodical holdings list to locate a specific issue of a periodical article. When you're not looking for a particular book or article but for information on a given subject, begin by defining the type of sources that you need and by searching through your course materials for any possible sources. After this preliminary work, your first task is to use the *Library of Congress Subject Headings* to identify possible headings under which material on this topic would be cataloged. A reference book can provide a good overview of your topic. Then look for books cataloged under the headings you've identified. Begin a working bibliography of possible books. From there, look for periodical articles by consulting an index like the *Reader's Guide,* and add a listing of possible articles to your working bibliography. Don't neglect other possible sources such as newspapers, government documents, and ERIC.

■
JOURNAL WRITING

1. What reference books do you have in your home? Catalog them and explain on what subjects they contain information.
2. How is your college library different from your local library? from your high school library?

■
ACADEMIC WRITING

Select one of the following topics and compile a working bibliography on it, finding:

a. An encyclopedia with information on the topic
b. Two books that have information on the topic
c. A reference book with information on the topic
d. Two indexes (the *Reader's Guide* and one other) that list articles on the topic
e. Two articles on the topic
f. A newspaper article on the topic

Topics:

Cognitive styles	Nurse midwives
High blood pressure	Sigmund Freud
Hypnotism	Asbestos
Caffeine	Mobiles
Anorexia nervosa	Black classical composers
The San Andreas fault	The Works Project Administration (WPA)

17

Tackling College Assignments

In this chapter, you will learn:

▲ how to analyze an academic assignment for what is expected of you
▲ how to plan your time and work
▲ how to think up a good topic for an assignment
▲ how to construct a preliminary outline and gather material
▲ tips on the writing process

In addition to tests, the other types of tasks on which grades are typically based are academic assignments: reports, term papers, lab reports, critical essays, research projects, oral presentations, and other assignments like these. This chapter and the next provide some useful ways to tackle academic assignments.

ANALYZING THE ASSIGNMENT

In one university writing lab, the writing tutors discovered that when students came to them for help with an assignment, the most common problem was that the students didn't understand the assignment that they had been given. Typically, students remembered what the instructor had said about how long the paper should be, but didn't recall any specifications about the sources to be used, the information to be covered in the paper, or the criteria for the final product. The first skill connected with your success in doing an academic assignment is analyzing the assignment.

Specifically, you should be able to answer most of the following questions:

Reprinted by permission of UFS, Inc.

1.   *What is the topic?* Sometimes the instructor will be very specific about the topic, saying, for instance, "Do a short report on the effects of caffeine on the nervous system." Other times, the instructor will give you a general area, but expect you to narrow down the topic some more. For example, if you were told to write a short paper on the effects of one stimulant or depressant on the nervous system, you would need to select what stimulant to write about. In other cases, the choice of topic will be left up to you. The assignment might be "Write a short report exploring any of the topics covered in this chapter in greater depth," for example.

2.   *What sources should be used for the paper?* Some assignments might call for you to use your own ideas exclusively, while others might ask you to consult your textbook and notes, to find and read books and articles in the library, to observe people or things, or to interview people. If outside sources are used, you need to know how many you should have, and any restrictions as to their date or type. For instance, the instructor might specify that you use at least three journal articles published after 1980.

3.   *What task are you being asked to do?* In Chapter 14, you studied the different types of essay questions. You can expect to see similar types represented in academic assignments. Some assignments will ask you to summarize or report information: others will ask you to analyze the steps in a process, to relate two different sets of ideas, to argue a position or evaluate something, or to apply knowledge to a new area. Knowing what type of task you're being asked to do makes a difference in how you write: there's a real difference between a paper summarizing Freud's view of the meaning of dreams, one comparing his view to another person's view, and one evaluating whether his view was correct or not. Figure 17.1 provides an overview of the subtasks involved in a writing assignment.

4.   *What process are you being asked to use?* Sometimes instructors will give you ideas on how to proceed with a writing assignment. They may ask you, for instance, to submit a preliminary outline or a first draft, or to organize the information you present in

Figure 17.1

A FLOW CHART FOR A WRITING ASSIGNMENT

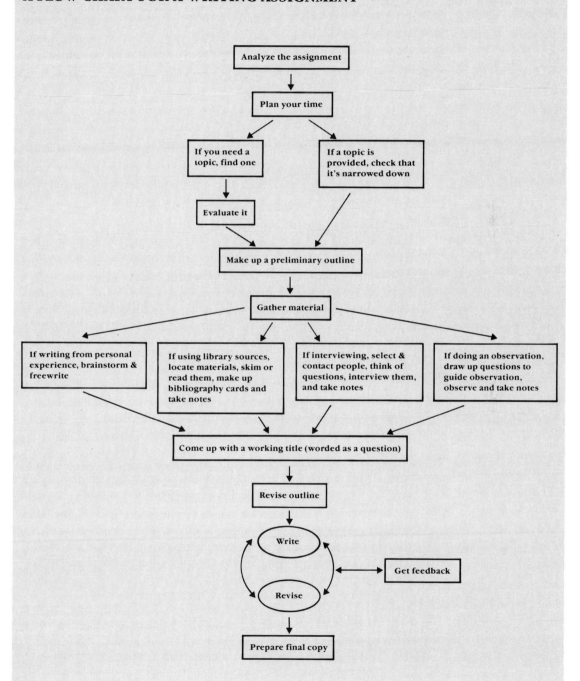

a certain way. All these suggestions give you advice in the steps you should undertake in planning and writing your paper.

5.   *What audience are you writing for?* Usually, the audience will be the instructor, or the instructor and your fellow classmates. But sometimes a different audience will be specified. For example, the directions may say, "Write an explanation of how the immune system works that could easily be understood by high school students."

6.   *What criteria will be used to evaluate your paper?* If you know what the criteria for grading will be, then you can write to fulfill those criteria. For instance, your instructor may say, "Your paper will be graded on whether you answer the question or not, your selection and use of sources, the quality of your writing, and evidence of your understanding of the basic underlying issues."

7.   *What should be the format of the final paper or report?* If it's a written report, should it be typed or handwritten, should it have a title page, subheadings, citations (references within the body of the text that show the sources of your information), a bibliography, any appendices? If it's an oral report, is there any standard order you should use in presenting it? For instance, if you were giving an oral report on an impressionist painter, the instructor might have specified that you should begin with a brief biographical sketch. You should also know if you are expected to hand in a written paper based on your presentation.

8.   *Finally, how long should the paper or oral report be, when is it due, and what penalties are attached to late assignments?* Sometimes, the instructor will distribute written directions for the assignment. Other times, the directions will be given orally. If the instructor gives instructions orally, take notes on what is being said. When you start to work on the assignment, you simply can't rely on the accuracy of your memory.

Whether the assignment is given in writing or orally, you should analyze it using the outline above to see what directions have been provided. Once you've done that analysis, you can ask the instructor questions about details of the assignment that haven't been provided.

Here's a sample assignment and an analysis of it:

> For this paper (3 to 4 pages), you are to investigate a child's understanding of an abstract concept, like colors, time, less and more, bigger and smaller, or good and bad. Your subjects should be two children close in age and of the same sex, both under the age of five. In your paper, summarize the information from the text and your notes on how children develop these concepts.

Then report your own observations, based on the children's use of these terms and based on some simples tests you devise for them. Finally, compare your findings with the current thinking about how and when children acquire these concepts. Paper is due December 8th.

Analysis:

1. Topic: child's understanding of one abstract concept (I choose which concept)
2. Sources: text, notes, and my observation of two children
3. Task: summarize information from textbook and from observations; compare the two
4. Process: no specifics given
5. Audience: not specified
6. Criteria: not stated
7. Format: not specified
8. Length: not specified
   Due date: Dec. 8th, penalties not known

This analysis highlights what the assignment does and does not specify, and could be the basis for questions to the instructor about the information not provided.

YOUR WORK PLAN

Any long-range assignment can be intimidating. There's a real tendency to procrastinate—to wait until the last minute to begin work. Unfortunately, most assignments done the night before they're due are doomed to failure. Instead, you should apply the skill you learned in Chapter 3: break the writing assignment down into a series of subtasks, then work out a realistic work schedule for yourself. (See page 23 to review how to break an assignment down into a series of smaller steps and how to plan your time for doing it.) Plan your time so that a writing assignment is finished far enough in advance to allow time for typing it. If you're working on an oral report, allow three days to a week after you finished writing it for rehearsal.

An additional advantage to breaking an assignment down into subtasks is that it makes the task of doing a writing assignment more manageable. It's less intimidating to do a series of smaller tasks than it is to tackle one large task.

Here's an example of how one student broke down the assignment on children's understanding of abstract concepts given above:

Breakdown:

2 days { 1. Contact Douglas's and Ryan's parents to make appointments.

1 day { 2. Review notes and textbook passages on children's development of abstract concepts and select one topic.

1 day	3. Take notes on one concept and write up summary (maximum one page).
1 day	4. Come up with some simple questions and tasks I can do when I observe—check them with the instructor.
5 days	5. Do observations.
	6. Write up observations.
1 day	7. Compare observations with my summary and write up conclusion.
2 days	8. Revise, type, and proofread paper.

Total of 2 weeks

■
_____
E X E R C I S E   1

Analyze the following assignment by using the eight questions above: look at its topic, the sources required, the type of writing called for, the process, the audience, criteria for grading, format, and length, and due date. Then devise a practical work plan for the assignment.

> Find a textbook in the library dated prior to 1960 and read the information in it about genes and chromosomes. Write a one-page summary of it. Next, compare that information to the information in your textbook. Using the library, research the discoveries that explain the differences in information about genes between 1960 and 1989. Find out what discoveries were made by scientists, when they were made, and who made them. (Your paper should have three parts and be 4 to 8 pages long. Due March 31st.)

FINDING TOPICS

If your topic hasn't been assigned to you, your first subtask might be to find a topic. Selecting a topic for a writing assignment is a real challenge. How do you go about finding a good topic—and what's a good topic anyway?

First, **a good topic is one that will allow you to explore a subject that you are interested in**. When you're asked to select your own topic, you've been given a chance to design your own learning task, and it makes sense to use that opportunity to learn something you'd like to know. For instance, one student in a psychology course had to write a research paper on some aspect of psychology. She had a cousin who was deaf and was interested in finding out how a handicap like deafness affected a person's personality, so she decided to write her paper on the psychological effects of deafness. Another student who had worked as an election judge chose to do a paper on fraudulent voting practices in his city for a political science course.

Secondly, **a good topic is within the guidelines of the assignment you have been given and is related to the subject matter of the course**. Recent efforts to control drug traffic would not be a good choice for a short report in psychology, even if one unit was on drugs (although this topic might be a good choice for a criminal justice course).

Third, **a good topic is specific**. It's actually more difficult to write or do research on a topic that's too broad than to work with one that's well focused. For example, a topic like "Education in India" is too broad for anything but a book. "Education of Women in India" is better, and "Higher Education for Women in India" is better still. In fact, after having done some preliminary reading on the topic, you might come up with an even more focused topic, like "Opportunities for Women in Higher Education in Modern India."

Fourth, **a good topic is practical**. In other words, a good topic is one that you can find information on and can write about. If you're looking for a research topic, look for one you can find information on written at your level. For example, it would not be practical to plan to write an essay about computerized music if you were totally ignorant about computers and would first have to learn the basic facts about them in order to read articles about your topic. If you're looking for a topic for a personal essay or speech, pick a topic you know something about or have ideas about.

With these criteria in mind, how do you go about finding a topic? Begin by thinking about topics that relate both to the course material and your personal interest or experience. The experiential knowledge you have is a good foundation for learning new information about the topic. Take your book and your notes to a quiet place and read over your notes and your underlinings. Make a list of any ideas that are possible candidates for your topic. Look at any study questions or suggestions for research at the ends of chapters in the textbook. For instance, these study questions from a humanities textbook could be the topics for writing assignments:

1. What purposes did Roman portraiture fulfill in public and private life?
2. How was art used as propaganda by the Roman emperors Augustus, Trajan, Hadrian, Marcus Aurelius, and Caracalla?
3. How did the Romans differ from the Greeks in their conceptions of architectural space and in the building techniques that they used?

Still another possibility is to spend a few hours browsing in the library. Look at reference books in the field, glance through some issues of current journals in the field, and look through the index to journals for that field. If you identify a topic in this way, you've also found at least one source for your paper.

After testing a possible topic against the criteria listed above, the best way to determine if a topic you've chosen is a good one is to check with the instructor. I recommend selecting two or three of your best ideas, writing them down with a short explanation, and asking your instructor to evaluate them.

■
_____
E X E R C I S E   2

Here are some topics students submitted to an instructor of a psychology class. The assignment was to do a short report investigating some aspect of memory in greater depth. Evaluate the topics for their suitability, giving reasons for your choice.

How to improve your memory
Memory for names
The effect of alcohol on memory
Long-term memory
How magicians trick your memory
Do people of different ages, sexes, and nationalities re-
   member differently?
Hypnosis
How memory works

MAKING A PRELIMINARY OUTLINE

When you studied how to write essay answers, one strategy you learned was to predict the parts of your answer (see page 200, Chapter 14). The same strategy is also useful when applied to academic assignments. For instance, if you were doing the observational paper on children's understanding of abstract concepts mentioned above and had decided to observe the child's comprehension of the concepts of less and more, you could predict the parts of your report from the assignment as follows:

I. Summary of what you know about this topic: What did we learn from lectures and our readings about the development of the concepts of less and more?

II. Summary of observations: What did I observe about Douglas's and Ryan's understanding of less and more?

III. Relation of observations to concepts: Does what I observed fit with current knowledge about how these concepts develop or doesn't it?

Note that, in addition to predicting the parts of the report, we also converted the subtopics into questions. These questions will serve several functions: they will be a useful guide to gathering information, they'll help you organize your writing, and they can be the basis of subheadings for your paper.

As you can see, it's possible to predict the parts of a writing assignment from the assignment, before you've begun to gather material on your topic. Later you may decide that there are other questions you want to answer in your paper or that you prefer to omit some of the original questions, and that's fine. Writers modify their preliminary outlines all the time.

EXERCISE 3

For each of the following writing topics, prepare a series of questions that you might expect to be answered in a paper on that topic. Try to keep your questions within the scope of the topic.

Example:

Treatments for schizophrenia
What treatments are currently being used?
Which are controversial?
What methods of treatments have been abandoned?
What evidence is there of effectiveness of different treatments?

1. How wild animals adapt to urban environments
2. Effects of loud music on hearing
3. The U.S. military budget compared to that of other countries
4. The use of older workers in minimum wage jobs
5. A history of newspapers in New York

GATHERING MATERIAL

You can't write a paper without material any more than a brick-layer can work without bricks. Depending on the assignment, you might gather material through **introspection** (looking inside yourself to learn what you think, feel, and have experienced related to a topic), by reading outside materials, by interviewing, or by observing.

1. Introspection.   For some college writing assignments, such as essays for writing classes or speeches for an introductory speech class, you will need to tap into your own memory, knowledge, and ideas. In gathering material for papers of this type, you can use prewriting techniques like brainstorming and freewriting. When you **brainstorm,** you write down any ideas related to a topic that occur to you. At this stage, you try not to judge ideas; you just list whatever comes to mind. The idea is to come up with more than enough material for a paper. You can eliminate points you don't need and add more points later.

When you **freewrite,** you set a fixed time (like 10 minutes) or a fixed length (like 3 pages) and write about the topic until you reach your set limit. Then you can go back and extract any useful ideas from what you wrote. Both brainstorming and freewriting are productive alternatives to staring at that blank piece of paper.

2. Reading Outside Materials.   Other writing assignments will require you to gather material from sources—either the text and notes from the course or from material that you find in the library.

When you search other sources to gather material for a writing assignment, your writing goal is very specific: you're looking for the information you need for the writing assignment. If you prepared a preliminary outline for the writing assignment, the questions you listed now represent your reading goals. For example, the student writing the observation paper on children's understanding of the concepts of less and more would use his first question, "What did we learn from lectures and our readings about the development of the concepts of less and more?" as his reading goal in reviewing his notes and readings. That means that he would search the text and his notes for information directly related to his question.

An assignment may require that you go to the library to locate outside sources on your topic. Chapter 16 provides instruction in how to find information on a subject in the library. Before you go to the library, think about the kinds of sources you will need. (Remember that it's easier to look for a specific book or article that the instructor mentioned or that's listed in a bibliography in your textbook than to start from scratch.)

3.   Interviewing.   Students often don't think of using people as sources for a paper, but often someone with firsthand knowledge on a topic is an excellent resource. For instance, if you were doing a paper on treatments for schizophrenia and knew someone who worked in the mental health field, you could ask that person whether she knew much about treatments for schizophrenia or whether she could direct you to someone who did.

When you identify someone with knowledge about your topic, you should call to make an appointment. To prepare for your appointment, make a list of the questions you're going to ask, using your preliminary outline as a guide. During the interview, take notes on the answers the person supplies. You might also consider using a tape recorder to supplement your notes, but, if you do, be sure to ask permission first. Some people feel nervous when they know that what they're saying is being recorded and will ask you just to take notes.

4.   Observing.   For some papers, you will be required to get your information by directly observing someone or something instead of by reading. For example, you might be asked to observe the behavior patterns of one species of animal at the zoo. When you are given an assignment of this type, prepare yourself for the actual observation by making a list of the elements you might observe. Get ideas by reviewing material from the text or your notes and suggestions the instructor gave you while presenting the assignment. For observing a species of animal, you'd prepare a list of behavior patterns to observe. It might look like this:

What activities do the animals engage in?

Do most of the animals stay by themselves or interact with other animals?

Do they show aggression? If so, how?

Do mothers interact with their young? If so, how?

What vocalizations do the animals make?

What do the animals eat?

How do the animals interact with their environment?

What variations are there in individual animals, in animals of different ages, in animals of different sexes?

These questions will guide your attention during the observation. Bring a notebook with you and take notes on what you observe. You should collect more than enough material for your report using this strategy.

TIPS ON WRITING THE PAPER

Once you've gathered your material, whether from your own mind, your textbook and notes, from library sources, from interviews with people, or from observations, it's time to begin writing. Start by reviewing your preliminary outline and your notes. Revise your preliminary outline to reflect any changes that you decide to make in the order of the parts of your paper. This is also a good point at which to review the assignment to make sure that you recall exactly what you were instructed to do.

Another suggestion is to come up with a working title for your paper, writing it in the form of a question. The purpose of writing the title at this point is to guide your writing: if you can come up with a precisely worded title to the paper, then your writing task is to express the answer to that question in writing. Here are some sample titles for examples used in this chapter.

How do children acquire the concept of less and more?

What behavior patterns are typical of captive lowland gorillas?

What treatments are being used today with patients with schizophrenia?

You might revise the title on your final draft, but for now it is a guide to what material you should include in your paper: if the material answers the question you posed, it should be included. If the material doesn't answer the question, it should be left out. Some students paste their working title on the wall over their desk while they're writing to remind themselves of what the focus of their paper is supposed to be, a trick you can try also.

Your first attempt to write your paper should be a **rough draft**—a first try at saying what you want to say. The process of drafting is similar to what artists do when they make preliminary sketches for a painting. You know that your first draft will not be perfect, and that you can make changes in it later. If you view your first draft as your first attempt to say what you want to say, you'll find it easier to start writing. Try writing on one side of your paper only, writing every other line, and leaving wide margins. Then you'll have room for adding material when you revise.

If writing that first word seems impossible, try talking through your paper before you start to write, a technique professional writers sometimes use. Look over your notes and your outline, and then talk through what you want to write as if you were giving a oral presentation to your class. Often this trick helps you to see what you want to say and frees up your writing hand.

Here's another tip for getting started: don't get stuck trying to write the introduction. One of the advantages of writing is that you don't have to write the parts of a paper in order. Your preliminary outline defined your paper as a series of sections. You can write each section separately and then, in your next draft, link the sections together. Look over your outline, pick the section that looks easiest to write, and start there. When you've drafted that section, go on to another section that looks easy to write, until you've written something about each subtopic on your outline. When you have a draft of the whole paper, you can work at putting the parts together and writing an introduction and a conclusion.

REVISING

When you have a complete first draft, read it from beginning to end to see whether it makes sense, whether it answers the question you posed as your title, and whether it fulfills the assignment. Make any changes that you feel you need, and keep working until you're satisfied with what you've written. You can cross out parts, add parts, and move parts around.

When you have a draft that satisfies you, consider asking someone else to read it and give you feedback. If you do, be sure to tell the person what kind of feedback you're looking for; otherwise your reader might just read to see if you have any spelling or grammar errors. You might say, for example, "I'm trying to write a description of the behavior of the gorilla colony at the zoo. Read it and tell me if you get a good picture of how gorillas act and if there's any part that's not clear. Don't worry about my spelling or grammar—this is just a draft." You can use the feedback the reader gives you to make further revisions in your paper.

When you've finished revising the paper, it's time to prepare a final copy. For most college papers, final copies should be typed.

Reprinted by permission of UFS, Inc.

They should follow the format that the teacher has specified. They should also be carefully proofread to eliminate grammar, spelling, and typing errors.

If you have used any sources in your writing—your textbook, a book or article from the library, or the comments of someone you interviewed—you need to **document** your sources. When you document a paper, you include references to your sources in a standard format as part of your paper. There are several standard formats for documentation: footnotes, MLA style (Modern Language Association) and APA style (American Psychological Association). In general, MLA style is used in the humanities and APA style is used in the social sciences. Figure 17.2 shows examples of passages using each of these systems. If you need to document a paper, ask the instructor which style to use and ask for a recommendation of a style sheet or manual on documenting.

LEARN FROM YOUR INSTRUCTOR'S COMMENTS

A final word: you can expect to become more skilled at doing writing assignments as you get more experience and more instruction in college. One way to grow as a writer is to learn from each writing experience. Be sure to get back every paper that you write and study the instructor's comments on it carefully, so that you can understand what you did right and what you did wrong.

SUMMARY

The foundation of doing an academic assignment is analyzing the assignment: knowing the type of topic, the sources to be used, the type of task, the process to be used, the intended audience, the criteria for evaluation, the format, and finally the length and due date. From this information, you can build a work plan—a list of subtasks for the assignment and a set of dates to estimate the time for each task. If no topic has been assigned, the first subtask may be to find a topic. Find a topic by considering subjects that interest you, or by browsing through your textbook, your notes, and related materials in the library. A well-chosen topic will interest you, will be within the guidelines of the assignment and the course, and will be both spe-

Figure 17.2

DOCUMENTATION FORMATS

MLA STYLE

Many guides to women's health, including The New Our Bodies, Ourselves (Boston Women's Health Book Collective 454) include a recommendation that women increase the calcium in their diets after they reach menopause in order to prevent or slow the development of osteoporosis. Advertisers also play a major role in publicizing recommendations that postmenopausal women consume at least 1500 milligrams of calcium daily.

> Reference in parentheses is to the author—in this case a group author. The number refers to a page number.

However, the scientific evidence to support a relationship between calcium intake and prevention of osteoporosis has recently been questioned. A recent article by G. Kolata (519-520) summarizes the research on this question. For instance, B. L. Riggs of the Mayo Clinic conducted a four year study of 107 women in Minnesota. When he compared the rates of bone loss of women who averaged more than 1400 milligrams of calcium per day and the rate of bone loss for women who averaged less than 500 milligrams per day, he found no significant difference between the two groups (Kolata 519). A similar study in Denmark found no relationship between a woman's calcium consumption and the density of her bones. Roger Smith, an orthopedic consultant in England, has concluded that "The effectiveness of calcium in reducing bone loss is slight or nonexistent." ("Extra calcium" 24).

> The article by G. Kolata will be listed in the bibliography. The numbers in parentheses refer to pages in the article.

> This study was mentioned in the article by Kolata on page 519.

> This quote is from an article whose author is not named, so instead a short form of the title is used. The whole title will appear in the bibliography.

Figure 17.2

APA STYLE

Many guides to women's health, including The New Our Bodies, Ourselves (Boston Women's Health Book Collective, 1984) include a recommendation that women increase the calcium in their diets after they reach menopause in order to prevent or slow the development of osteoporosis. Advertisers also play a major role in publicizing recommendations that postmenopausal women consume at least 1500 milligrams of calcium daily.

Reference in parentheses is to author—in this case a group—and to the year of publication.

However, the scientific evidence to support a relationship between calcium intake and prevention of osteoporosis has recently been questioned. A recent article by G. Kolata (1986) summarizes the research on this question. For instance, B. L. Riggs of the Mayo Clinic conducted a four year study of 107 women in Minnesota. When he compared the rates of bone loss of women who averaged more than 1400 milligrams of calcium per day and the rate of bone loss for women who averaged less that than 500 milligrams per day, he found no significant difference between the two groups (Kolata, 1986). A similar study in Denmark found no relationship between a woman's calcium consumption and the density of her bones. Roger Smith, an orthopedic consultant in England, has concluded that "The effectiveness of calcium in reducing bone loss is slight or nonexistent." ("Extra calcium," 1987, p. 24).

Since the author is mentioned in the sentence, only the date appears in the parentheses.

This study was mentioned in G. Kolata's article.

Since no author was given for this article, a short form of the title was used instead. A page number is mentioned as well as the article's date because it is a quotation.

cific and practical. Before you begin to gather material, construct a preliminary outline based on the assignment, and use that to guide you. Depending on the assignment, gather material through introspection, through reading outside material, or through interviewing or observing. Plan to write several drafts of the paper. If getting started is hard, try talking through your paper, or start by writing a middle section instead of the introduction. Finally, study your paper when it's returned to learn from your instructor's comments.

■
JOURNAL WRITING

1. What do you like and dislike about writing?
2. Make a list of ten topics related to the courses that you are taking now that you would like to find out more about.
3. Analyze the way you went about doing your last writing assignment. Be as specific as possible—describe all the steps you can think of—when you thought, when you wrote, when you revised, when you procrastinated, anybody who had a role in the writing, how you felt while you were writing, and so on.

■
ACADEMIC WRITING

Write a report on how students actually handle one of the topics covered in a chapter in this textbook. In addition to reviewing the material in the chapter, look at another book on the topic for background information. Then talk to five people you believe to be good students and ask them to tell you their strategies and tips on the topic. Summarize their advice into a two-page paper that details the best advice you found.

18

GIVING ORAL REPORTS

In this chapter you will learn:

▲ how to tackle an oral report
▲ how to write or "script" an oral report
▲ how to rehearse your presentation
▲ tips on delivering your oral report effectively

While oral reports aren't as common as written assignments, you can expect that some of your instructors will assign oral reports. Typical assignments might include:

Make yourself an expert on one Impressionist artist from the list below, and prepare a five-minute presentation on him or her.

Next week, we'll have debates on several controversial issues in current American foreign policy. You'll be assigned one side of the issue to debate. Prepare a three-minute presentation of the arguments for your side.

After you've done your research paper in psychology, prepare a five-minute presentation of your research for oral presentation to the class.

To give a successful oral presentation, you need to know how to plan your speech, how to rehearse your speech, and how to deliver it. Many of the skills needed for oral presentations are similar to those you've learned for doing written assignments; therefore, some of the material in this chapter will be a review. Other points, such as voice quality, are unique to oral presentations.

TACKLING THE ASSIGNMENT

As with a writing assignment, the first step in preparing an oral presentation is making sure that you understand the assignment exactly. Specifically, you need to know:

1.   *The topic.* If no topic is provided, you can find your own topic by using the same techniques you learned for finding a topic for a writing assignment (see Chapter 17).

2.   *The sources.* Should you develop your own ideas, use material from your textbook and lecture notes, do library research, do observational research, or interview someone?

3.   *The task.* Are you to inform people about a subject, convince them of a position, evaluate something, or perhaps teach them the steps in a process?

4.   *The process.* Is any advice offered on how to proceed in planning your speech?

5.   *The audience.* In most cases, your audience will be your classmates. Spend some time thinking about what they know and don't know about your subject and how they can be expected to feel about it. Your answers to these questions will help you decide how to present your information and ideas.

6.   *The evaluation criteria.* On what criteria will your oral presentation be graded?

7.   *Format.* Is there any standard order you should use in presenting your report? For instance, if you were giving a report on an Impressionist artist, the teacher might have specified that you should begin with a brief biographical sketch. You should also find out if you will be expected to hand in a written paper based on your presentation.

8.   *Length and presentation date.* When should you be prepared to give your speech? How long should your speech be? The length for a speech is usually given in minutes. An average rate of delivery is around 150 words per minute so for a five-minute speech, estimate that you would write a 750-word draft. Expect that you might have to increase or decrease the length of your speech after you time yourself actually giving the speech.

YOUR WORK PLAN

Once you've found out all you can about an assignment, your next step should be to break the assignment down into a series of smaller tasks. In general, you'll do this the same way you broke a writing assignment down into a series of smaller tasks. The only difference is that you need to plan to finish preparing your speech three days to a week before your presentation date in order to allow yourself time to rehearse it. To rehearse effectively requires frequent practices spaced over several days.

PLANNING YOUR ORAL REPORT

Start by preparing a preliminary outline of your oral report. Your preliminary outline should be a list of questions that your speech will answer. As with a preliminary outline for a written assignment, your preliminary outline can then be a guide to gathering material for your speech.

Since you'll be presenting your information orally, try to keep your preliminary outline simple. It's best to focus on a limited number of questions. Of course, this will depend on the assignment, but if you can limit yourself to three or four points, do so.

You'll gather material for an oral report in the same way you do for a writing assignment. Depending on the assignment, you might use brainstorming and freewriting as aids to gathering your own ideas, or you might look to outside sources, such as your textbook and notes or library sources. For other oral reports, you might use observation or conduct interviews. Suggestions for all these techniques for gathering materials are included in Chapter 17.

Additionally, look for anything you might include in your oral report to make it come alive for your listeners. Oral reports provide a unique opportunity for sharing materials with the class. For example, with an art report, you might show reproductions of some of the artist's work. For a linguistics report on differences between men's speech and women's speech, you could play a short tape to illustrate a difference that you noted. For a report on an experiment you did in psychology, you could display a chart of your results. Any kind of demonstration, real example, or visual aid you can include in your report will make your message more memorable, and will also have the virtue of shifting your audience's attention to where you want it—on your subject instead of on you.

WRITING A DRAFT

In drafting your speech, use a two-stage drafting process, in which the aim of the first stage is to get your ideas down, and the focus of the second stage is to revise what you've written for oral presentation.

Chapter 17 has suggestions for starting to write your first draft (see pages 263 and 264). Begin by reviewing what the assignment was. Next, revise your preliminary outline in light of the information you've gathered on your topic. Try to formulate your topic as a question, so that you can use the question as a guide to your writing. When you write, write about one point on your preliminary outline at a time. Remember that you don't have to write the parts in order. Keep working on the first draft until you're satisfied with it, and only then turn to adapting it for oral presentation.

How would you revise a written paper for oral presentation? Think about how readers receive information differently from listeners. Readers can control the pace at which information is received by speeding up or slowing down, and can also go back and reread parts of a text when questions arise. Listeners have to process information as it's being spoken, cannot go back to review parts, and can only ask questions when invited to do so. In many respects the task of listening to learn is the more difficult one. There are several ways in which you can make the listener's task easier.

1.   *Use a simple organizational plan.*   Because your listeners need to follow your presentation of points easily, stick to an organizational plan that's easy to preview. For instance, if you were reporting on an Impressionist artist, you could have three main parts: a brief biography of the artist, a discussion of the characteristics of the artist's work, and an evaluation of his or her contribution to the art world.

2.   *Provide an overview of your organizational plan to your listeners.*   Write into your introduction a brief preview of your organizing plan that tells your reader, in a sentence or two, what the main parts of your presentation are and the order in which you'll present them. At the beginning of your presentation, you can also list the parts of your speech on the board.

3.   *Use transitions when moving from one point to another.*   Whenever you move from one point to the next, make it clear that you are doing so. A **transition** is a bridge from one part of a text to the next. Examples of transitions are phrases like, "My next point is . . .," "The third reason why the U.S. should not give military aid to counter-revolutionary forces in country X is: . . .," or questions that you will then answer, like "Next, what features are typical of Mary Cassatt's paintings?"

4.   *Use simple, straightforward language.*   For instance, you can begin simply by saying, "My report today is on tests designed to assess differences in learning styles among people." The language of an oral report needs to be more direct than that of a written report; it can also be more informal.

5. *Provide plenty of examples.*   As mentioned earlier, any kind of visual aid or demonstration you can incorporate into your oral report will increase your listeners' interest and make your points more clearly. Oral reports provide an opportunity for "show and tell" that written reports do not. If your assignment doesn't lend itself to any kind of visual, you can still make your subject real to your listeners by providing examples to illustrate verbally each point that you make.

6. *Use your conclusion to briefly summarize what you have said or to reemphasize your main point.*   Your conclusion can be short and to the point—just a few sentences will do. You can either summarize the points you've made in several sentences or re-state your main point. If your working title was a question, your con-clusion could simply be the answer to that question, stated in a sentence or two.

PRACTICING FOR ORAL PRESENTATION

Take several days after you complete your draft to prepare yourself for the oral presentation. First, you'll want to decide what kind of notes you want to use. You may decide to read the oral re-port as you wrote it, but reading will make it difficult to maintain eye contact with your audience as you talk. If you decide to work with your script, use a highlighter pen to signal the main ideas and the transitional sentences so that you won't lose your place if you depart from your script.

More often speakers prefer to talk from a detailed outline, one that indicates all main ideas, supporting information, and examples, but doesn't record them in complete sentences. When a speaker works from an outline, the language sounds more spontaneous, and it's easier to look at the audience while speaking. Your outline can be on 4×6 or 5×8 index cards, with one point outlined on each card and one card each for your introduction and conclusion, or it can all be on standard size paper. In either case, make sure that it is typed or written neatly and clearly so that you can read it easily as you talk.

After you've prepared your notes, prepare any visual aids you will use. If you plan to write something on a blackboard, write it out in your notes. If there is something you want the class to look at while you talk, you can prepare a dittoed handout or an overhead transparency. An overhead transparency is a sheet of clear plastic on which something can be reproduced and then projected. Transpar-encies are surprisingly simple to prepare. If you have information you'd like to convey in this way, such as a table of data or a chart, ask your instructor to direct you to someone who can show you how to put your information on an overhead and how to project it.

If you are using any equipment, such as a tape recorder, a slide projector, or overhead projector, be thoroughly familiar with how it operates and bring backups of any parts that might fail without notice, like batteries or a projection bulb. Set up the equipment in the room ahead of time and check how it will be seen or heard by your audience.

Now is the time to rehearse. Go through your report several times, spaced over several days. Work with the actual notes and materials you'll use in your presentation. Don't memorize your report word for word, but practice until you're not completely dependent on your notes to remember what to say next. The first time that you rehearse the entire presentation, time yourself. Your report should take slightly less than the allotted time. If it's much shorter or much longer, you'll have to do some revision. The day before you will give the report, do a dress rehearsal. You can ask a friend to listen to your presentation or you can tape it yourself and play it back.

Rehearsing has a side benefit—it helps you with the nervousness that accompanies any speech. Everyone feels nervous before addressing an audience, but if you're well prepared, nervousness is less likely to impair your presentation.

GIVING YOUR REPORT

When you deliver your report, you want to keep your audience's attention focused on your message. To do so, you need to pay attention to your style of delivery. Think about where you will stand and where you will have your notes while you are talking. If there's a lectern available (a speaker's stand with a slanted surface for your notes), try it out before you speak to see if you're comfortable using it. While you're speaking, avoid nervous behaviors that can sidetrack your audience's attention—fiddling with a ring, twisting your hair, or tapping your foot. Look directly at your audience, not at the ground or over their heads. If you can't handle direct eye contact easily, try to maintain eye contact with a few people in the class that you know.

If you're using visual aids or equipment, have them set up and ready to go beforehand. But don't actually display them until the point at which you want your audience to pay attention to them. If you distribute a handout before you begin talking, students will be reading the handout when they should be listening to your introduction. If you plan to show students an example of a painting and it's displayed too soon, your audience will be examining it when you want them to be listening.

While you're speaking, pay attention to the quality of your voice. Speak at a conversational rate. If you speak too quickly, you may slur over your words, and you give the impression that you're trying to rush through the speech so you can sit down. If you speak too slowly, your audience's attention is likely to drift away. Speak loudly enough to be heard without shouting. Emphasize some words in your sentences so that your tone isn't monotonous.

Perhaps the most important point about your delivery is to speak with enthusiasm—if your voice communicates that you find your topic interesting, your audience is likely to have the same attitude. If you've taped your report while you were rehearsing it, review how your voice sounds, and practice varying your delivery until you're satisfied with your rate of delivery, the level of loudness, the variation in your voice tone, and the enthusiasm your voice conveys.

SUMMARY

Begin work on an oral report by finding out as much as you can about the assignment, including the topic, the sources, the task, the process, the audience, the evaluation criteria, the format, and the length and presentation date. In planning and gathering material, keep your report focused on a limited number of central points and look for any materials that could be used as visual aids. Draft your report, and then work to adapt the draft for an oral presentation. To do so, use a simple organizational plan and give your listeners an overview of it, include transitions when you move from one point to another, use simple, straightforward language, and provide plenty of examples. Make your summary a brief restatement of your main points. Prepare a detailed outline of your report on cards or paper and begin practicing. Frequent practices over several days are best. Prepare your visual aids and plan when you will distribute them. When you present your report, monitor how you're delivering it. Pay attention to your voice quality, avoid nervous behaviors, and speak with enthusiasm.

■
JOURNAL WRITING

1. As a student, you're in a position to observe speakers every day—your professors. Which instructors give effective oral presentations? What qualities do you like? Which professors are less effective and why? Based on your observations, write about the qualities you think make an instructor an effective speaker.
2. Write about the experiences you've had speaking in front of an audience. What were the occasions? What kinds of subjects did you talk about? How effective did you think your presentation was? How did you feel about it?

■
ACADEMIC WRITING

Prepare a short (under 5 minutes) oral presentation reviewing the information in one of the chapters in this book, rehearse it, and present it to the class.

APPENDIX

The following is a sample textbook chapter taken from *Explorations in the Arts,* an introductory humanities textbook. This chapter is about the arts of theatre and film. Use this sample chapter along with the exercises in this text's chapters eight, nine, and ten to practice surveying a chapter, reading actively, and studying.

Components of the Composite Arts

Unlike the arts we have been considering, which exist primarily either in space or in time, the theater and film belong to the *composite arts,* which are both spatial and temporal. Theater and film unfold before our eyes in a defined playing space or on a screen, sharing many of the qualities we associate with the spatial arts. In addition, they relate a story over time, have a plot enacted through the dialogue and movement of its characters, and therefore share many qualities associated with the temporal arts. They require our attention to the individual stage or screen images, as well as our use of memory and anticipation, the mental habits necessary for understanding a narrative.

61 Stage set, Act I, Scene 2, for *Victoria Regina,* 1935. Designed by Rex Whistler. This box set with its overstuffed furniture, heavy draperies, numerous pictures, and elaborate ceiling gives the appearance of a mid-19th-century English parlor.

Theater

In addition to the components of the spatial and temporal arts we have already discussed, theater has several distinctive features. Most fundamentally, it consists of an actual performance, enabling us to witness the events as they occur; we are observers of the action as it happens. Furthermore, theater has a special playing space and a special kind of stage time.

The Stage as Playing Space

The playing area, the spatial component of the theater, is in many cases defined by the proscenium arch, which surrounds the opening of the stage and separates it from the auditorium. In effect, this arch is a frame, setting off the playing space as if it were a picture. Theaters with a **proscenium stage** are usually designed to accommodate fairly elaborate sets. Using backdrops, wings, and even false ceilings, the **box set** [61] can create the illusion of reality, of looking into a room as if a wall had been removed. The plays of Henrik Ibsen (1828–1906) and George Bernard Shaw (1856–1950), with their detailed directions for locales and furnishings, were written for this type of theater. However, such elaborate sets limit the number of locations that can be shown in one play.

The playing space of a theater can also be less precisely defined. Shakespeare wrote his plays for a much more flexible stage, one that did not attempt to recreate specific locations through scenery. Because Shakespeare and his contemporaries used only a few movable objects—such as a throne or a bed—they relied on language to paint the setting of each scene. As a result, Renaissance English playwrights were free both to vary the locales of their drama and to change their settings rapidly. Moreover, the bareness of the stage encouraged the writing of glorious, descriptive blank verse.

The fluid staging of the Elizabethan theater makes greater demands on the audience's imagination than is usual in a proscenium theater. But audiences are capable of exercising a good deal of imagination, and they are usually not troubled by indeterminate or unlocalized scenes. The audience may not know or care where the action is supposed to be occurring, since this information may not matter. Samuel Beckett (b. 1906) in *Waiting for Godot* (1952), for example, calls for a single tree on an otherwise bare stage; that is the only visual indication of place.

Such flexible use of the playing space is accomplished less easily in proscenium houses than in modern *experimental theaters*. Here the spectators often sit on three or even four sides, surrounding the playing area. This arrangement limits the painted scenic effects that can be used, but has the advantages of permitting actors to enter or exit from various sides and of creating an intimate relationship between the audience and the play being performed. Although we associate such seating with the post–World War II theater, it is derived, in fact, from patterns established by the **amphitheaters** and coliseums of ancient Greece and Rome.

Regardless of how precisely or vaguely defined the playing area is, the audience must use its imagination. For the playing space is hardly ever identical with the place called for by the playwright. No matter how many trees and even live rabbits are placed on the stage, for instance, we must still supply the imaginative act that transforms these into the forest of Arden in Shakespeare's *As You Like It*. Some theorists believe that we, as spectators, experience what Samuel Taylor Coleridge calls "the willing suspension of disbelief"—that we ignore the reality of the stage and its sets. Most of us actually have a double experience, simultaneously appreciating the physical reality of the theater and enjoying the fictional world of the play. Indeed, *play*—with its double connotation of "imaginative playfulness" and of "drama"—is the appropriate word for what we experience in the theater.

Stage Time

But theater, we have said, is an art of time as well as of place. Just as space or place has two meanings in theater productions—being both the physical stage and the fictional location for the action—so time has a double significance. It refers to both the actual time taken by the performance of a play and the fictional time experienced by the characters in the plot.

The actual time of a performance is limited. In this respect, plays differ from novels, which may vary according to the wishes of the author. A more significant difference between experiencing a novel and a play is that a performance cannot be interrupted at the spectator's will. A novel can be picked up and put down, and can also be reread. A play in the theater can be experienced only in the order in which it is performed. Consequently, we as spectators cannot go back and must rely even more heavily on our memory and attention than we do as readers. In general, theater provides a more concentrated experience than novel reading, perhaps because we are caught in the excitement of witnessing an actual performance. We are called upon to use the same mental habits and we feel the same excitement when we watch such related arts as opera and ballet.

Unlike real time, stage time can be either longer or shorter than the duration of the actual performance. In most plays the action is compressed so that the events cover a greater span than the time taken to show them on stage. For example, in only three hours of playing time, *The Tragedy of Dr. Faustus* (1592) by Christopher Marlowe (1564–1593) presents incidents that occur during the twenty-four years of Faustus's pact with the Devil. Then, at the end, the play takes only a few minutes to present Faustus's agonizing last hour. Indeed, this last hour is compressed into one soliloquy: "Now, Faustus, hast thou but one bare hour to live." The preparation for this moment, the intensity of Faustus's emotion, and the brilliance of Marlowe's poetry make the audience forget that far fewer than sixty minutes are elapsing.

A still more flexible use of stage time can be found in *Waiting for Godot*. The audience cannot know whether the second act of this two-act play really occurs, as the stage directions claim, "Next day. Same time." Although the characters talk as if only one night has passed, the tree, bare in Act I, has sprouted leaves; one character has gone blind; and another character has become dumb. This ambiguous treatment of time is used deliberately by Beckett to suggest at once the monotony and the radical changes brought by life.

Some experiments in stage time resemble those made by novelists, who can freely manipulate the time sequence of their narrative. The American playwright George S. Kaufman (1889–1961) in *Merrily We Roll Along* (1934) and the English dramatist Harold Pinter (b. 1930) in *Betrayal* (1978) both begin their plays at the end of the story and move backward in time in the succeeding scenes. The effect is strong dramatic irony, for the audience sees the characters play out the resolution, and then watches them at earlier moments in their lives when they are still ignorant of their futures.

Like other storytellers, playwrights have also adopted the device of beginning **in medias res**, "in the middle of things," moving backward in some scenes while still generally moving forward in their plot development. But stage scenes, unlike those in prose fiction, present their material before our very eyes and exist, so to speak, only in the present tense. In this regard, they resemble film. Some modern playwrights have, in fact, taken over a cinematographic device for dramatizing earlier moments in time—the **flashback**. This device, which we will consider at greater length in the next section, is used with special effectiveness in *Death of a Salesman* by Arthur Miller (b. 1915). Although the main action occurs at the end of the life of Willy Loman, a frustrated and pathetic traveling salesman, earlier moments are introduced as Willy remembers them. One powerful scene dramatizes the time years earlier

62 Scene from *Death of a Salesman* by Arthur Miller, with Mildred Dunnock and Lee J. Cobb as Willy Loman and his wife and Arthur Kennedy and Cameron Mitchell as their sons, 1949. Directed by Elia Kazan. Setting and lighting by Jo Mielziner.

when Biff, Willy's son, discovers Willy committing adultery. The set, which presents two levels of a house, helps the audience to understand the differences in time. When the action takes place in the present, the characters move through conventional door openings. But when the action takes place in Willy's memory, the characters move through wall areas that are only suggested by the framework of the house [62]. Interestingly, the time of the various scenes is indicated by the way in which the space is used. This example reminds us of how intimately space and time are related in the theater.

Film

Although the theater, along with opera and dance, can present space and time with considerable flexibility, film is a still more fluid and flexible medium. Like the theater, film provides visual images and can also dramatize events in space over a period of time. After 1928, when the sound track was invented, speech, music, and other sound effects could be included, bringing this medium still closer to the theater.

In a crucial respect, however, theater and film differ. The theater presents an actual performance by actors on the stage, and even the same company of actors will inevitably present slightly different performances from night to night. Motion pictures, on the other hand, present a filmed performance by actors on the screen, and the actors' performance can never vary because it is recorded. All copies of any film are basically the same.

In its use of cameras to record the action, film is also related to and an outgrowth of still photography. As such, it shares some of the technical advantages of the latter art form. But as the term *motion picture* implies, film differs from still photography in being able to present movement.

Indeed, the distinctive feature of film is that it can record motion by showing us characters moving from one place to another over a period of time. In doing so, it gives a vivid impression of how we actually experience time and space in our own lives—simultaneously. We are, after all, always conscious of motion, and we measure it at once spatially, in a physical setting, and chronologically, by the clock. That is, we measure motion by both the distance and the time it takes to get from one point to another—"It's a two-hour trip." By recording motion that shows space and time operating simultaneously, film comes closer than the other arts, including theater, to recreating reality as we normally experience it.

Yet film is not limited to recording aspects of reality. Like the theater, it has the capacity to manipulate space and time. And it has the additional capacity to create images representing thoughts or dreams. Indeed, film can present images that are imaginary or fantastic. Moreover, the fact that we can watch the images, often larger than life, while sitting passively in the dark makes our experience of film close to dreaming.

That motion pictures can create an illusion either of reality or of fantasy is amazing if we consider that the camera can take only two-dimensional shots, while we see the world in three dimensions because of our binocular vision. The camera, with its single opening, cannot as readily record depth as can our brain, which combines images entering at different angles through our two eyes. But by skillful use of technical devices, the director can overcome the limitations of the camera in order to fashion the entire film into a coherent and artistically meaningful whole.

Treatment of Space

The technical devices film can use to capture both space and time in motion are so numerous that only the most important can be considered here. In terms of space, the size of objects or people can be determined by the distance between them and the camera: the closer they are to the camera, the larger they will appear. In *Notorious* (1946), for instance, Alfred Hitchcock (1899–1980) photographs a cup of drugged coffee first with normal dimensions but then menacingly larger as the camera moves closer. The term *close-up* is used for the shot of an object or even just a part of an object taken at such close range that it fills the screen. In *Apocalypse Now* (1979), Francis

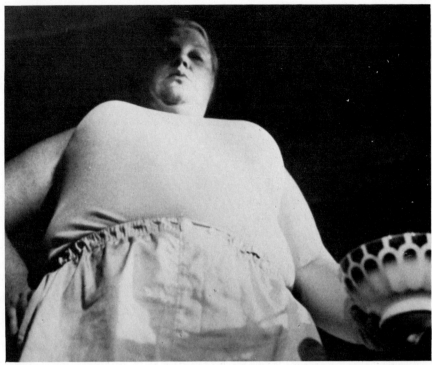

63 Scene from *Seven Beauties,* with Shirley Stoller as the sadistic commandant of the concentration camp, 1976. Directed by Lina Wertmüller.

Ford Coppola (b. 1933) at crucial moments emphasizes the harshness of the American colonel in Vietnam by focusing only on his stern and brutal face, which looms gigantically before us.

Size can also be determined by the angle from which an object or person is photographed. An upward shot makes the image appear large; a downward shot makes it appear small. In *Seven Beauties,* directed by Lina Wertmüller (b. 1930), the sadistic concentration camp guard Hilde is photographed at a sharp angle from below so as to appear monumental and threatening [63]. Conversely, her pathetic victim is photographed from above so as to appear smaller and helpless. Crowd scenes must be taken at a downward angle in order to include a sufficient number of people, and the individuals in such crowds always appear tiny.

Depth in motion pictures—the troubling problem of creating the illusion of three-dimensionality even though the camera can only record two dimensions—can be achieved not only by camera angles but also by the lighting of a scene and even by the choice of lenses. Although the focusing of the camera is usually taken for granted by the audience, only the technological advances of the 1930s have made it possible to establish an extensive "depth of field"—that is, the amount of space including both foreground and background that is kept in sharp focus. Mike Nichols (b. 1931) in *The Graduate* is able to capture not only the silhouette of the young hero in the balcony of the church but also the figures at the altar and even the natural setting beyond [64].

The choice of camera angles and focus as well as lighting are all available to still photography and motion pictures alike, but the latter have the additional possibility of creating depth through movement. In the technique called **panning**, the camera can film in an uninterrupted horizontal sweep by rotating from a fixed pivot. In the technique called **tracking**, the camera films while itself in motion. For instance, panning can record the progress of a train through a landscape by photographing the train from a fixed location; tracking can record it by moving with the moving train. Both techniques enable the camera to move about, capturing various aspects of a scene and throwing objects into relief. In addition, these techniques allow the audience to become participants in the space, not mere spectators as in the theater.

While simulating motion, film also presents a series of isolated images in space because everything is seen within the rectangular shape of the screen. The darkness that surrounds the screen can serve as a frame—just like the frame of a picture or like the arch that separates the proscenium stage from the theater audience. In the movies, we are so absorbed in the action that we are usually not conscious of such a "frame," but directors use the device of **framing** to organize their shots. They can select and order their material as if it were a painting, paying attention to symmetrical and dynamic

left: 64   Scene from *The Graduate,* 1968. Dustin Hoffman is shown at the church trying to stop the marriage of the woman he loves (Katherine Ross) to Brian Avery. Directed by Mike Nichols.

right: 65   Scene from *Ivan the Terrible,* Part I, with Nikolai Cherkassov in the title role, 1943-1946. Screenplay and direction by Sergei Eisenstein. This shot, carefully composed, uses framing to balance the close-up of the tsar's profile on the right with the queue of Russian peasants at the left. Here the size of the figures is directly related to their closeness to the camera.

balance, light and shadow, and other patterns of composition we have observed in the spatial arts. By lingering over such shots—for instance, the brooding face of the tsar with the masses of Russian peasants behind him at the end of *Ivan the Terrible* [65]—Sergei Eisenstein (1898–1948) gives tremendous emphasis to the scene, which sums up the relationship between the fatherly ruler and the Russian people.

Treatment of Time

The director can manipulate the time elements of a film with as much freedom as the spatial elements. For one thing, film is always highly selective, moving quickly from one significant moment to the next. In Alfred Hitchcock's *Spellbound* (1945), we see the heroine in a sanitorium in Vermont, reading a letter that mentions a Manhattan hotel; and in the very next shot, we see her in the lobby of that hotel. Her intervening trip is omitted.

Large spans of time are also frequently omitted in films that record such factual happenings as a process of growth. Using a technique called *lapse time,* the camera may photograph flowers only at set intervals of, say, four hours. When shown uninterruptedly, such shots make us ignore the omitted time and actually give the impression that the flower is unfolding before our eyes.

The abrupt transition from one significant moment to the next, known as **cutting**, is one of the most common devices used in motion pictures. So common that we are usually not aware of it, cutting can be used quite deliberately for dramatic effect. It is especially memorable when it takes the form of **cross-cutting**, or the back-and-forth movement between shots. In *Apocalypse Now,* Coppola juxtaposes shots of the murder of the American colonel, who has become a tribal chieftain and demigod, with shots of the sacrificial slaying of a water buffalo. These two bloody acts are shown alternately in quick succession, indicating that they occur simultaneously and implying a close parallel. The skillful combining or juxtaposing of images is known as **montage**, a term derived from the French *monter,* "to mount" or put into place.

More gradual and less abrupt transitions between scenes than those made possible by cutting can be achieved by the devices known as **dissolves** and **fades**. In a dissolve the image disappears gradually while a new image emerges; for a brief moment the two images are superimposed on one another. In a **fade-out** the image gradually dims and finally disappears into blankness; in a **fade-in** a new image gradually appears out of the blankness. Early in the action of Orson Welles' *Citizen Kane,* as the camera focuses on Kane on his deathbed, the script calls for both devices:

[Scene No. 14] The Foot of Kane's Bed
The camera very close. Outlined against the shuttered window, we can see a form—the form of a nurse as she pulls the sheet up over [Kane's] head. The camera follows this action up the length of the bed and arrives at the face after the sheet has covered it.

Fade Out

Fade In
[Scene No. 15] Int[erior] of a Motion Picture Projection Room.
Herman J. Mankiewicz and Orson Welles, *The Citizen Kane Book: The Shooting Script*

The rest of Scene No. 15 focuses on the newsreels that give background material on Kane, whose life story is the basis of the film. This example suggests how well the fade-out, fade-in technique can be used to mark a change in both place and time.

The motion picture also can manipulate time quite literally by reversing, stopping (or *freezing*), speeding up, or slowing down the action. Keystone Cops movies use *accelerated motion* in their chase sequences to intensify the excitement, crowding far more activity into a short time than is humanly possible. In the frolic sequence in *Hard Day's Night* (1964) Richard Lester (b. 1932) shows the Beatles running at impossible speeds, leaping up and then floating back to earth with a languor that defies gravity. Both the fast and the slow motion delightfully capture the mood of exuberance.

The director can not only manipulate relatively short periods of time by expanding, contracting, and even on occasion stopping the film, but can also manipulate larger units of time in telling a story. Such treatment is often necessary because film narrative can depict action only in the present tense, since the action always unfolds before our eyes. In this respect, film is more limited than prose narrative, which tends to be expressed in the past tense, but can also use the present and future tenses. Film does not even have a cinematographic means of including time references such as "Earlier that day," "In the meantime," or "Later on."

To overcome this limitation in treating time, film can use the device of the flashback, breaking the chronology of the narrative by shifting to a scene set at an earlier time. This earlier scene, however, unfolds in the present tense. Such a scene is often introduced not by an abrupt cut, but by a dissolve or a fade-out and fade-in calling attention to shifts in time. When the chronology shifts to the future rather than the past, the scene is known as a *flashforward*.

Michael Curtiz (1888–1962) uses flashback memorably in *Casablanca* (1942) when the tough adventurer Rick, played by Humphrey Bogart, sits drunk in his Casablanca nightclub and recalls his earlier meetings with the beautiful refugee Ilsa, played by Ingrid Bergman. The script reads:

The camera closes in on Rick. From his expression you know that he is thinking of the past. Slowly the sounds of an orchestra join into Sam's [the club pianist's] playing as the scene dissolves.

It is Paris in spring. A shot of the Arc de Triomphe is followed by one of Rick driving a small, open car along the boulevard. Close beside him, with her arm linked in his, sits Ilsa.

On an excursion boat on the Seine. At the rail of the boat stand Rick and Ilsa. They are transported by each other. Ilsa laughs.

Inside Rick's Paris apartment, Ilsa fixes flowers at the window. Rick opens champagne. Ilsa joins him.

These quick visual flashbacks, introduced by a dissolve, are followed by scenes of dialogue in Paris in which Ilsa promises to elope with Rick in order to escape from the invading Nazis. The sequence ends at the train station as Rick learns that she will not join him. Transition back to the Casablanca night-club is achieved by a dissolve as "the steam from the engine clouds over the scene."

Ingmar Bergman (b. 1918) uses a more elaborate flashback in *Wild Strawberries* (1957), in which two different times in one man's life are presented simultaneously. The central figure, an elderly widower, indulges in memories of his youth. Flashbacks show the girl he loved as young as she was at the time he is remembering, but show him in the same shot as old as he is now. This flashback goes beyond the bounds of human possibility by combining two different times in the same image. It demonstrates that film can convey complicated psychological experiences in direct visual terms.

Not only can film record events or memories of events but it can also focus on the workings of a character's mind. In the nightmare sequence of Hitchcock's *Spellbound,* the camera presents an actual dream as if we were witnessing the processes of the hero's unconscious. As we shall see in the section on stream of consciousness (in Chapter 4), our minds, especially in a dream, function in visual images, and a film-maker can present the workings of the mind directly in those visual images.

Films, especially on science-fiction subjects, can even make us witness totally fantastic spectacles. Stanley Kubrick (b. 1928) in *2001: A Space Odyssey* [66] and George Lucas (b. 1945) in *Star Wars* (1977), can make us feel that we are traveling on futuristic space ships and engaging in epic battles beyond the solar system. By enlarging photographs of miniature models and using computers, mirrors, and other means of achieving special visual effects, film-makers can make the most implausible scenes seem real. The accompanying sound—overwhelmingly loud, clear, stereophonic or even quadrophonic—often intensifies the experience in such films.

66 Scene from *2001: A Space Odyssey,* 1966. Keir Dullea (unseen, in space exploration vehicle) attempts to retrieve the body of Gary Lockwood. Produced and directed by Stanley Kubrick. Screenplay by Stanley Kubrick and Arthur C. Clarke, based on Clarke's story "The Sentinel."

Sound

Sound is an important component in many modern films. This later addition to film technology, which became practicable only after the development of the sound track in 1928, makes possible the synchronizing of the image with spoken words, special sound effects, and music. Some critics have suggested that sound is not as essential to the film medium as are the visual images. We might argue, however, that it certainly enriches the art form. Especially in the dialogue, through which much of the story is usually told, words and facial expressions can reinforce each other, as is vividly demonstrated in *The African Queen* (1952) directed by John Huston (b. 1906). When Humphrey Bogart as Mr. Allnut flippantly asks Katharine Hepburn why she has come to such "a God-forsaken place," her indignant retort that "God has not forsaken this place" is emphasized by her tone as well as by her disdainful look.

No less than in the case of visual images, film has special devices for manipulating sound. Because the sound track operates separately from the images on the screen, a voice can be heard without our seeing the lips of the speaker. This technique is called **voice-over**. The voice need not be that of the person we see on the screen, but can belong to a narrator. *Citizen Kane* opens with a disembodied voice commenting on the newsreel shots that depict Kane's life.

Voice-over is especially useful as a means of expressing the character's innermost thoughts. Known also as **interior monologue**, this device uses the sound track to let us listen in on the character's thinking while allowing the camera to show that the actor is not speaking. In doing so, film can express private thoughts more believably than a play, for in drama such thoughts can be delivered only in a **soliloquy**, a monologue spoken by an actor alone on the stage. Appropriately, Laurence Olivier [67] used voice-overs to translate the soliloquies of both Hamlet and Henry V to the screen.

Again because the sound track can be separated from the visual image, voices can be *dubbed;* that is, someone else's voice can be synchronized with an actor's lip movements. This device is useful not only in translating films from one language into another but also in substituting the voice of a professional singer for that of a nonsinging actor. In *My Fair Lady* (1964), George Cukor (1899–1983) gave the visually enchanting Audrey Hepburn the appearance of delivering songs that were actually recorded by the singer Marni Nixon.

The sound track also makes it possible to-enrich a film with special sound effects. We are all familiar with the shrieks, groans, and echoing footsteps in horror movies—all of which may either accompany an image or merely be audible while the camera focuses on a frightened face. A much subtler use of sound detached from the image occurs in the film *In Which We Serve* (1941) about the British navy in World War II written and directed by Noel Coward (1899–1973). As we watch the English captain picnicking peacefully with his family while on leave, we hear the ominous sounds of fighting planes offscreen and realize that the war is beginning in earnest.

67 Scene from *Hamlet,* with Laurence Olivier, 1948. Olivier sits immobile in deep contemplation as his voice is heard delivering a soliloquy. Produced and directed by Laurence Oliver.

One of the most frequently used sound effects consists of music that is written especially to accompany some of the action. Often such music becomes the theme song of the film and is totally identified with the characters. "As Time Goes By" is inseparable from Rick and Ilsa's love relationship in *Casablanca,* just as Paul Simon and Art Garfunkel's "Mrs. Robinson" is identified with the older woman in *The Graduate.* These theme songs do much to establish or intensify the mood, as does orchestral music adapted or especially composed for a film.

Varied effects can be achieved by either paralleling or contrasting the music with the visual images. The delicate lyricism of Mozart's *Piano Concerto No. 21 in C Major, K. 467,* contributes to the idyllic background of the poignant and poetic love story in *Elvira Madigan* (1967) directed by Bo Widerberg (b. 1930). On the other hand, the equally lyrical excerpt from Mozart's opera *Cosi Fan Tutte* forms an ironic counterpoint to the irresolvable love relationship in *Sunday, Bloody Sunday* (1971), directed by John

Schlesinger (b. 1952), in which the two main characters can never achieve the balance and harmony established at the end of Mozart's opera.

From this discussion, we can understand that film draws on all the elements of both the spatial and the temporal arts and can unite these in unique and complex ways. In fact, film is probably the richest and most flexible of the composite arts. No wonder it is so popular in our day.

To sum up, both plays and films can manipulate space and time in distinctive ways. The stage need not define precisely the location for the action, and the plot of the play need not unfold in simple chronological fashion. Stage place and stage time can even be interrelated by the staging. Film is still freer in treating space and time. With its special devices of the close-up, panning, and tracking, film can alter the size and spatial relationships of objects on the screen. With its special devices of cutting, cross-cutting, montage, and flashback, it can also rearrange the time sequence of the story. Although theater and film have much in common—since both present narratives in space as well as time—each of these art forms has distinctive possibilities of its own.

Two other art forms closely related to theater also exist in both space and time. Opera combines drama with music, vocal as well as orchestral; dance combines bodily movement with music. Both of these art forms unfold before our eyes in a defined playing space. They develop narratives or, in the case of some ballets, abstract patterns over time. And they share the distinctive feature of the theater in that they exist in performance. Rather than analyze their components further here, we will consider opera in Chapter 9, on genres, and dance in Chapter 5, on performance.

Questions for Study and Discussion

1. For a dramatization of Edith Wharton's "Roman Fever" (see page 85), what stage designs would be appropriate in a proscenium house and what different designs for theater-in-the-round?

2. In a dramatization of "Roman Fever," what problems of stage time—if any—would have to be solved? If the play version begins exactly when the story begins, how could a playwright dramatize the earlier events that Edith Wharton conveys through the reflections of her characters?

3. In a film version of "Roman Fever," what special devices—such as close-up, angle shots, panning, tracking, framing, cutting, cross-cutting, dissolves, fade-out, fade-in, freezing, accelerated motion, flashback, flash-forward—could be used? What sound effects—voice-over, off-screen sounds, theme music—could be included?

4. Because "Roman Fever" takes place in only one setting and in a short period of time, it seems to lend itself more readily to dramatization as a stage play than as a film. Agree or disagree.

5. In the next motion picture you see, find examples of as many of the special devices of film—such as close-ups or angle shots—as possible. In each case, consider what the use of the device contributes to the film.

GLOSSARY

Absolute statement   A statement asserting that something is always true, or if it is a negative absolute statement, that it is never true.

Abstract   A brief summary of a periodical article, often appearing either at the beginning of the article or in an indexed collection of abstracts in the library.

Academic probation   A status for students whose grades fall below a certain minimum standard. Students on academic probation typically are offered academic support and given a limited time in which to raise their averages.

Acronym   Use of initial letters to create a word that stands for a phrase. Examples: FAA (Federal Aviation Administration), BART (Bay Area Rapid Transit).

Appendix   A section in the back of a textbook that contains reference tables.

Back matter   Sections of a textbook placed after the last chapter; back matter might include glossaries, appendixes, and indexes.

Bibliography   A list of books related to the subject of a book or article, often included as an appendix.

Brainstorming   Listing all possible ideas that might be included in a paper as a way to gather material.

College organizer   An assignment book that combines spaces for recording daily assignments, study grids and a term calendar.

Cornell System   A two-column system of notetaking with the right column used for notes and the left column used for study aids.

Directed reading   Reading with a specific comprehension goal in mind.

Discussion leader   In a small group discussion, the person who directs the flow of the conversation and keeps the group on target.

Documentation   Any method of indicating the sources of information in a written text to readers.

Freewriting   Writing on a subject without stopping for a preset time or length: a technique for focusing ideas or gathering material.

Front matter   The material in a textbook in front of the first chapter, including the preface and the table of contents.

General vocabulary   Words in everyday use that are not tied to a certain academic field.

Glossary   A listing of technical terms in a textbook along with their definitions.

Grade point average   An average of your grades in all your college courses, computed by dividing the total number of grade points you earn in each course by the total number of credits attempted.

Hearing   The physical activity of perceiving sound waves.

Index   An alphabetical listing of people and topics mentioned in a textbook, along with page numbers for each item.

Inference   A logical guess as to a word's meaning, based on your understanding of the context.

Introspection   Looking inward to discover your ideas and feelings on a certain subject.

Learning journal   A notebook of private writings related to the subject matter you are studying.

Listening   The activity of comprehending an oral message.

Listening worksheet   A page of notes in preparation for listening to an academic lecture: will include brief summaries of the notes from the previous class and of the readings for the present class, as well as a list of specialized vocabulary that might be used in the lecture.

Mapping   A simple visual aid used to represent the relationships between ideas, such as a flow chart.

Margin notes   Notes written by a reader in the margins of a text to aid comprehension.

Mnemonic aid   Any device to help you memorize information, such as visualization or the use of acronyms.

Morpheme   A linguistic term for meaningful language units. Simple words, prefixes and suffixes are all morphemes.

Options   In a multiple choice question, the choices that are offered as possible correct answers.

Organizational chart   A study sheet that arranges related information visually into rows and columns.

Paraphrasing   Restating an author's idea in your own words.

Periodical holdings   A library's collection of newspapers, magazines, journals, and other texts issued at regular intervals.

Preface   (pronounced PREF-us) A preview of a textbook written by its author.

Prefix   A syllable attached to the front of a word. Examples: *un*usual, *dis*interest.

Prerequisite   A requirement that you must have taken a certain course or achieved a certain skill level before you register for a particular class.

Proofreading   Rereading your written work carefully before submitting it, checking for typing, spelling, and grammar errors.

Reading goals   Comprehension goals for reading.

Reciting   Speaking or writing to yourself to learn and retain information.

Recorder   The person in a small group discussion who is responsible for writing down the group's ideas.

Rehearsal   The repeated recitation of information to be learned until it is fixed in your mind.

Reporter   The person in a small group discussion who is responsible for relaying the group's ideas orally to the class as a whole.

Rhetorical question   A question that a speaker asks without expecting an answer: used so a listener can anticipate the next point.

Root   A meaningful syllable that forms a word's center. Examples: psychology (root is *psyche*, meaning *mind*).

Rough draft   A first or intermediate attempt at a writing assignment.

Scanning   The process of rapidly surveying a chapter to locate a specific piece of information.

Skimming   Glancing over a text rapidly to get an overview.

Specialized vocabulary   Terms used in an academic field; also called technical vocabulary.

Stem   In a multiple choice question, the part of the sentence that appears first and that you must try to complete correctly by selecting the right option.

Study plan   A weekly plan for distributing your study time.

Study sheets   Notes written while studying that summarize the information to be learned for an exam.

Suffix   A syllable attached to the end of a word. Examples: coach*es*, as-sign*ment*.

Surveying a chapter   The process of previewing a chapter to orient yourself to the material and to note the study aids.

Surveying a textbook   The process of looking through a textbook, reading its preface and studying the table of contents in order to understand the book's features and organizational pattern.

Syllabus   A handout that presents an overview of the class, including information concerning topics covered, course requirements, and grading policies.

Table of contents   A listing of the topics and subtopics for each chapter in a book in the order in which they appear, along with page numbers.

Technical vocabulary   Terms used in an academic discipline; also called specialized vocabulary.

Term calendar   A calendar with space for recording significant dates in an academic term; can be used to set a series of intermediate deadlines for a long-term project.

Textbook   A book specifically designed to teach its readers a subject.

Thesis   The central idea or communicative goal of an essay.

Trade book   Any book written for a wide audience.

Transition   A word or phrase that orients readers to how a text is organized and how ideas in it are interrelated. Examples: "My second point is . . .", "On the other hand, . . ."

TTD list   An acronym for "Things To Do" list. A list of tasks to be accomplished on a certain day.

Visualization   The use of mental images as a memory aid. Example: remembering a person named Mr. Farmer by depicting him wearing overalls.

Word families   Words that are related in meaning and form, often sharing the same root. Examples: psychology, psychoanalyze, psychic.

Working bibliography   A list of books and periodical articles that are potential sources for your research paper, along with the information needed to locate them in a library.

INDEX